OH GOD, WHAT NEXT?

Oh God, What Next?

Hugh Montefiore

Hodder & Stoughton
LONDON SYDNEY AUCKLAND

Copyright © Hugh Montefiore

First published in Great Britain 1995

The right of Hugh Montefiore to be identified as the Author
of the Work has been asserted by him in accordance with the
Copyright, Designs and Patents Act 1988.

10 9 8 7 6 5 4 3 2

All rights reserved. No part of this publication may be
reproduced, stored in a retrieval system, or transmitted,
in any form or by any means without the prior written
permission of the publisher, nor be otherwise circulated in
any form of binding or cover other than that in which it is
published and without a similar condition being imposed on
the subsequent purchaser.

British Library Cataloguing in Publication Data
A record for this book is available from the British Library

ISBN 0 340 64222 X

Typeset by Hewer Text Composition Services, Edinburgh
Printed and bound in Great Britain by
Mackays, Chatham, Kent

Hodder and Stoughton Ltd
A Division of Hodder Headline PLC
338 Euston Road
London NW1 3BH

CONTENTS

For Teresa, Janet and Catherine

FOREWORD

I first started writing about my life and family at the suggestion of one of my daughters; she thought that our grandchildren would be interested. Then, after Mary Loudon had interviewed me for her 'Revelations', it occurred to me that, as John Peart-Binns' biography is no longer in print, what I have written might be of interest to a wider public. I have tried to avoid criticising by name anyone still living.

At any rate, here it is.

Hugh Montefiore
St Hugh's Day, 1994

Chapter One

BEGINNINGS

I was sixteen years old at the time, and it happened to me about 5 pm one dark wintry afternoon in 1936. I was sitting alone in my study in School House at Rugby School – all older boys had studies of their own: pillboxes, really. What happened then determined the whole future pattern of my life. I was, as I remember, indulging in a rather pleasant adolescent gloom. I suddenly became aware of a figure in white whom I saw clearly in my mind's eye. I use this expression because I am pretty sure that a photograph would have showed nothing special on it. I heard the words 'Follow me'. Instinctively I knew that this was Jesus, heaven knows how: I knew nothing about him. Put like that it sounds somewhat bare; in fact it was an indescribably rich event that filled me afterwards with overpowering joy. I could do no other than to follow those instructions. I found that I had become a Christian as a result of a totally unexpected and most unusual spiritual experience, although that was not how I would have put it at the time. I was aware of the living Christ, and because of that I was aware of God in a new way. People ask me why and when I decided to convert. I did not decide at all; it was decided for me.

I was not at the time under any special pressure or suffering from depression; in fact I was leading a normal schoolboy's life. I had been modestly interested in other faiths. I remember buying *Benn's Threepennies* on Buddhism for example; but I was not in any way dissatisfied with Judaism – in fact I had even thought of becoming a Rabbi, but I had rejected the idea because it seemed to me at the time (perhaps wrongly) that I would be too much under the thumb of a congregation.

I knew nothing about the Christian Church. I knew too little about Christianity to pass any judgement about it, negatively or positively; but I suspect that I thought of it in the same kind of way as many Christians think of Islam – a decent offshoot but not the real thing. I had some good Christian friends at the school but they never attempted to proselytise me, and they did not discuss their faith with me. I did not feel isolated as a Jew among Gentiles; I was not the only Jewish boy in School House, and I think some boys were slightly jealous because I did not attend chapel! I did not perceive the slightest whiff of anti-Semitism any of the time I was at Rugby.

I had never in my life attended a Christian service of worship, either in a church or in a school. I had never read the New Testament, except for a few sentences at my prep. school when I was starting Greek, because it was such easy Greek. (Funny that I should remember that.) I shall never forget the wonderful experience of reading the Gospels for the first time; I felt that I had come home. I find it hard to describe this experience, because words cannot do justice to it. Any verbal description sounds rather bare and banal. Deep religious experience is always indescribable, and usually incommunicable. I also fear that I may cheapen it by speaking of it too often. Not for one moment do I think that this is a better way of becoming a Christian than any other. It was simply the way it happened to me, and it is still vivid in my memory, nearly sixty years later; and I have to begin this book by writing about it, because otherwise the rest of it would make no sense. It shaped the whole future of my life.

Of course I had to tell my housemaster, who was also the headmaster; and he was kindness itself. Of course I also had to tell my parents, and that was going to be much, much more difficult, as they were devout and practising Jews, and it would pain them dreadfully. It was simply out of the question for Jews to become Christians. It is difficult to explain to Gentiles how Jews feel about this. It was like treason; it was a spiritual betrayal, as Jews see it, of all that earlier Jews had lived and died for. (According to the present law in Israel, it is not possible for a Jew to become a Christian, so they have to call themselves 'Messianic Jews'.) No doubt there are folk memories of those Jews who had been baptised to escape persecution or to better themselves, as well as bitter feelings about the way that Christians have persecuted Jews ever since Constantine the Great gave them the power to do so. Jews, or at any rate the Jews among whom I was brought up, were intensely aware of their Jewishness. They formed a community of their own. Of course they had Christian friends but that was different. What would they think of me? I was aware that my parents loved me; but how would they react? How could they be anything but terribly wounded?

I can remember to this day holding the letter over the slit in the letterbox before I dropped it in. As can be imagined, there was nothing more to be said; the matter had been settled. I could no more deny my experience than deny myself. I have of course often reflected upon it since then. I suppose there were psychological dynamics behind it, but I do not know what these would be. I was somewhat hurt to hear a well-known Christian writer dismiss it as being in the same class as the various reported appearances of the Blessed Virgin Mary in southern Europe, some of which seem to me to be fantastic. There was nothing fantastic at all about what had happened to me: all I knew was that God had communicated with me through what I had experienced, and that was that.

My parents came down to see me. They asked me not to be precipitate, as any parents would in such a situation; and I agreed. But they did not attempt to dissuade me: it was settled. I felt sorry for the man who came down from London, stayed at a local hotel, and gave me and another boy religious instruction every Sunday. He ceased to come, and I eventually lost touch with the boy. I was too hot for the school to handle. I was sent to see the Vicar of Rugby. He was a nice and good man, who later became Bishop of St Edmundsbury and Ipswich, and when he died his wife gave me his pectoral cross. That was how I became a member of the Church of England. He told me that he supposed that was what I wanted to do. I said I supposed it was. How could I know the differences between the churches? There was a Roman Catholic seminary up the road with interminable tolley bells, which hardly warmed me to that church. In any case I just wanted to be a Christian in England, not special in any way, not out of the ordinary. So I joined the Church of England. I still think I made the right decision and for the right reasons.

What would this mean for me? I did not know. Would there be radical change? I remember lying in bed at night in my dormitory and fantasising about being thrown out of home. In fact my parents, though hurt, were very loving. Life went on more or less as it always had, except that it was transformed. I waited a year before I was confirmed.

Although my conversion is the dominant event in my life story, I did not begin then, and I am what I am partly because I was what I was. So, before I continue with my story, I had better explain how it was that a person called Hugh Sebag-Montefiore ever came into existence and how he found his way as a schoolboy into that Rugby study. I have already mentioned my parents, and I need to say something about their Jewish family in which I was born.

I was the youngest (by five years) of three brothers. My father was a very successful stockbroker in the family firm begun by my great grandfather, Sir Joseph Sebag-Montefiore. My mother's father had also been a stockbroker, a common occupation for Jewish families long established in this country. My mother's family arrived here in the days of Oliver Cromwell from Spain via the Low Countries, and my father's from Livorno (Leghorn) in Italy in the middle of the eighteenth century. After their two centuries in this country, I feel thoroughly British, but at the same time rather cosmopolitan. Although the two families came from the same branch of Judaism (Sephardim, in contrast to the Eastern European Ashkenazim), they had different origins and different histories. Because these family traditions have played a great part in my life, and still do, I must briefly sketch them in. Even if they are intrinsically more interesting to me than to others, I cannot be understood without reference to them.

So far as I know, I have not got a drop of Gentile blood in my veins; or, as I suppose we would say nowadays, all my genes are Jewish, and I am the only member of my generation in my immediate family who has 'married out'.

My mother's family name was de Pass, which is a translation of the Hebrew *shalom* (peace). Her family has a long history, the name being spelt in almost as many ways as Shakespeare spelt his. It is still one of the hereditary names of the kings of Spain. The Moors had treated the Jews well in Spain, and they attained positions of eminence. At first the Spanish conquerors did the same, because they were invaluable as doctors, diplomats and financiers. But the Jews became disliked for their culture, dignity and wealth, and this dislike was hidden under the guise of religious fervour. Finally Queen Isabella banished all the Jews from Spain in 1492, and a lot of those who had achieved high positions preferred to convert to Christianity, while still secretly continuing their Jewish customs. They were known as Marranos (pigs). de Passes became Marranos. The family spread right over Europe and beyond: you name it, they were there – France, Germany, Holland, Italy, Gibraltar, Martinique, Jamaica, USA, Australia, and South Africa. One branch was known at Livorno in Italy, where Montefiores lived: how strange if the families knew one another centuries before my parents met. This cosmopolitan spread of the family has had quite an impact on me; it tends to make one feel more than merely British.

Among de Passes in Spain were diplomats (one was in Rome in 1535, persuading the pope to stop confiscating the estates of 'new Christians'). There were de Pass poets and playwrights too, and de Pass officers in the army. The tradition has remained: here in

England many have been in the armed forces, and we are proud of a posthumous VC in the First World War. Cryspyn de Passe invented the modern method of copper engraving in Amsterdam around 1600 – I have a facsimile edition of his *Hortus Floridus* – which encouraged me as a boy to do etching. At least one de Pass is known to have perished in the Inquisition. Although he had been baptised, he was heard reciting the Shema (the Jewish equivalent of the Lord's Prayer) as the flames engulfed his body. This death of an ancestor at the hands of the Roman Catholic Church has deeply affected me.

But of course it is the English branch of the family which really concerns me. There was a certain Shalom of Chichester hanged in 1278, accused of clipping gold coins, a common anti-Semitic charge. I hope he wasn't an ancestor of mine, known by the Jewish form of the name. After persecution and even massacres, Jews were banished from England in 1290, but they came back in the time of Oliver Cromwell. Two branches of the family then came to England. Two de Passes contributed capital when the Bank of England was founded in the seventeenth century, and the rules of the Royal Exchange were changed to admit a member of the family along with eleven others; so there is a long history of finance behind me; on both sides, actually.

My own branch of the family seems to begin about 1600 with Alvarez de Pass, a scholar and publisher in the Low Countries and France. I have been encouraged to find that this preoccupation with books goes back a long way! In the next generation his son was a wealthy merchant in England in 1663, professing Christianity; yet this merchant's son was bar mitzvah (the Jewish rite of passage marking coming of age) at Bevis Marks synagogue in the city of London in 1682. That was the way of Marranos! As we shall see, on my father's side the commitment to Judaism was always strong, but on my mother's side there was a tendency to adapt their outward religion to the temper of the times. As a result, today de Passes as a family can no longer be regarded as practising Jews; and one of them is actually a lady-in-waiting to the Queen.

At one time the British branch lived in King's Lynn, because of the sugar trade in the West Indies. Many West Indians today still bear the family name, taking their master's patronymic when they were liberated from slavery. There is a nice story of my grandfather, Charles de Pass, visiting an island in the West Indies. 'What is your name?' he asked the West Indian rowing him ashore. 'Charles,' he replied. 'No, I mean your real name,' he said. The man replied 'de Pass'.

In Victorian times, however, they returned to London. My grandfather de Pass was a convinced Jew, and my mother was brought up as a practising Jewess, although Christianity was not a closed book to her, since as a girl she was allowed from time to time to attend Christian worship with her friends if she wanted. She was the eldest daughter of a family of one son and three daughters. The son, William Hugh de Pass was killed in the First World War. I was called Hugh William after him. The family lived in a huge house in Queen's Gate, now part of the Kuwaiti Embassy, which I used quite often to visit as a small boy for Sunday lunch.

Although we never saw many of our de Pass cousins, I was always rather proud of their long and continuing history, just as I am of the Montefiores'. Again, my father's family goes back a long way; the earliest mention is in 1460. Research is taking it back still earlier, and it is beginning to look as though the family did not migrate to Italy from Spain, but was a 'leftover' from the Jews living in Italy in the days of the Roman Empire. I should rather like to think that my forebears were among those with whom St Paul talked when under house arrest in Rome, even if they did not accept his message.

There are three villages called Montefiore in Italy, and obviously the family name comes from one of them. Archives show Jews in one of the villages, but we cannot directly trace our line back beyond a certain Judah Leone Montefiore who married Rachel Olivetti in 1605. In the following century, after one branch came to England, they spread, like the de Passes, to many parts of the world, including planters in the West Indies; but they specialised usually, like so many Jews, in banking. One, the first Jewish commissioned officer in the British army, remarried in America at seventy-three, and then begat seven children before dying at eighty-one! Another opened the first bank in Australia, in Hobart. Yet another was among those who decided on the site of the city of Adelaide. One, however, was forced to migrate to Australia. His father married a well-known opera singer, and finding his son from an earlier marriage inconvenient, left him to the butler, whose idea of education was port and prostitutes! When he was found in their bed with one of them, he was despatched to Australia. In rather the same way one of my mother's de Pass cousins had to 'sail before the mast' to New Zealand. Some fared better: the Princess Royal has married Commander Timothy Lawrence, RN. The family name used to be Levy, and one of his forebears married a Montefiore. These were exceptions; most of us remained middle class.

The family had arrived in England in the 1750s from Livorno (Leghorn), trading in marble and straw hats, and settled in Stockwell.

now in South London (the house has been demolished). I have a family print of 1797, with Joseph Elias sitting very upright, and his wife wearing a hat of monstrous proportions, surrounded by (as yet) four children. Six-year-old Moses would grow up to be the famous Sir Moses Montefiore, who haunted my childhood.

Moses Montefiore was the family exemplar, because of his distinction and his religious exertions. He started from scratch, beginning by walking every day into the city from Stockwell, apprenticed to a grocer. But fortunate marriage connections enabled him to become one of the few Jewish brokers allowed in the city of London. He prospered, and retired from the city at the age of forty, after making a fortune, and determined to spend the rest of his life (he lived to be 100) in helping his fellow-Jews. However, he still took an active part in some business affairs, helping for example to organise the loan for the liberation of slaves in the West Indies. In addition to his house in Park Lane, he bought an estate, East Cliff Lodge, between Ramsgate and Margate (now demolished); I can just remember, as a small boy, visiting my grandmother there. Princess Victoria was then living in Ramsgate with her mother in somewhat reduced circumstances, and Moses befriended her and (so the story goes) gave her a gold key to the estate. She did not forget that kindness.

Moses was given many honours in this country, but his journeys abroad made him famous, at a time when foreign travel was fraught with danger, discomfort and disease. He became a kind of ambassador-at-large for world Jewry. Jews in Damascus were accused of ritual murder: Moses went there and defused the situation, and procured from the sultan in Jerusalem a kind of 'Magna Carta' for Jews within the Turkish Empire. In 1846 he went with his wife in a coach-and-four to Russia to tell the Czar to stop pogroms against the Jews (there are horrific stories of cracking ice as he crossed rivers), and went on to visit Jews in the 'pale' of Poland where his visit gave new hope to the Jews there. His mission on their behalf was, for a time, successful. Twenty-six years later he went back to Russia to see a different Czar; he also visited Morocco, Rumania, and Iran on behalf of the Jews there. His visit to Rome about a forced conversion was less successful.

Moses made no fewer than seven pilgrimages to the Holy Land (the last when he was eighty-two; he was dissuaded from making another in his nineties) under difficult travelling conditions. He helped to alleviate the Jews' terrible poverty there, sited a hospital, kept meticulous records of the plantations he originated, and gave the famous windmill for grinding corn in Jerusalem in 'the

Montefiore quarter', still on view to tourists today, although I am told it has never worked. His hundredth birthday was attended by great celebrations in London and Ramsgate.

In a sense he was almost a founding father of Zionism, with a great love of the Holy Land; this formed part of his deep religious devotion. But he was also a patriotic Englishman, and Lord Lieutenant of Kent. He was also a sheriff of the city of London, and would drive to banquets bringing his own kosher chicken with him. He elected to be buried with Judith his beloved wife in the mausoleum which he had built, together with a synagogue, on his Ramsgate estate, to which the family still makes pilgrimages. Today no one has heard of Moses Montefiore, but in Victorian times few had not.

Well, not quite no one today; we were never allowed to forget him. It was 'Sir Moses this' and 'Sir Moses that'. His picture, solemn and grave, hung on the walls of the house; it hangs on the wall of the room where I am writing these words. His ethos of service and devotion was always before us. We had to live up to the standards of Sir Moses. Although we might joke about 'Old Sir Mo' and 'Old Sir Jo', trying to live up to these standards was no joking matter; that is why I have spent so much space describing him.

Moses himself had a long and happy marriage to his beloved Judith, but they were childless. Moses' favourite niece had married a Soloman Sebag from Morocco ('Bab-el-Sebagh' or 'the gate of the dyers' still exists in Mogador, now known as Essaouira, on the west coast of Morocco). The inheritance, but not his baronetcy, went to Soloman's son Joseph, my great grandfather. With the inheritance he adopted the name of Montefiore, so that our branch became Sebag-Montefiore, not unsurprisingly a little looked down on by the senior branch.

It was to this other branch of the family that my cousin Claude Montefiore belonged. He died when I was a schoolboy at Rugby. He founded the Liberal Jewish Movement in this country and wrote a great many books on religious subjects including rabbinics; and he was also the first Jewish scholar to write commentaries on the Christian Gospels and about Pauline thought. Although sympathetic to Christianity, he always remained a convinced Jew. He was a really great scholar, much respected by Christian scholars because he was a person of high integrity. I was always asked by them what relation of his I was. He was also a philanthropist like Moses, helping to establish the Froebel Institute and Southampton University. He was rather a hero of mine. I always regret that I was never allowed to see him, because he was regarded as dangerously liberal in his religious views by our branch of the family.

I never knew my Montefiore grandfather: he died early of diabetes. I can only just vaguely remember my Montefiore grandmother. She was rather a matriarch and a bit of a martinet; perhaps she needed to be, widowed early with seven boisterous children to bring up. I am told that she used to order the coach for twenty-three minutes past the hour; perhaps that's how I come to have my fetish for punctuality.

My eldest Montefiore uncle was killed during the First World War, and so my father, the second son, had to act as head of the family. He had to enter the family firm early and could not go to university, so he was anxious that his sons should. He had three sons, and I was the youngest by five years. And that is how I come into the story, and this is the story of the genes I have inherited from both these two families.

I know that the question of genetic inheritance is a vexed one. Are we affected most by our nature or by our nurture? As the human genome project proceeds, it is said that more and more will be seen to depend on our particular combination of genes. On the other hand, these so-called traits are really only potentialities, and our actual characters are formed in a far more complex manner. In this, the way in which we were brought up in our formative years must surely play a large part. To this I now turn.

Chapter Two

Nurture

I was born in Paddington just north of Kensington Gardens. The house, 35 Palace Court, is still standing, but I have only a hazy recollection of living there. My first clear memory is of being in a pram in Kensington Gardens, near our home, and being lifted out of the pram by my nanny in order to be shown off to someone else. I can even remember where it happened: near the north-west corner of the Gardens, by what used to be playing fields, roughly opposite the back of the Russian Embassy. I must have been only a few months old. Why do I remember that, and nothing else of such a very early period? I do not know. After all, the cortex in my brain was then still developing. Perhaps some neurotransmitter made a particularly good connection. I can only hope the reason is not because I have always had an innate love of showing off or being shown off.

I remember one of my elder brothers frightening me at night by pretending to be a cat (for which thereafter he earned the nickname 'Meum'). My night nursery looked out into the rather inferior Ossington Street. I do remember seeing a lot of furniture one morning there on the pavement. Looking back over nearly seventy years I have a clear recollection of a washbasin in the street; I suppose some family must have been turned out of their house. I suspect that a feeling of despair on behalf of the homeless began right back at this episode.

I was looked after by a nanny. When I was very young, my brothers, who were five and seven years older than myself, were also nursery children, and so at that time there was a nurserymaid as well, who later actually became the nanny to one of my brother's own children. It is hard nowadays to communicate what it was like to live in the nanny culture of the 1920s. The nursery was a little empire of its own, disliked by the servants (who had to carry upstairs all the nursery meals) and distinct from one's parents' domain. When I was young I slept in the night nursery where nanny slept. (She continued *en famille* as a kind of family retainer even when I was away at prep. school.) The day nursery was my living-room. My parents of course visited the nursery: in the morning, my father came briefly before going out to work and my mother, when she was well, for perhaps half an hour. In the evening I was allowed 'downstairs' for an hour after tea; and my mother 'heard' my prayers. Otherwise there was apartheid, except when the whole family was on holiday together.

It was only a few years before my brothers graduated to the 'schoolroom' (their downstairs living-room), and so I was really left alone with nanny who in many ways became my mother substitute. She was devoted to me, but hardly a stimulating companion. She lived a lonely life without any real friends of her own. She came from a working-class Norfolk family: her father was an agricultural labourer, and she had had little formal education. Obviously she would consort with other nannies also exercising their charges in the Gardens, and those with Jewish children tended to congregate. My social life therefore as a small child was really determined by my nanny. With practically no contact with my brothers, and with very little contact with my parents, I was very dependent on her; and it is hardly surprising that I was a very lonely child.

As I look back now, and contrast how we brought up and nurtured our own daughters, it seems almost incredible that this way of bringing up children was not merely tolerated, but taken for granted in the kind of upper-middle-class family into which I found myself born. What terrible privation my parents must have (quite unconsciously) suffered from such a regime! And of course there is bound to be privation for the child subjected to this nurture without much contact with his peers (except for those whom he happened to meet in the Park, and who were occasionally invited back to tea in the nursery). This privation is increased by the habit of sending away children at a tender age to a prep. school and later to a public school.

Our family fortunes must have thrived, for we soon moved into a vast house near Kensington Palace in a private road called Palace Green, sometimes unkindly dubbed Palestine Green. Our house has since become the Israeli Embassy. It gave me a funny feeling when the Embassy was bombed in 1944. The house had once been the home of William Makepeace Thackeray, the famous Victorian novelist whom Virginia Glendinning, Trollope's biographer, describes as 'reconstructing an ambitious Queen Anne mansion in a Palace Green in Kensington'. However, the description of the house which has most surprised me I found in one of Jeffrey Archer's thrillers. In *Honour Among Thieves*, Hannah was summoned to the Israeli Embassy and told 'Top of the stairs, the door straight in front of you.' She climbed the wide staircase, and (in the story) found herself talking to the chief Mossad agent in London. Unknowingly she would have walked straight into my old night nursery. Actually I did once visit the house when it was the Israeli Embassy, when Israeli ten pound notes were issued with Moses Montefiore's face on them. We were each given one. (Can you believe it? Each one was overstamped 'Specimen'!) On that occasion I did ask to see my old bedroom (my mother had innocently moved me to the maids' landing when I needed a room of my own – but no dalliance took place). Not unnaturally the bedroom was then an office. Strangely enough, from the pictures, it seems to have borne the brunt of the 1944 bomb.

It was indeed a large house, with the chauffeur's flat at the end of the garden: a large garden for London, with a conservatory which produced luscious black grapes. There were (not counting the chauffeur and nanny) eight servants: a butler (who got drunk in the local pubs where he was known as 'Lord Kensington'), a parlourmaid and an underparlourmaid, a head housemaid and an underhousemaid, a cook and a kitchenmaid, and an 'odd man' (which referred not to his character, but his doing odd jobs about the place). They all had meals in the servants' hall in the basement where they seemed to sit in some kind of hierarchical order. One of my vivid memories is the only time my father ever beat me, because I had assaulted the cook for not voting in a recent General Election. Evidently my political interests started young, but I cannot remember whether then I had any party preference. I do remember the General Strike of 1926, with soldiers camped in Kensington Gardens, and the only newspaper the single sheet of the *London Gazette*. In my mid-teens I used to complain to my parents that I was ashamed to bring my schoolfriends to this vast mansion; that was, I think, one of the reasons why at the beginning of the Second World War they moved to a smaller house in Addison Road (now demolished). However, it could not have been as small as all that, because it later became the Ceylonese High Commission, in the days before the country was called Sri Lanka.

At Palace Green we were fortunate in having fascinating next-door neighbours. No. 3 was a small cottage hidden behind large bushes, the old home of the washerwoman of Kensington Palace in the time of Princess Victoria and her mother. In it lived Estella Canziani, an artist of some distinction, who had painted the then well-known picture, much reproduced, called 'The Piper of Dreams'. I have got the original of a water colour she painted in a 'college' collection, of the garden of my Oxford college, complete with its 'burning bush plant'; Her old father too was a painter. He was also psychic. My mother remembered standing in their large studio, when the old man said: 'My goodness! Look who's just come in through the window!' My mother, of course, saw no one. I liked Estella because she used to invite me to her bubble parties in her garden in the summer. We all blew bubbles and ate strawberries and cream. Of course this wonderful and historic old cottage has now been pulled down and a huge and hideous millionaire's house put in its place.

My childhood was not particularly exciting. I remember my first venture into journalism, producing a ghastly tabloid called the *Jazzy Paz*. My father, before he went to the office each day, had taught me to read reasonably accurately in a book entitled *Reading Without Tears*. My schooling started with Miss Manville in the schoolroom. She spent her life instructing the children of leading Anglo-Jewish families and impressed on me that I was among the most fortunate of all children, belonging to the most famous of all nations with the largest of all empires, and at the same time a member of the Jewish race and so one of the 'chosen people', marked out by God as heir to all the privileges of divine election (although of course she did not use that kind of theological language to a five year old).

At about the age of seven I went to a private day school in Orme Square – Wilkinson's. When I was nine I had my first taste of anti-Semitism. I was friends with another Jewish boy called Friedlander, and we both worked hard and so were not overpopular. On one occasion I was seized, and a hot poker from the fire applied to my leg above the knee joint. When I showed it to my mother during the lunch hour, she sensibly insisted that it be dressed, and my stocking pulled up over it (I was still wearing shorts) and that I returned to school as though nothing had happened. Times have changed. There are no open fires today, and even if there were, I doubt if that would happen.

It was my first experience of anti-Semitism, but I don't think that that was how I thought of it; at the time it just seemed like bullying. It was only later that I recognised it as anti-Semitic. Jews expect a degree of this; after all, Christians have discriminated against them now for some sixteen hundred years. In those days the Holocaust had not been imagined – how could you imagine the deliberate murder of a whole people? Although Britain was a country to which Jews had escaped from pogroms in their own countries, from Russia and the Balkans, and although in the period when I was brought up there was not much open hostility against Jews – Sir Oswald Mosley and his Blackshirts came later – nonetheless some clubs and golf courses would not admit them to membership; and in any case the memory of anti-Semitism lies deeply embedded in the Jewish folk memory. Jewish families celebrate every year the festivals of Purim and Hanukah, and these festivals commemorate the hostility of Gentiles towards Jews.

This made a Jewish boy very sensitive about jokes against Jews, and the often unconscious anti-Semitic language that was common in the days when I was young; phrases like 'Don't behave like a little Jewboy.' I remember the shock that I felt when the Principal of my theological college used the phrase to 'Jew it', meaning to behave in a grasping way. It did not help when, on an other occasion, someone, realising that I am a Jew, added hastily to some anti-Semitic remark 'Of course I don't mean you': that only made things worse.

When I was about ten I was sent to a residential prep. school in Minchinhampton, called Beaudesert Park. There we were well taught, and I was happy. We could play golf on Minchinhampton Common, and I had the place to myself on Sunday mornings when everyone else had to go to church. The school is now a trust and going strong. It's funny the things that one remembers from one's prep. school: the headmaster playfully pulling my cheek by way of rebuke, wet Sunday afternoons when we had to rack our brains for something to say in our compulsory weekly letter home, doing nothing in a dormitory with measles for what seemed weeks, and the headmaster's wife saying in a cheery voice to the natural history enthusiasts on beetles 'Come along now, you buggers'; and a very mature boy who was seduced by the matron (authority never found out, but we were all agog). The rest of us were very ignorant about sexual matters; the current view was that babies were born with the mother sitting on the lavatory seat. I can't believe that twelve year olds today are so innocent.

What about the holidays? When I was very young, I was taken to Littlehampton, and later I went away with my nanny at Easter to board and lodgings at Swanage, and I can remember boring high teas, blustery weather, and foam spuming over the Old Harry Rocks. Sometimes I went with a very distant cousin, Catherine Joseph, because our nannies were great friends. When we were young we were bathed together. When we grew a few years older, we were both interested in, but ignorant of, the other's peculiarities (she from a female family and I from a male); and I remember we once showed them to each other behind a large tree at Ken Wood Towers by the swimming bath (the home of my Waley Cohen cousins). Later still in my early teens, after complaining to my mother that I never saw any girls, I went on a cycle tour in Brittany with her and her mother and sisters. After we grew up we had nothing in common, I thought; but I noticed one of her sons was called Hugh. She is now dead.

Occasionally when I was older the whole family went touring in a car in France or the Ardennes. My oldest brother was away, and I was made to share a room with my other brother who objected very strongly to the smell of my oil painting. (At Rugby I was then spending most of my spare time in the Art School.) To keep the peace, my father had to go to the expense of giving us separate rooms. My father's French was rather rudimentary, but that did not inhibit his fluency in a somewhat polyglot style, in which even Hebrew words might be interspersed, to the great delight of his family.

In the summer we went as a family to Scotland. I loved the overnight train journey, lulled to sleep by the rhythm of the wheels, and then real porridge for breakfast on Aberdeen station. In those days the Deeside line to Ballater was still in action, and I was fond of flattening pennies on the line. Sometimes I and my nanny would accompany the chauffeur in the car, an old Studebaker. Everything went at a sedate pace in those days, and we would spend two nights travelling. My father was a keen salmon fisherman on the Dee, and first we used to stay at the Huntley Arms Hotel at Aboyne by the village green, and later on at Profeits Hotel at Dinnet, five miles further up the valley. I remember how I and my nanny would make a fire by the side of Dinnet Loch behind the hotel, and bake potatoes in it. I would also be allowed a little trout fishing up the Gairn on picnics.

In my early teens my father bought a holiday house one mile east of Dinnet, called *Tygh-na-Bruaich*, with stained pine walls. We had it for a good many years. I loved it there. It was only one acre in extent, but somehow a tennis court was made, and this meant social life. I could now make friends with people who lived nearby, go to tennis parties and picnic dances, and – oh the bliss of it – meet girls, who were almost entirely lacking in our nearly all male household. Some of them I even grew quite fond of, and I can still remember their names: Anne and Heather and Almora, to start with. People were wonderfully friendly. I learnt to dance 'Strip the Willow' and 'Dashing White Sergeant' and to do a foursome reel, as well as shuffling round in the foxtrot and quickstep. It was all very innocent and great fun. And there was swimming in

Loch Davan and glorious walks in the heather: Dinnet Moor was a showpiece.

The events of the season were the Aboyne Ball (which at fifteen I was considered too young to attend), the Aboyne Sheepdog Trials and the Aboyne Games. I remember thinking we must have 'arrived' when my father became a patron of the Games. The Marquis of Huntly was chief of the Gordon clan. The 'Cock o' the North' was an impoverished Highlander forced to marry an American millionairess. I persuaded him to give me written permission to wear a Gordon kilt, as we had a house within Gordon 'territory'. However, Mr Youngson, the tailor at Aboyne, refused to make one for a Sassenach like me. We all had a new pair of plus fours for the Aboyne Games every year, and as they had more than a year's wear in them, they tended to pile up. In the fitting room, Mr Youngson would dash around me, making marks with tailor's chalk and muttering 'A wee bitty here, and a wee bitty there'.

I was never considered old enough to go with the rest of the family on the really tough mountain walks, to Ben Macdhui, or through the Larig Ghru pass to Speyside. By that time, as I have mentioned earlier, I had begun to be fascinated by painting. A schoolmaster from Aberdeen Grammar School called Winckley brought a caravan on his annual Deeside holiday, and did really quite good watercolours, some of which I still possess. I used to go out painting with him, and learnt a lot. I remember one occasion when a quite terrible thunderstorm came down the side of Morven mountain, and forked lightning was all around us: we abandoned our pushbikes and despite the downpour went ahead and lay down in the heather. Thunderstorms seemed to abound in those days. On one occasion when two thunderstorms met over the house one night, balls of fire ran along the telephone wires and Bella the cook started running around shouting 'I be affeerd, I be affeerd'. No wonder.

We had frequent troubles with our water supply which tended to dry up in summer until my father had a 'ram' put in at a spring below the house. (A ram is an ingenious machine which uses the force generated by a fall of water to pump it up to the house.) This water shortage gave us a quite undeserved reputation locally of being people who 'washed up in Malvern water'. We only drank it on these occasions. One year my father took some rough shooting, but his temperament was too excitable. One day when a rabbit ran back, he unfortunately shot at it, and peppered one of my brothers, who claimed that only a cigarette lighter in his waistcoat pocket had saved him from being shot in the heart; but my eldest brother regards this as an exaggeration. At any rate the story went around that this was the father who had shot his son. As a result, he had a near nervous breakdown, and had to be packed off to South Africa for a time with his doctor as his companion.

Throughout this period my mother was subject to regular bouts of illness. It was never clear exactly what was the matter. Lumps came up on her body, and went down again. She went off to quack nursing homes for cures – twenty-eight days once on orange juice. There was not just homoeopathy, but tissue salts and other strange medicaments. Much time was spent in bed, and silence often had to prevail in the house. I can remember in Scotland my father trying to bribe us to silence by offering twopenny bars of chocolate. A room for her had to be built at the back of the house in Scotland, where she could have rest; and in London she complained so strongly of a smell in her bedroom (which no one else could detect) that my long-suffering father put in air conditioning before its time. It was very sad, because, due to all this illness, I saw little of her. When she was well, she was great fun, full of good humour with an attractive giggle, and people grew very fond of her. My father, who was pre-eminently successful in his stockbroking business, would have been Lord Mayor of London, but of course he had to withdraw from the *cursus honorum* on account of my mother's health. She grew interested in women's freemasonry and in astrology; but of course she had nothing to do, except manage the household with the help of all those maids. During the war she came into her own working with the WVS (Women's Voluntary Service). She loved that and was really happy.

It was not until after the war that her periods of elation and depression grew worse and she was diagnosed by the specialist Dr Yellowlees as a manic depressive. For short periods she even had to be 'sectioned' and put in a home where she was forced to have electric shock treatment which she very properly hated and feared. During this later period she would blow very hot and cold with her children. In a sense it was a relief when another brother was out of favour, because it meant that one was safe oneself; but we all knew that we would cop it in turn. Also, it was extremely unwise to regard any present she might give (and she was very generous) as a permanent gift: it might be required back at any time. When she gave money away it usually had strings to it in the form of a trust, so that sooner or later it would return to the family. Perhaps this was no bad thing! On one occasion, after the war, when she was over the top, she once bought up the entire contents of a shop full of Chinese antiques! Fortunately my father persuaded the owner to take them back again.

After the war she and my father moved for a time to a flat in Roehampton. She then decided to live on her own at Bexhill. My father's doctor had advised him that it was too much of a strain on him for them to live together. She had Betty to look after her, who lived in a large caravan in the garden. She did not want to live in the homes of any of her three sons: she said she did not want to be a burden to them; and in any case it would not have worked. She had become very fond of Dorothy Kerin the healer, who had herself been miraculously healed – there is no other word for it but that. Dorothy had also adopted nine children. She had little idea how to look after them, and I think my mother gave her some practical advice. Dorothy was very good to her. She made her permanent home in a bedroom at Burrswood, Dorothy Kerin's lovely home of healing which still flourishes today; and she gave the organ to its chapel.

It was, I am sure, due to Dorothy Kerin's influence that my mother became a Christian. She was baptised, although this was not publicised in the family. Dorothy had been able to help her where I could not. I am sure that it was not on my account that this happened, although my example may have helped her. Looking back now, I blame myself that we were not more intimate, but there was this psychological blockage. I think she was a little in awe of me as a priest. I loved her dearly, but it was a love mixed with continual guilt. She seldom actually scolded me (it was the same with my father); but she could exude an almost visible aura of disapproval. Although it sounds awful to say, I'm afraid that I did not really feel free until she was dead. I was with her when she did die in 1972 at the age of eighty-one: her blood pressure was very high (it could go up and down like a yo-yo), and she had had a stroke. It was the first time I had held someone's hand when that person actually died. Her death was the most peaceful thing in the world: she simply stopped breathing. I hope and pray that in the next world she is rid of the dreadful imperfections of her human body, and able to be her true self, which was a rare spirit when she was normal. I am glad that her troubled years ended serenely at Burrswood, where she was cared for with great love and forbearance. There was something very bizarre about her funeral, which she had requested me to take. Apart from the undertaker, the only people present besides myself were my two brothers, both of course practising Jews, which made me feel very selfconscious. I took the 1662 Funeral Service just as it stood. There seemed something extraordinarily appropriate about the phrase 'delivered from the burdens of the flesh'.

My mother and father were really ill-suited, in fact she had thought of breaking off her engagement, but she was dissuaded, as wedding presents had already started arriving. (I am glad she didn't, as I would not have existed.) My father was restless and energetic, my mother more interested in music and the arts. But they were both genuinely fond of each other. My father was the senior partner of the family broking firm. At Clifton College he had been in Polack's, the Jewish house, and although he always played for the First XV at rugger, he could not get his colours, because he could never play in the main school matches which took place on Saturdays. This, thankfully, made him resolve never to send his sons to Clifton. My two brothers went to Wellington College, and, as I shall recount, I went to Rugby School.

He was a superactivist. He captained the Wasps, the well-known Rugby club. Before his marriage he spent a lot of time at the Victoria Boys' Club in the East End, and went on camps with them; and from time to time he preached. Nothing was too much trouble for him; he looked after all the needs of his extended family. He went to committee after committee meetings of Jewish voluntary organisations. One of his great loves was Finnart House School in north London, an 'approved' school for offending Jewish boys, which was very successful. A Christian chapel had to be built because there were not enough Jewish delinquents to fill the place! He was always at odds with what he called 'those stupid fellows at the Home Office'; and it is said that this was the reason why he was rewarded for a lifetime of social service only with an OBE instead of a knighthood. He also built up a most successful broking firm and he was very popular in the city of London. When he joined it, 'Sebags' was a small family firm dealing mostly with trusts: when he left it, it was among the half dozen largest brokers in the city, with a vastly increased number of partners and concerned with bringing out many new issues. After he retired, the lack of his leadership was apparent; the firm lost its way, and had to stop trading.

At home he was always a kind father, although we did not see much of him except on holidays. He was wonderfully forbearing of my mother's illness. He would say to us 'Your mother's rather seedy today'; and we knew that trouble was ahead. I never once heard him complain. He had a large tummy, and it must be said he was very fond of his food. His attempts to lose weight seem ludicrous by today's standards and seemed to consist mostly of eating cotton-wool-type rolls instead of bread. He could usually be lured out of gloom (and my mother's health gave him much cause for gloom) by tempting him with food. Even on holidays the firm seemed supreme: salmon landed with difficulty from the

Dee in Scotland were tied up in a 'bass' bag and sent off to key customers. Shopping with him was quite an experience. The name of Sebag-Montefiore was so distinctive that salesmen tended to assume there could be only one person of such a surname; and accounts tended to be mixed up. When my father's birthday present to my mother, bought at Harrods, was charged to my mother's account, my father really blew up. He cancelled his account and opened another in the name of Julius Caesar to ensure no further mix-ups. It used to cause me acute embarrassment when the salesman would ask my father, with his pencil poised over the bill, 'What name, sir, please?' and my father would respond 'Julius Caesar'. Sometimes the man thought my father was joking.

My father loved entertaining in Palace Green in the huge dining-room with Adam and Eve carved in wood on each side of the fireplace; but I fear my mother found it a great burden before she became too ill to attempt it. My father was not naturally a tidy man. He spilled so much food on his clothes that my mother used to call him a walking menu. The *Illustrated London News* called him the worst dressed man in the city. I fear it is a case of 'like father, like son'. Towards the end of his life, when he lived in the flat in Roehampton, arterio-sclerosis set in, and not enough blood got through to the brain. He became silent and morose, and had to be led in front of his portrait to remind him who he was. He died in 1960 a few years after a recurrence of cancer which had first appeared earlier. Before his death I had never heard a death rattle (and I hope never to hear it again). His body was laid to rest in the Jewish cemetery in Ramsgate, alongside the rest of his family. (I suspect my mother knew that, because she had been baptised, her body could not be laid to rest alongside his, and so she had asked for hers to be cremated.) Jewish funerals in the open air have a pleasing informality lacking in our Christian equivalent. One of the great honours that can be given to a Jewish man is to be a Lavantadore, one of those who washes and lays out the dead. Christians pay undertakers to do it. Another pleasing feature is that Jews have to be buried in a simple coffin. We were given hard-boiled eggs afterwards to remind us of resurrection.

We were brought up as a religious family, both my parents being genuinely religious. My father, whom I admired greatly, took a great interest in community affairs, and was president of the Spanish and Portuguese (Sephardi) congregation in Lauderdale Road. We used to go to synagogue there most Saturdays. However, Lauderdale Road was a long way from where we lived, and we would drive nearby and walk the last two hundred yards, so as not to offend the stricter members of the congregation who kept to the 'sabbath day's journey'. One wasn't really expected to be present when the service began.

We were modestly 'frum', keeping to the biblical rather than the rabbinic kosher rules. Any part of the pig was utterly forbidden, rabbit never appeared nor did shellfish. But I remember my brother, after consuming 'fruits de mer' one night on a holiday in Brittany, coming down to breakfast next morning looking very white and muttering 'Moses knew best'. We were not finicky about food. Of course we kept Tabernacles as a kind of harvest festival and waved around our 'lulabs' (boughs of willow and palm and a lemon). We lit the lights of Hanukah. Naturally, we had been circumcised, a matter not without interest to my Gentile schoolfellows. Synagogue worship was pleasingly informal compared with its ecclesiastical equivalent. Women were upstairs in the gallery, and the men below would wear a white shawl or 'taleth'. There was a certain amount of chatter both downstairs and upstairs; but generally the atmosphere was devout. When we did not go to synagogue, we usually had family prayers which my father led. In Jewish thinking, a father acts as priest to his family. Judaism is basically a family faith, not an institutional one. I cannot help thinking that the family spirituality of a Jewish family is more intimate and preferable to the more formal kind of spirituality often found in Christian families.

The Day of Atonement, the day of fasting when Jews ask for divine forgiveness for their sins, was a big effort. The service went on all day, and there was a very great deal of confession: 'Ashamnoo, vagamnoo, haramnoo' (we have sinned, we have erred, we have gone astray . . .). We came home to a meal of immense quantities of cold fried fish, so that I always doubted whether there was a net debit of food on the day. We kept the Seder Service on Passover Eve, a lovely informal occasion; and sometimes, as the youngest present, I would say the 'Manishtanah' ('Why is this night different from other nights . . .'). One of my brothers always got helpless giggles when an exercise in Jewish numerology (which is always read out at the service) managed to increase the number of the Ten Plagues to 150. Unfortunately the family is not musical, so the chanting of the Hallel (the joyful psalms) was cacophonous, to put it mildly. The occasion is really a meal with a service within it, in contrast to Christian Holy Communion, which is the other way round. At the conclusion of the service, the family has a tradition of reading aloud an excerpt from Sir Moses Montefiore's diary. It recounts how the ship in which he was travelling was going to be wrecked in an awful Mediterranean storm, when he scattered on the waves a piece of last year's Passover Matzah (which is always retained as a talisman), after which the sea abated and there was a great calm.

Of course I was bar mitzvah. This is a rite of passage when one comes of age in the Jewish community, around the age of thirteen. A male Jew becomes a 'son of the commandment', liable to the duties of the law and responsible for carrying out its injunctions. The ceremony is marked by reading a portion of that part of the Law of Moses set in the lectionary for a particular sabbath. Usually this is chanted by the minister, and customarily people are 'called up' to the dais in turn to witness the chanting; but on this occasion the bar mitzvah boy has to chant it himself. This is a great ordeal for a thirteen year old. There are two particular snags. The scroll of the law in Hebrew characters is not vocalised: the chanter has to provide the vocalisation. (Some bar mitzvah boys simply learn it by heart phonetically without knowing any Hebrew at all.) So far as I was concerned the great difficulty was the chanting, for I am, if not stone deaf, very unmusical. (Later on even the great Sir David Willcocks could not get me to sing even the Anglican versicles in tune, and my later attempts have brought distinguished choirs to a total standstill.) After the service there is a great feast, and many presents, some of which I still have. I was prepared for my bar mitzvah by the minister, the Revd David Bueno de Mesquita. When attired in his liturgical gown and top hat, he looked like his name, every inch a Spanish grandee, even to twirling mustachios. He was a real gentleman and also a man of God. I doubt whether he liked being at the beck and call of the congregation who had hired him.

We often went for Passover to the London flat of my Aunt Ida. We also used to visit Thorne, her estate in the West Country. She had been married to Robert, my father's elder brother, the head of the family: she was a Samuel, the daughter of Lord Bearsted. She had two sons: Arthur, and James who was a blue baby before the condition could be cured. He was a brave man who, despite his condition, raced at Cowes before he died. Arthur, the elder and the heir, was a daredevil; jumping over stone walls onto roads when hunting, motor racing at Brooklands and flying aeroplanes. This activity eventually was his undoing, because he crashed at Manston, leaving a young wife, Jackie, who married again, and two small children, both of whom have settled outside Britain. I remember being driven by Arthur down narrow Devonshire country lanes at breakneck speed, bottling up within myself mixed feelings of hopelessness and helplessness.

My father's mother, who died when I was four, was a Beddington, a branch of the Moses family who changed their name to that of an old English village. (Many Jewish families when they settled in England sensibly anglicised their surnames, of which I suppose the classic case is Montagu Samuel becoming Samuel Montagu.) My father was one of six children. His eldest brother, who died in the war, has an exhibition at Balliol College Oxford in his memory, and there used to be the Robert Montefiore Jewish aided primary school in the East End, also named after him (he had been a keen member of the old London County Council).

Of my father's two other brothers, one was a soldier, a gunner, who had once been peacetime adjutant and later became Honorary Colonel of the Royal Bucks Yeomanry, the regiment in which I served during the war. His wife was a sweet gentle lady, but her husband's bluff army ways must have been too much for her: she committed suicide. (Once when he was staying with us in his widowhood, he took off his socks on the sofa, pushed his foot towards my mother and said: 'Muriel, cut my toenails'. She did. One did not lightly disobey his orders.) There were three children of the marriage: the eldest son was a brilliant Eton scholar, but tragically he got pneumonia at school before the days of antibiotics and died. A daughter was also very bright, and got a First in History at Cambridge and married a professor of Sinology in California who sadly drowned on holiday. The other son has been a regular soldier. My uncle had distinguished himself in the First World War with a DSO and bar. He liked horses and had jumped for the army, but he could never reconcile himself to the motorisation of gunner regiments. Because he refused to go to Staff College he never reached the higher ranks of the army, but he was a well-known and much-liked army character.

My father's other brother was an agent at Lloyds during a period when this was a safe job, unlike today. He had five children. His parents-in-law also lived in the same road as us, next to the Russian Embassy. My father also had two sisters. The husband of one of them was an honorary consultant to the zoo, and one never knew what one would find in their house in Westbourne Terrace: I remember once a marmoset. My mother felt she was not always taken very seriously there. On one occasion when she went to tea, my aunt said to the maid: 'The second best tea service will do for Mrs Montefiore.' One of her children was one of my few real boyhood friends to come from the 'nanny network'; sadly he was killed in the war. My father's second sister at one time lived in Barnet, and I used to see something of her children. She was always somewhat short of money. Her husband did not earn his living, or rather he lived by shooting and fishing, and selling what he shot or caught. This naturally took him from home for most of the time, a factor which I suspect was important to him.

There were no first cousins on my mother's side, only two aunts. My uncle William Hugh I never knew, because he was killed before I was born. My grandfather was a most unpsychic kind of person, but during the battle of the Somme he heard his son cry 'Daddy, Daddy' and knew that he was dead. Charles de Pass had been a stockbroker, like my father. I suspect that my father's great success in that profession did not altogether commend him! My maternal grandparents used to live in a huge corner house in Queen's Gate. I can remember that, when I went there for Sunday lunch, at times there was straw in the street, to soften the noise of traffic outside for a very sick person.

We had lunch in a large dining-room with a great silver centrepiece on the table, waited on by Goddard, who had been their parlourmaid for years. After lunch my grandfather would take me into his study, seat me opposite his large safe, put on his skull cap, and tell me stories about Good Dog Fido. He also used to hold out a five pound note, and tell me I could have it if I guessed the numbers. I was very peeved once when I got all the numbers right except one, but got nothing. His wife Mabel was a Benjamin from New Zealand. She came over to marry him, but her sailing ship was six weeks overdue, and when she did arrive everyone was in mourning, thinking the ship had been lost. I got the impression, perhaps wrongly, that she was an ineffective person who never had anything to do, and that she was completely dominated by my grandfather. She was very sweet natured. They used to holiday at the Station Hotel Strathpeffer in Scotland (in those days all station hotels were very comfortable), and occasionally, when my parents and brothers were at our holiday house in Aberdeenshire, I would go north and stay a couple of nights with them. I can only remember the absolutely scrumptious hotel breakfasts.

My grandfather lived in a purely female establishment, which he must have found rather difficult. He had quarrelled with his synagogue over the dues which were required of him, so he did not attend worship; but he never in any way renounced his Jewishness like some others of his family. Esme, the youngest of his daughters, like her mother, never seemed to do anything and sadly died of cancer. Her sister Kathleen was a top class skater, who used to spend most of her time at the Westminster Ice Rink; she was a friend of Sonya Henye and the other champion skaters of the time.

She turned down many offers of marriage, but eventually married Hans, an Austrian, who was employed to dance in an Austrian hotel. This greatly distressed my grandfather, who decided that he had given his daughters enough, and left all his money to 'charitable and benevolent uses'. My two aunts challenged the will in court, on the ground that the phrase was legally meaningless – and won. They took the lot. The ex-skater's husband was locked away with other aliens in the Isle of Man during the war, and no one could get him out. She followed her husband's faith, and became a Roman Catholic. They had no children, and settled near Taunton, where they farmed. I visited them very seldom because of their ferocious Doberman pinschers to which they were devoted.

The effect of my becoming a Christian did, I think, alienate me from my family somewhat, although it did not make me feel less Jewish; more so, if anything. After all, Jesus was a Jew, and I could only understand Christianity as the fulfilment of Judaism. My affection for my parents was undiminished, and theirs for me; but there was, I think, a certain restraint between us, of which I was aware on the few occasions when I was at home during the holidays. But this may have been due perhaps to 'adolescent revolt' and to a more radical political outlook. (I remember once at Palace Green having to retire to my bedroom with a palpitating heart because of some deep disagreement over social matters.) I did not in any case see much of my two brothers, Oliver and Denzil, who were much older than I was; in a sense I was rather like an only child. In any case they both married soon after I became a Christian. Certainly in later years there was on two occasions a complete rupture of relationships with one of them, first when I was at a Cambridge college and I went to Israel on sabbatical leave without telling him; and secondly because I preached at Eton College when his son was at school there (but he did not attend chapel). Happily I am now in a warm relationship with him – our wives managed to smooth things over.

My aunts, uncles, cousins and grandparents had formed part of the environment in which I grew up. Jews tend to have an extended rather than a nuclear family. Their presence added to my security, and helped me to find my identity. But since I have become a Christian I have over the years seen little of them. I do not know what most of them think of my conversion; but I know that at least one of them thinks I have disgraced the family name. Over the years we have inevitably been out of contact. First I was away at school, then at university, then in the army, and after the war my ministry for many years was outside London where most of them lived, so opportunities for meeting have been rare. But this could not have been the only reason for our not meeting, because during this period I have had warm and supportive relations with my wife's family wherever they were living, and I was in a quite close relationship with her mother when I was in Cambridge and she in St Albans. Since I retired, contacts with some of my family have happily been resumed.

But this is to anticipate the future. Back in my prep. school days the headmaster's youngest son who was my contemporary won a scholarship to Eton, and I was keen to go there too. (We met up again later in the same regiment during the war.) Although I got on to the Eton Scholarship Roll, I was too far down it to be offered a place in college, and it was not possible for the school to accommodate me as an oppidan scholar; I suspect this was not unconnected with my Jewish blood. At any rate I went to Rugby School, and thank God I did! It was one of the happiest times of my life. My first year I went to a kind of waiting house, with a master called Jim Bruce, his sister Marjorie and his mother looking after four or five of us. In fact this was a good preparation for the rigours of School House which lay ahead.

Initiation ceremonies still took place as in *Tom Brown's School-days*, but in those enlightened days one was only tossed in a blanket in the corridor. I was of course a fag; actually Freddy Temple's, the nephew of Archbishop Temple, chairman of the governors. I had to clean out his study and do his errands. If there was a fag call, we fags had to run into the yard, and the last one to arrive got the chore. As School House was a warren of corridors, steep steps and alcoves, and as there was a certain amount of jostling, the race was not without dangers: I can remember one boy breaking his leg. Naturally all such practices have now been stopped, and a successful appeal has gone out for School House to be completely re-styled inside.

As the headmaster was the housemaster of School House, a lot of the work of running the House devolved upon the head of House; and there were also two tutors. Anyone in the sixth form had the powers of a prefect; and that included the power of beating, with the permission of Head of House: three goes with a fives bat. And of course there might be beatings from the staff, but these were rare. People ask today 'Wasn't it humiliating?' But, no, it wasn't. Faced with 'one hundred lines' (writing out something one hundred times) or a beating, the latter though more painful was quickly over; and one's bottom could be judiciously padded. However, some of the penalties for which a beating was prescribed I found extremely trivial, like leaving one's bicycle under the wrong arch of the quadrangle!

I know boys can be beastly but they can also be friendly; and I made many friends, a few of whom still remain today, sixty years later. Exercise had to be taken every afternoon; if not games, then a run (the shortest was known as Billy Belch, allegedly after Archbishop William Temple). I passed into a middle school form, and I realised that I had entered a new world when my form master the first day, sitting on a dais in the formroom, announced: 'My name is Frank William Odgers, I live at No. 1 Hillmorton Road and I go to the lavatory twice a day.' I was still young enough to sit for an entrance scholarship, which I duly won, and was given a double remove into a class with the other scholars, with whom I moved up the school.

The staff at Rugby then were superb; in fact they were too good, because they tended in turn to disappear to become headmasters of other schools. Over a dozen left in this way. Having started on Greek and Latin at my prep. school, I naturally drifted into the Classical stream, which I thoroughly enjoyed. Of course we looked up all the dirty words we could find in the Latin and Greek dictionaries, but most of them seem to appear naturally when doing the classics, especially if one is reading Aristophanes. I can still hear one of the Classical masters lisping: 'Will you pleath go on conthtrue, Thebag-Montefiore?' We were well taught: eight of my year won Classical awards at Oxbridge colleges. Many of the staff had a considerable influence on me, but I must mention one, Roger Roberts, who was pre-eminent. In my time he taught the 'Upper Bench' at Classics. A brilliant young scholar and a convinced Christian, he made us analyse the Sunday sermon in chapel, not always to the advantage of the preacher. Although later he behaved most oddly as a disastrous headmaster of Blundells, I am personally very grateful to him. He sowed in me the seeds of a passion for Christian truth and the need to ask awkward questions while remaining firmly convinced as a Christian. This has had a profound effect on me for the whole of my ordained ministry.

We were worked very hard at Rugby, and I am grateful for that too. I can remember school before breakfast in the summer, and a cold 'tosh' every morning before breakfast, with the penalty of a beating if it were skipped. We were at one stage required to learn the whole of Milton's *Lycidas* by heart. I am so glad I was made to learn by heart at Rugby: it is sad that this has now gone out of fashion in education. The best lessons I learnt from the school were honesty and hard work. Of course there were games, but the sixth-form power system prevented an athletocracy. I was a keen rugger player, and ended up by getting my colours in the school rugger XV to my infinite satisfaction. I was, in the kindly words of the XV coach, 'on the whole more of a threat to the other side than to my own'. Boys were expected to join the Officers Training Corps, and field days with blanks in our rifles were in more senses than one a day out. It was fun pulling the trigger with the barrel under water. Looking for a soft option I decided to join the aircraft section, which was admirable until, against all expectation, parts of an aeroplane appeared. I was in charge of the section, so I retired hastily into the Scouts, which was happily an alternative to the OTC.

I greatly enjoyed being in the School House because it meant that we saw a lot of Hugh Lyon, the Headmaster, his wife Nan, and his two daughters Eleanor and Barbara. Hugh had a rare combination of virtues which meant that he was a great encourager as well as a shrewd teacher and counsellor; he was also an administrator, pastor, preacher and poet. His unpretentiousness got through a small boy's reserve, and he and his wife's hospitality prevented one from feeling that one was locked away in an institution. I owe to him more than I can say. For example, one summer he took over a prep. school, Fyling Hall School, near Scarborough, and invited not only members of his extended family but some of us boys: we had a marvellous time walking and bathing. He took parties of us to the League of Nations Summer School in Geneva. He was not just a headmaster: he was genuinely interested in people.

People always say that public schools are sinks of iniquity; but I can't say that this was true of Rugby in my time, at least not in School House. One boy who was caught with another *in flagrante delicto* when the headmaster came into his study was passed over for head of House: another could not control his feelings for another; and that is all I can remember that is out of the ordinary. Of course we enjoyed dirty stories; it would have been unnatural not to have done so. My parents, hardly surprisingly, were quite unable to tell me about the facts of life, and it was left for the headmaster to do this in a private talk, which came, alas, after puberty had begun. It was, of course, deeply frustrating being educated in an all-male establishment, especially as there were no girls at home; and I would not have wished to send any son of mine to such a set-up. It made me very awkward with girls for a long time.

Stimulated by those sketching lessons in Aberdeenshire, I spent most of my spare time in the Arts School, where there were two outstanding art masters, R. B. Talbot Kelly (well known for his studies of birds) and Denys Watkins-Pitchford (who became well known for his illustrations of books). I learnt oils, poster painting, water colours and etching; and also a bit of pottery. I only wish that I had kept up these skills after I left, for I got enormous satisfaction from these activities, even though I was not very good at any of them. In the summer, when I no longer had to play cricket, I used to go sketching in the Warwickshire countryside.

I have already told the story of my becoming a Christian at the age of sixteen. I then started going to chapel and attending religious education lessons in class. The feeling of religious exaltation gradually wore off, but it left me with a warm glow in my heart and an abiding conviction. I started reading the New Testament. I was no theologian; I remember my tutor, preparing me for confirmation, talking about the pre-existence of Christ, and it made no sense (it still doesn't). I continued with all my other school activities, with a feeling of heightened purpose and endeavour. Do many people make lasting friends at school? Mine have lasted – mostly from the form room rather than from School House. One, Hubert Monroe, became a distinguished tax lawyer and QC before dying prematurely of a heart attack. Another, Patrick Rodger, was in turn Bishop of Manchester and of Oxford. A third, Robin Barbour, with whom I went on a wonderful holiday in Greece during a summer holiday at school, became Professor of Theology at Aberdeen, and took his turn as Moderator of the Church of Scotland. And there are others. Friendship is sadly underrated in today's culture; it is one of the loveliest of God's gifts.

I tried for a Classics scholarship at Corpus Christi, Oxford, to which my uncle after whom I had been named had belonged; but I was unsuccessful. I stayed on an extra term to have another shot, and incidentally this meant that I was Head of School House for that term. As Head of House I was invited to meet the distinguished visitors who came to speak at the school. The two who stick out in my memory are Harold Nicholson and Archbishop William Temple. The latter, as chairman of the governors, came fairly frequently. I recall in his Speech Day oration long periods flowing effortlessly from his mouth, with subordinate clauses folding and unfolding like Ciceronian prose. He had a huge infectious laugh and a wonderful capacity for friendship with the young. (Everything about him was huge: it is said that his surplice came back from the laundry itemised as a 'bell tent'.) He invited me to come and stay a weekend at Bishopthorpe, an invitation which I was later to take up.

To my surprise (and I think others' too) I landed a major scholarship at St John's College, Oxford. Roger Roberts suggested that college because his brother was a Classics don there; not that

I ever had much to do with him. By the time I went up the war had started, and as a papyrus expert (he discovered the earliest fragment of St John's Gospel) he was very properly taken off to Bletchley to crack German codes. I saw more of him when I returned to the college after the war. Later he ran the Oxford University Press.

I am glad that I went to Rugby; I am very grateful to the school for what I was taught, how I was taught, and how I was treated. Certainly in those days the message of service came through loud and clear. But was I not brought up in a world apart, a world of the élite and the well heeled? This was the time of terrible unemployment in the 1930s, when there was ghastly poverty and despair, especially in Wales and the north of England. Were not we gilded youths given privileges which we neither deserved nor should have had? Well, yes, I suppose we were; but things being as they were, how could it have been otherwise? And Rugby did make some efforts. I remember the headmaster organising a trip to Wales and Durham. In Wales we were in the Rhondda Valley. I and John Hoskyns (a fellow-priest today and still my friend) were billeted in the house of the corporation dustman. Why? Because he had a steady job, and could afford to have us, while those out of work lived too near the bone. We spent the days with the unemployed at the 'levels'; that is to say, the holes that they had been allowed to drive into the hillside to get out coal for themselves and for their families to keep themselves from freezing. What these good and kindly men must have thought of us heaven only knows; but at least we were not patronising. We were there to learn, and it certainly opened our eyes. On another occasion we went to Durham to see conditions there, but all I can remember of that is sitting in Dean Allington's study and thinking that he had a grave but remarkable face.

I am not in favour of levelling down education to the lowest common denominator. If there are schools where boys can be really well taught, where they can be happy, where they can genuinely learn the lessons of service which go with privilege, then let parents pay the fees and I hope such schools can prosper – so long as they are not single-sex schools. Such views may not be so fashionable today; but times have greatly changed, and it is only too easy to make judgements about education out of context.

I left school in December 1938. I was not due to appear at St John's College until 1st October 1939. What was I to do? It was arranged for me to spend the spring term at a well-known prep. school, the Dragon School in Oxford. It is a co-educational establishment with a high reputation where the girls play rugger with the boys (they tend to be stronger at that age), and where far more liberty is given than

in most such institutions. I was detailed to teach spelling – the lowest
of the low – and Latin Verses (the highest of the high). I did not like
teaching and did not have any skills for the job. I had friends who
had not stayed on that extra term who were also in Oxford, but as
undergraduates. It was a strange experience at the Dragon School,
and it was made clear to me that, of all things I might ever do with
my life, teaching in schools was unlikely to be one of them.

And then what? Storm clouds were gathering over Europe, but my
father kindly arranged for me to spend the summer with a family in
Lausanne and attend the university there as an *auditeur*. I lodged at
72 Avenue de Bethusy with a family of decayed gentlefolk who lived
in a large house. There was little money, and the only people of
my age were Belgians who could not speak English; I *had* to
speak French. I was very lonely indeed, and I was glad that I had
brought with me some hefty books to read. I remember reading and
re-reading Evelyn Underhill's great book on mysticism, and William
Temple's *Nature, God and Man*. Both books had and still have a big
impact on me; I still have the pencil underlinings over fifty years on.
It is a pity that they are not popular today.

I tried to make friends through the English church, but it didn't
work out. Rugby had been bad enough, in the sense that it was an
all-male school, and one was never in the company of girls. It was
the same at home in the holidays, except in Scotland. And, even
in Lausanne, it still seemed to be the same. For a young man of
eighteen this was a most unnatural situation, but I survived; and
the countryside all around was glorious. I got home only a very few
weeks before war was declared.

It was clear that there would be a war. I was staying with a
great schoolfriend (who was killed in the war) whose father was
what in those days was called a 'gentleman farmer', the real family
income coming from making gin. (It is a monstrous phrase because
it suggests that ordinary farmers can't be gentlemen.) I used to go
out into the fields in the early morning to watch sheep, to see if they
were itching and had the tick. War had by then been declared. This
gave me solitude and time for reflection: should I fight or should I
not? How can it be Christian to take other people's lives? But then
I reflected on the fate of my fellow-Jews in Germany; and I realised
that I was prepared to let people lose their lives on dangerous seas
to bring food to me so that I could survive. In that situation I felt I
had no option but to do my best to stop such an evil monstrosity as
Nazism; I still think the same. So I went to the recruiting centre at
Oxford and received the King's shilling and became a member of the
army. It was something of an anti-climax after all that agonising to

be told that I would be called to the colours when I was wanted, and that I should go away again, for my first year at Oxford University. There was nothing for it but to obey. It was, as it were, my first taste of army discipline.

Chapter Three

WAR

To be a student at Oxford seemed like the fulfilment of a dream. It used to be said (in more sexist days) that an Oxford man walks the streets as though they belong to him, and a Cambridge man walks them as though he doesn't care to whom they belong. I certainly felt from the first moment that I belonged to Oxford and Oxford belonged to me. This was the city of dreaming spires, the seat of learning and a key centre of Anglicanism. When I arrived as an undergraduate, I felt that I had indeed 'arrived'. The High, the Broad, the Turl, the Sheldonian, Christ Church and Magdalene's beauties, Blackwell's bookshop – the list goes on and on, and they were now all part of my inheritance. Of course I had been in Oxford earlier in the year, teaching at a prep. school; that was north Oxford, and this was the real thing. Or was it for real? I fear that it was somewhat of a fantasy, and the reality was otherwise.

Oxford in wartime was very different from Oxford flourishing in a time of peace. Dons were away in the Services, or undertaking some work for the government. My own college had a consignment of 'fish and chips' – 'men from the ministry' evacuated from London, in this case the Ministry of Fisheries and Agriculture. Many clubs were in abeyance. Extravagance was out. Even if it was as yet the 'phoney war', people felt a little guilty at still pursuing 'education, religion, learning and research', Oxbridge's four official aims. The dons at Lady Margaret Hall were actually 'digging for victory' on their allotment.

I knew very little about St John the Baptist College before I arrived. I had not realised that it is one of the wealthiest colleges in Oxford, owning as it did then almost the whole of north Oxford (since then it has turned a lot of this into cash), with the names of its streets called after college livings. At the same time it was a modest college, with an intake largely from grammar schools, and with a reputation for hard work which later put it at the top of the league table. As a major scholar I was given a wonderful room in beautiful Canterbury Quad which you pass through to get to what must be the loveliest and largest of all Oxford college gardens. Canterbury Quad had been built by the famous Archbishop Laud as a public relations exercise to show off to the king. Laud had been President of the College, and was Chancellor of the University when the king and queen attended the feast to show off the new quad. It must have been some feast, as the cost of this occasion was more than half the cost of the building.

As a classicist I was doing a specially shortened Classical honour moderations, to be completed in a year. This meant a great deal of hard work, and the new experience of working on my own. However, there were quite a few 'freshers' doing the same subject, in particular men who had come from Merchant Taylors School in London. They seemed to have rooms all around and about me. The school was on the same foundation as St John's, with closed scholarships and a special connection. Our college prayer rather quaintly mentioned our joint founder, 'Sir Thomas White, Knight, and the ladies his wives . . .' (the wives were serial, not polygamous). I can't remember much about the lectures I attended, and I don't think I went to many of them; but I do remember Dr Roger Mynors' famous lectures on Virgil's *Eclogues* in Balliol, and E. R. Dodds on Greek Religion and Philosophy.

There were undergraduates who did not strike me particularly at the time, but who later made a name for themselves: a rather squidgy little English scholar called Kingsley Amis, people reading philosophy called Tony Flew and Peter Strawson, and a certain John Wain, who later wrote novels. I played for the college rugger XV – we were very proud of our full back, who was a Blue – and occasionally for the Greyhounds, the university Second XV, but clearly I was not in the top rank. I remember having fun at archery – there was an ancient college archery society, and fortunately the lawn in the college garden stretched into the distance for muscular long bowmen. I had to sit at the scholars' table in hall, and I was introduced into the folklore of sconces: if a person was accused of talking politics or religion at dinner in hall, and the challenge was allowed by high table, one had to drink a pint of ale in one long gulp to escape the penalty.

I was surprised at the very large complement of dons who came every Sunday evening to the college chapel. On the whole dons were friendly, among whom I must include Bill Moore, the modern linguist, W. C. Costin, the historian, and John Mabbott, the philosopher, the two latter subsequently becoming presidents of the college. The president at the time was a cadaverous-looking man of few words (and those spoken in a deep bass), Sir Cyril Norwood, who had formerly been Headmaster of Harrow School. The Chaplain, S. L. Greenslade, who later became Professor of Church History, was a nice man but so shy as to be useless as a chaplain other than for taking services.

Fortunately there were two or three stalwarts of the chapel who introduced me to the SCM (Students' Christian Movement). This organisation was later taken over in the 1960s by radicals, and politicised. In my day it really was a going concern. It took the Christian faith seriously, and had a fine tradition of spirituality; but it was not frightened by modern criticism and it was really interested in the getting at the truth of things rather than handing on church tradition. What is more, it was run by students, not even by its Oxford University chaplain, although Hort, a relation of the famous Cambridge New Testament scholar of the same name, was a great inspiration during my time. The SCM also gave one an opportunity of making friends of both sexes outside the college. Rachel Bailey (now Rachel Moss) was a leading light. I became very caught up with the movement, and in wartime Oxford I quickly became a member of the executive. There was a certain undergraduate from Lady Margaret Hall, Elisabeth Paton, who was co-president for the year. We made friends, and she later became my wife. Not for nothing was SCM sometimes said to be an acronym for the Society for Courtship and Marriage!

Another outside group which made a great difference to my wartime Oxford was the Colloquy, a gathering of a few students collected by Canon Dick Milford, the Vicar of St Mary the Virgin, the university church. Dick was an extraordinary man, who went on later to be Chancellor of Lincoln and then Master of the Temple in London. He was an original thinker, who lived then in Holywell Street. He had a great knack of making intellectual connections, a wonderful insight into people, an extraordinary gift of constructing gadgets, as well as a mind well stocked in theology and philosophy. He suffered, alas, from accidie, and with this lethargy he never got round to writing more than a pamphlet, which was a great pity because if he could ever have been able to write a book, it would have become a classic. He seemed impervious to cold; a thin, bony man with execrable clothes, he would sit in his ill-heated house, wearing mittens with his hands blue with cold and a drip at the end of his nose, producing gems of wisdom in a somewhat lugubrious voice. I grew to love him dearly, and I met people there who later became my friends; for example Ingram Cleasby, later Dean of Chester, then a ruddy open-air type with a love for the Yorkshire moors.

Classical honour moderations are concerned with literature; it is only later that the syllabus progresses to philosophy and history. A great deal of Greek and Roman literature had to be read quickly, including Silver Age writers. This meant memorising the meanings of a great number of words; for example, the intricate details of food in *Trimalchio's Feast*. With Colin Roberts away in Bletchley for the duration of the war, my tutor was a junior don called Moerig-Davies. He was very eccentric, and became more and more so; finally ending up, to the consternation of his wife, living in his garden shed. Of course by this time he had ceased to act as Classics tutor. The college, when it woke up to this sad fact, had to farm us out to another college. I was sent to a well-known Classicist called Page, but it was all very unsettling. When it came to exams, I just missed my First. I was told that the smallest increase in the mark of any paper would have earned it for me, but a miss is as good as a mile. I was not much comforted by the conviction that the strange behaviour of my tutor had something to do with it. It was a failure which very greatly irked me, as I had worked very hard, and I was sure that a First was within my grasp; but perhaps it was good for me to come to grips with failure for the first time. In any case it was wartime and my mind was soon preoccupied with matters of greater moment.

What was one to do in wartime Britain during the vacation? The college owned Bagley Wood, and the bursar, who was always one to turn a quick penny, offered us board and lodging in college if we worked on timber there. I gladly accepted the offer. I even went camping in the wood with a certain George Series, who later became a professor; and I still preserve a snap of my presiding over a very home-made scout-type camping site that I had made in the woods. However, vacations were not simply for relaxation. The college had a nasty custom of 'collections' which meant examinations on the vast amount of reading one had been given to do in the vacation.

When I left Oxford at the end of the summer term (no commem. balls in wartime), I went home to our new house in Addison Road. The staff were enormously reduced, with just a butler and an Austrian maid-of-all-work to assist my mother. It was the time of the Battle of Britain, but one saw little of it in the London skies. The papers wrote up the numbers of shot-down Messerschmitts as though a game of cricket was being played. But it was a very deadly game, and it was an enormous relief when we appeared to have won the battle. Churchill's words: 'Never in the field of human conflict was so much owed by so many to so few' may sound old-fashioned today, but it was a heartfelt tribute to the RAF shared by all.

We live today in a 'culture of contempt', when politicians are (not altogether unfairly) disparaged. It is hard to communicate the 'infection of a good courage' conveyed by the speeches of Churchill, and the esteem and goodwill in which he was held by the population as a whole. Again, politics today are so polarised that it is hard to imagine that in those days there was a national government containing both Tories and Socialists. There was a feeling of unity and patriotism which enthused the whole country and brought us all together in a common cause, in marked contrast to national feeling today.

I had enrolled in the army the previous year, and during the summer I received my call-up papers. I was to go to a camp on Blubberhouses Moor a few miles outside Harrogate, to be transformed from a civilian into a soldier. I had opted for the Royal Artillery, partly because my uncle was a gunner, and partly because I preferred the idea of motorised transport to the pedestrian infantry. I owned a very small Standard car (the make is now extinct) which I called Esmeralda, because she looked rather sleek outside, which belied her true character. I took her up to Yorkshire with me, and left her, like a mistress, a discreet distance from the camp, which was situated on the bleak moors. Doing guard duty there, especially on a biting cold winter night, when it was obvious that no one was going to be fool enough to attack an army camp for raw recruits, was absolutely ghastly. So far as I can remember, it had no comforts for the troops, other than a NAAFI which sold nothing more exciting than small hot pies.

It was very good for me that I had refused to join the Oxford OTC (Officers' Training Corps) as in that case I would have begun immediately by training as an officer. As it was I had for the first time in my life a taste of the real world. The officer in charge of the camp was a big man with a yellow face, appropriately called Colonel Coleman (I was told that he was a member of the mustard family). I was put into a long barrack room, alongside other young men of the same age. We had endless square drill and rifle drill, all done by numbers. Once we had a written test, and some walked out: poor men, they could not write. We had to lay out our kit perfectly in the barrack room each morning, and 'bone' our boots so that they shone; and believe it or not we actually had to polish the coal in the coal scuttle to please the inspecting officer. I can remember in our squad a tall Geordie we called 'Lofty' whose broad accent I could never begin to understand. Little did I imagine that I myself would, in a few years' times, be living in Newcastle-on-Tyne.

There was only one other Oxford man in our squad. He was from Balliol, just over the wall from St John's, and had just finished Mods and Greats and had got Firsts. His name was Dennis Healey. If you had seen him on parade as a recruit, you would never have guessed that he would later become Minister of Defence. We used to play dominoes together when we 'fell out for a smoke' during the endless squarebashing. Unfortunately he got appendicitis – I remember bringing him some goodies in hospital – and then got posted elsewhere.

I found myself, rather surprisingly, able to make friends, and about four or five of us used to knock about quite a bit together. My twenty-first birthday took place during this primary training, and I remember that we had a night out in Ripon. We had to conserve our petrol, which was rationed. There was plenty of army stuff around, but it was all dyed red, and woe betide anyone caught in a civilian car with army petrol. I know we were only undertaking preliminary training, and it was probably sensible to condition men to blind obedience in square drill and in other ways, so that on the field of battle they would obey orders however horrific these might be. But it did seem to me at the time a curious way of spending one's life, cut off from all civilisation, doing square drill and rifle drill by numbers, during a time when one's country was grievously threatened. Night by night horrific bombing was taking place in the city of London, and elsewhere; but on Blubberhouses Moor we appeared entirely secure and never once heard the drone of enemy planes.

While I was at Uniacke Barracks on Blubberhouses Moor, I used a weekend leave to take up Archbishop Temple's invitation to visit him at Bishopthorpe Palace. He and his wife were kindness itself, and I was deeply impressed by their courtesy to a humble Gunner. My chief memory of Bishopthorpe is the extreme cold. As it was wartime, the Temples seemed to confine themselves to one living-room in that vast house. When I returned there for a night fifty years later, before preaching in the Minster at a consecration, it was quite a different temperature. Archbishop Temple took me with him in his car on his Sunday outing. He preached three different sermons in various churches, one I remember in Hull, and spent the time talking to me in the back of the car between these engagements. It was a wonderful break, and he made a profound impression on me. I realised that intellectual rigour could co-exist with deep faith and commitment. I am sure this must have helped me later to find my vocation.

During my time as a recruit I was up for an officer's cadet board, and I was recommended to proceed to an OCTU (Officer Cadet's

Training Unit). I suppose it was only natural that I should be sent to the nearest such gunner centre, at Ilkley. Unfortunately my distinguished uncle had come out of retirement and was Colonel-in-Charge. As soon as I arrived, he summoned me. 'Well, Hugh,' he said in his bluff way, 'I don't want to be accused of any nepotism here, and so I've given orders that you will be given the worst jobs.' Fortunately I think we were all treated the same. Here we were no longer actually on the moors, but in the town, although the town was considerably smaller than it is today, and Ilkley Moor was adjacent. One of the advantages of going into the Gunners is that there is a lot to learn; not only how the gun works, but also the problems of getting the gun directly on line, co-ordinating it with other guns, taking into account wind and temperature in calculating the trajectory of the shell, and so on. It was also necessary to be skilful at maps and an 'artillery board', so that distances to targets could be measured with accuracy, and also to get used to a 'director' which enables guns to be put on line. Since guns were not far behind the front line, and officers served in OPs (observation posts) with the most forward infantry, it was necessary to have in addition the normal skills of war. There was a lot to learn. I was impressed by the logic of army thinking, requiring strategic and immediate aims to be verbalised before going on to consider methods and finally orders. Taking this in conjunction with the way officers were taught to look after their men, it seemed to me that, in those days, the army was miles ahead of industry in the way in which it went about its business. Just as well too.

I didn't have a lot to do with my uncle during the time when I was under his command, and that was right and proper; but he did occasionally take me out for a drive, and his love for the old days of horse artillery was obvious when he was going up hill – he used to urge on his steering wheel by leaning backwards and forward as once he had urged on his horse. He had a distinguished staff to instruct us. One of them, I remember, was Captain Bonamy Dobrée, who later became a well-known Professor of English. Another was Captain Verney, who later became Sir Ralph Verney, the inheritor of Claydon in Buckinghamshire, where Florence Nightingale lived for many years. I got to know the whole family after the war. His youngest brother Stephen I met at theological college, and he became a lifelong friend; Elisabeth was godmother to one of his daughters. Another brother, now the Recorder of London, later joined the same regiment as I had. A sister married Dick Hare the philosopher who was Head of the School when I was at Rugby. Ralph became an influential environmentalist, and I conscripted him on to our Environmental Panel when I became Chairman of the Church of England's Board for Social Responsibility.

Training continued at Ilkley, although I can remember little of it now. I used to escape in Esmeralda occasionally up to some friends in one of the Yorkshire dales. It was glorious countryside round about, and a lovely walk over the big hill to industrial Skipton. There was one good restaurant in the big hotel in the town. Of course we had to wear khaki uniform all the time, and we had to keep it clean which I found a bit of a strain.

Then the time came for posting to a regiment. I was to go to the Royal Bucks Yeomanry, which was also the 99 Field Regiment RA. I suspect that I got this posting because my uncle was its Honorary Colonel. The regiment was under the command of Lt Col. J. P. Whiteley, MP, and most of its officers were still the original territorial officers drawn from the landed gentry of Buckinghamshire, and the men came from the county, many of them having known one another in peace time. The officers were pretty well heeled, and it was difficult to avoid all the gambling in the mess. I remember, for example, the colonel betting the quartermaster how many nails he had in his boots. And there were cards in the evening.

We seemed to have a surplus of beer in the regiment. One officer was a Tetley, another a Hanbury, and Brian Bonsor (father of the chairman of the present House of Commons Select Committee on Defence) was a Watney. The two Weatherby brothers owned the well-known betting establishment. Arthur Stewart-Liberty owned the famous Liberty's in the West End, and so on. When I joined the regiment in June 1941 it had recently come down from Filey where it had been put on coastal defence after losing all its equipment in France and escaping via Dunkirk. It was part of the Second Division, and felt proud that it was the only territorial unit among the gunners in the division. It formed part of 6 Brigade, which had within it famous battalions of Royal Welsh Fusiliers, Royal Scots and the Royal Berkshires.

I was posted to Gate Hemsley, on the road a few miles north of York, to 394 Battery, under the command of Major Hughie Vandervelt, a charming, decent and efficient officer who had been a stockbroker and who knew our family firm of course. I was initially put in C Troop under the command of Captain Graham Pank, another charmer who was in the wine trade and so knew what was what in that important department of life. After a bit, I was transferred to D Troop which was detached on a location three or four miles away, in a village called Stockton-on-the-Forest. There were three officers in the troop, and we were billeted in the local big house, Stockton Hall, where there was a widow who had no idea what treasures lay in her wine cellar; very decently, we told her. I was under the command of Captain Ralph Merton, at that time a dapper and decisive man (the brother of the well-known painter) who always said he would make a fortune after the war out of seaweed (he did).

It is somewhat frustrating being on active service as a gunner as one can only actually fire the guns at practice camps. And of course we did go to them, at Otterburn, Larkhill and Okehampton. The rest of the time was spent in fitness training, gun drill, map reading, and the like. There were things called TEWTs (Tactical Exercises without Troops), a sort of glorified school field day. Vehicles were troublesome. They tended to conglomerate in convoys on such occasions, and sometimes they got lost. We were often allowed home 'Method B' (each making his own way back independently). It is a phrase that has stayed with me. The army at that time had a crazy system of maintenance called 'The Task System' which meant that every driver had to tinker with every part of his vehicle once a month. Of course they went wrong.

One of the first things I had to learn in my regiment was that I must really know about the men on my troop and the names of their wives and children if they were married, and it was essential to care for them and to look to their welfare. Furthermore, no officer coming back from an exercise could sit down to a meal until he had seen the guns put away, the vehicles washed and his men fed. This was splendid pastoral training for my work in the ordained ministry. It was not surprising that the armed services were the best recruiting ground that the Church of England has ever had. Young men, cut off from the securities of home and school and university, and brought up for the first time against the harsh realities of life and death, and made to care for the men under their command, often found God a reality and wanted to spend their lives in his service and caring for his people. The army also gave me knowledge of what it is that makes ordinary people tick, and forced me into close contact with all kinds of people.

Part of the time was spent on army courses. Some of these were residential, and were shared out as fairly as possible. I remember being sent on a residential physical fitness course at Catterick Camp, which was not far away. It had its unpleasant side, such as going for a run in a gas mask. But such courses make a pleasant break from the monotony of army routine. The mess secretary at Catterick was an elderly officer, Captain Westerman. My interest was aroused when I noticed that his initials were P. F. 'Are you *the* P. F. Westerman, the person who writes all those children's stories?' I asked. 'Yes,' he said. He was a most unassuming kind of person, very different from what I had imagined this popular writer of many boys' stories to be. As a boy I had read all his books, but I don't suppose that boys nowadays have even heard of him.

I have not so far mentioned Elisabeth during my time in the army, but she was very much in my thoughts and in my correspondence. We saw a good deal of one another in Oxford, and then she got a First in English (she was two years ahead of me, even though she is only six months older). I continued to see her on my leaves when I could after I had been called up, although I was too scared of my parents to tell them of my attachment, which was I suppose silly. I was not intimate with them, and I did not know how they would react to her being a Gentile; but I felt I had to spend part of my leaves at home with them. When I was in Burma I purchased a local opal stone and had it set and sent it to Eliza as an engagement ring to formalise our 'understanding'. My parents knew about it by this time, and used to invite Elisabeth to the house, and grew (naturally) very fond of her: she shared with my father his love of gardening. The two sets of parents met and got on well together.

During my leaves I also stayed at her home in St Albans. Washing up after meals was a social occasion. I participated in it there for the first time in my life, such was the way I had been brought up! Her father was at home on only one of these occasions, and alas I only ever spoke to him through the door of his bedroom because he was laid low with flu; and I never saw him again, because of his premature death of a burst ulcer, brought on by chronic overwork and a very hearty appetite. He was a very special person indeed, known as 'the Protestant pope'. He was Chairman of the International Missionary Council and was constantly on world tours. A Presbyterian minister, he was the Free Church equivalent of William Temple (and a friend of his). He later became with Visser t'Hooft Joint Secretary of the World Council of Churches in formation.

Elisabeth's mother had become a Roman Catholic. She also had started life as a Presbyterian, then became an Anglican, and then went over to Rome because she heard a raw curate in St Albans Abbey (where the family worshipped) saying from the pulpit that God became man in order to gain experience (yet as a Roman Catholic she remained sufficiently Anglican to expect the Dean of St Albans to call on her!). Her children did not follow her to Rome, and detested the fiercely patriotic Irish priests who served her church. She herself finally attended Mass in a nearby convent. Here was a Presbyterian father, a Roman Catholic mother, and six good Anglican children, with two of them to be ordained in the Church of England.

Elisabeth's mother was a bit of a saint. She had an understanding with the police to put up any couple for the night stranded in St Albans (even though this once involved her in someone's divorce proceedings) and she seemed to spend most of her time running what the family called 'the Hell Hole', a 'British Restaurant' (wartime cafe) opened in the Roman Catholic hall.

Elisabeth, after her First in English, could have stayed in Oxford to do research. She thought that during a war she ought to do something more practical than a higher degree in English, and she opted to become an almoner (she would now be called a medical social worker). This meant she had to do a preliminary year at LSE which had been evacuated to Cambridge. She stayed with the Mortons who were family friends. He was the Presbyterian minister in Cambridge and went on later to be leader of the Iona Community in Scotland. The Mortons put me up too when I stayed; and it was while I was there that Elisabeth and I had an understanding that we would get married after the war.

Was that wise? Should we not have got married in a hurry like so many other couples? Perhaps. But I did not expect to come back from the war, and I did not want to leave Elisabeth a widow, still less to leave behind a single-parent family. Nor, until Hitler was beaten, did I want her to marry a Jew, for her own safety's sake. And if we had got married we would have seen practically nothing of each other, with a couple of days' honeymoon. Married men in the division were not allowed to lodge with their wives; and very soon I would be abroad. Better wait, and if I did come back, we would be married. So we thought, and I still think we were right.

How would the Royal Bucks Yeomanry and the rest of 2 Division be used when it came to fighting? Speculation was rife. Then we were ordered to mobilise ready for battle, and so it seemed clear we would not be waiting for the Second Front. Embarkation leave was completed, and we moved south to Tewkesbury in December 1941. The regiment more or less took over the town, which had at that time more pubs to the hundred yards than any other town I have ever seen. The men made many friends among the girls of the town. When we went abroad, it fell to the lot of officers to censor the outgoing mail of their men except for the 'green envelope' they were very sparingly allowed (which was censored at base). I could not help noticing that throughout our time overseas many letters were sent to the girls of Tewkesbury. It was also a very 'olde worlde' kind of place. I was quartered in a lovely house in the shadow of the

Abbey, near the old mill. We went there for church parades, and very beautiful the church was.

I was part of the advance guard that had to load our guns and vehicles at Birkenhead; but we still did not know where we were going. In May we boarded the *Empress of Canada* which had been converted into a troop ship. As we had been issued with thick woollen vests we thought we might be going to Persia, or Iran as it is called today. We were part of the largest military convoy that had yet been assembled. Originally we were bound for Suez to join the Eighth Army, but the 'Quit India' campaign had started in India, and that was where we went.

We had to go the long way round. We moored off Freetown, where we were visited only by the native mosquitoes, and went far across the Atlantic to avoid the U-boats. Officers had to take turns on the watch looking for conning towers, which we imagined we could see by the dozen at night. In fact if they had been close enough to be seen, nothing would have stopped them launching their torpedoes; but luckily none came round us, although some ships in the convoy were lost. Officers were comfortably ensconced in cabins, but the men had to sleep below deck in hammocks, which then had to be cleared away by day for training; not that much could be done. Officers spent part of the time becoming proficient at Morse code. Of course wireless was used for communication between guns and observations posts and we spoke 'in clear'; and I suspect we had to learn Morse code to give us something to do. I took the opportunity of the journey to assert my manhood by growing a moustache, but I shaved it off on arrival, as I thought it looked ludicrous.

We stopped briefly at Cape Town, and were allowed ashore just long enough to enjoy a day's hospitality given by public-spirited South Africans, and then we were whipped off to a camp for exercise after confinement on board ship, including the ascent of a 2,000-feet-high kopje. This greatly irked us, but the story had got around, quite falsely, that Singapore had fallen because the previous convoy had arrived there shortly before it fell, and the troops were out of condition. The next time we landed was at Bombay in great heat, shortly before the monsoon. Our brigade went to Ahmednagar, where Nehru was under house arrest, and the rest of the division was in the Poona area some fifty miles away. We went to a peace-time camp, Minto Lines, in greater comfort than we had expected; but because of the riots, we were not allowed to employ any local bearers, although the officers' mess had a khansama, or Indian cook.

I wanted to find out about Indian culture, and I soon got into trouble by employing a munshi (a language teacher) to learn some Urdu, which was forbidden, in case we would be posted away into the Indian army from the only all-British division in India. I also had a propensity to lose my revolver, which as officers we had to carry outside camp. This was a court martial offence, but fortunately the regiment always closed ranks, and the quartermaster managed to find others without any trouble from the 'G 1098' (the stores). Fortunately we were not called on, as were the infantry, to police Bombay during the anti-British riots. When I went down to Bombay it was to play in seven-a-side rugger competitions on brick-hard ground. We liked staying at the grand Taj Mahal Hotel and having lobster thermidor for dinner. We were also granted honorary membership of the extremely posh Royal Bombay Yacht Club, with its entrance guarded by turbaned flunkeys.

It takes time to get used to the poverty and stench of India, with cows wandering around the streets and masses of hideously deformed beggars, excited vendors and lots and lots of shouting. There is an energy and colour missing in our colder climate. Religion is evident, and holy men walk about totally naked. Curry is everywhere; but the British troops were given a very English diet, including the hated 'soyalink' sausages. The Indians were very lovable and their country vast, and I found it all very attractive. I would love to return there; but I expect a lot of it has changed now.

A happy relationship usually grew up between Indians and British soldiers, although the officers were likely to be more peremptory. Of course we were the occupying power and India wanted to be free. But, despite the fact that we profited hugely from our trade with India, and the people were not allowed to determine their own future, I think on the whole the Raj really did help to develop the country and to provide education. There are still Indians who look back with nostalgia to the peacefulness and comparative prosperity of the British Raj. I know we did many shameful things in our imperial past, but it is a pity that we, as a nation, are so ashamed of our former Empire.

Previously British troops in India had worn the topee, a kind of constable's helmet in light khaki, keeping out the fierce rays of the sun. However, we were issued with the Australian bush hat, which looked rather splendid and was popular with the troops; I still have a film-star photograph of myself wearing one.

At the time I was Assistant Gun Position Officer in my gunner troop. The regiment began some training for combined operations, and had to learn how to use 3.7 howitzer mountain guns, after we had been trained to work with 25-pounders. In November 1942 two of our three batteries moved down to Juhu beach on the outskirts of Bombay to continue practising combined operations landings. When we were there, 'passion wagons' were organised to go to a certain 'safe house' for sex-starved officers (the men could and did fend for themselves). Despite enthusiastic reports from my fellow officers about luscious Anglo-Indian girls, I determined to keep myself virgin for Elisabeth. Whether in fact it is better to come to the marriage bed totally inexperienced in these matters is, I realise, debatable. Strictly speaking, those officers who were married were committing adultery. But it is hard to equate this kind of sexual relief, however culpable, with full-blown adultery. I learnt early on to be cautious before making hasty judgements on sexual matters.

We learnt that most of the two batteries on Juhu beach were to go to the Arakan, on the coast of India bordering Burma, in order to take part in a combined operations action against the important port of Akyab. By this time Mark Maunsell had taken command of the regiment, and he chose me to be his intelligence officer at Regimental HQ, when we went with the batteries to the other side of India. This really meant being his dogsbody or ADC, whatever you like to call it. As I liked and admired him, I was glad to do the job.

We went by train in January 1943. It was a long and tedious journey, because we were often shunted into sidings; however, the men had reasonable travelling accommodation. At one stage we stopped to give the troops char from the boiler of our steam engine, which unfortunately took it off the boil, and we had to wait quite a time to get up steam again. I regret to say that the officers ate at restaurants at stations by the way. The train would wait while the meal was ordered and cooked, and then start up again. This sounds deplorable, but then it was the 'raj' and Britain was the imperial power, and the army symbolised this. After crossing the Brahmaputra by boat, we got on to another train which took us to Chittagong. Unfortunately we were there during the dreadful Bengal famine. We were forbidden to give food to Indians, and it was awful to see the women rummaging in our dustbins. In stark contrast to this, the army supply of razor blades ran out. As intelligence officer I was ordered by the CO to go round the Chittagong bazaars buying up as many blades as I could find to form a regimental pool. The colonel insisted that every man should shave, if necessary using the regimental blades. Nobody did.

From Chittagong we went on down the coast, often on an apology for a road with Bailey bridges over the many chaungs, and finally ended up at an extinct hamlet called Maungdaw (I could only see the remains of a small wharf). Beyond Maungdaw was a peninsula, leading to a point; and across from that was Akyab, our combined ops objective. We never got there; and just as well, we realised, when the underwater defences were later discovered. Many years later, when I visited Japan for the Episcopal Church there, I met an ex-soldier who had been in Akyab, and who is now ordained. We shook hands.

The Allied troops were held up at a small village called Donbaik, where there was a narrow strip of coastal flat, and then jungle-clad steep hills with a kind of sierra edge. Absurd as it may sound, the whole brigade group was held up here by an immensely strong point, known as Sugar 5 from its artillery target number. It was strengthened with steel doors and steel internal reinforcement on which direct hits made no impression. The battle was being run from Delhi, over one thousand miles away! Thousands of shells were fired at it, and infantry attacks in First World War style were repulsed with terrible losses. (When Field Marshal Lord Wavell came down to have a look, he was heard to say: 'This is not what I ordered.') Meanwhile there were even greater casualties from malaria. Officers had to see that their troops took a daily dose of Mepacrine. I never took it because it was (wrongly) said to affect one's virility. I didn't get malaria myself, but the troops most certainly did, especially as at one stage the Mepacrine supplies ran out.

While our British and Indian troops were failing to make any progress, the Japanese did what we had not yet learnt to do (and could not yet do, with our reliance on motorised transport). They went round through the jungle and the sharp-topped ridged hills, and encircled us. The Indian troops had simply not been taught jungle warfare, and while most of them fought bravely, some ran away. Almost as fearsome as the advancing Japanese was the sound of tigers roaring at night. As we retreated, Brigade HQ was overrun. We were lucky to get out intact. The first Arakan campaign was a ghastly failure, but through it important lessons were learnt, especially the need to learn jungle warfare, and to go round rather than attempt to overcome these impregnable Japanese strongpoints.

When we returned to the other side of India in June 1943 to rejoin the rump of our regiment and the rest of the division, we were encouraged that our Colonel Maunsell had been awarded the DSO. As his intelligence officer naturally I saw a lot of him. I did not see much of the fighting, but I do remember going on a motor cycle through the old railway tunnels between Maungdaw and Buthidaung

to find out if the Japs had arrived there. It was eerie going through a
tunnel not knowing what one would find the other side.

When we returned, I found myself made the Regimental Survey
Officer. My task was to see that all the guns of a regiment pointed in
exactly the same direction with only a five minutes tolerance, and to
know precisely where they were on the map. This was a responsible
job, as even a small error could mean that all the guns of the regiment
were concentrated on our own troops! It certainly weighed heavily
on me. In a country where mineral deposits could produce a 23°
variation in magnetic north, this operation could seldom be done
by compass. It was necessary to do it by azimuth, which involved
using the nautical almanac and measuring the degree of the sun at
a particular time. The army provides forms with a proforma for a
multitude of tasks, thank goodness, including azimuth shots! The
troops had been so affected by malaria, with over 100% casualties
(when those who had it more than once were taken into account)
that we were sent to a beautiful hill station 4,000 feet high called
Mahableshwar, seventy-five miles from Poona, to recover. My
survey section had nothing to do, and as there was no map of the
place, I determined that we would make one. It was good practice
for us all. We did it by means of taping distances and 'traversing'
and checking our accuracy by closing the traverse. I enjoyed this
small command, because there were only twelve in the section, and
we got to know each other and worked well together as a team.

Further jungle training ensued when we returned to Ahmednagar.
Lord Louis Mountbatten, C-in-C SEAC, paid us a visit. I remember
the quartermaster looking around for a box which had actually
contained soap. Mountbatten insisted on this for his oratory, which
certainly stirred the men. For further training we camped in the
jungle near Belgaum, where I learnt that there was something far
more frightening to British soldiers than the Japanese. One day a
huge snake moved at great speed through the camp. The troops ran
away like men possessed!

Perhaps I should at this point mention something about leave. I
think we were allowed a fortnight every three months. When we
were in Burma it was a fortnight at destination, so of course most
of us went to Kashmir, which took a week to get to, and a week
to get back, giving four weeks away. We would go in couples. In
Kashmir we would stay on a houseboat in Srinagar, and the country
around about was simply marvellous, as was the lake on which we
were living. Unfortunately there was a tendency for the houseboys
to throw sewage into the lake and then to use lake water for cooking
and drinking. This meant that on one occasion I had to go into the

Srinagar Hospital with dysentery, fortunately not the amoebic type. In those days the only medication for this was the sulphonamide 693, but it did the trick. Otherwise I was fortunately in rude health all the time that I was out East. Some people got infective hepatitis badly, or malaria. We had to take precautions against tick typhus. Jungle leeches could cause septic spots, especially when pulled out, because the leech's head was left in. Better to apply a cigarette to the pest. Any cut easily turned septic. Also men suddenly went down with 'fever n.y.d.' (not yet diagnosed – and never was).

To return to our leaves, Kashmir was the favourite, with visits from Srinagar up to the ski resort, Nedou's Hotel at Gulmerg. On one occasion I went to Delhi to be inspected by Elisabeth's brother David, back from China where he had been chaplain in universities. I once cadged a lift on a Dakota to Ceylon, where my brother Oliver was serving on Mountbatten's HQ SEAC staff. I managed to see the Temple of the Tooth at Kandy, and I had a wonderful holiday up in the hill district at Neuralia. On another occasion I went to Ootacumund, a famous British hill resort; and of course there were leaves in Calcutta, an enormous city, with the famous Chowringhee street. On one occasion I stayed with the Oxford Mission to Calcutta, an impressive house with a chapel where everyone took off their shoes when they entered. These 'local' leaves were an enormous refreshment, and travel on Indian trains first class was very comfortable. Although there was no air conditioning, enormous blocks of ice were installed which cooled us off quite efficiently.

When I was at Ahmednagar again I finally decided that I must be ordained. I still had no idea whether I would be alive when and if the war ever ended. I did not particularly want to be ordained, because this would mean that in a sense I would be 'different' from other people, wearing a dog collar, etc, and in the army I had learnt to treasure my solidarity with my fellow officers and men, and to enjoy their company. Also I had no idea what the ordained life would entail. After all I had never been in a parish set-up, and I had had no experience of parish life. Why then did I make this decision? I simply felt deep in myself that I had to, that this was what God was ordering me to do, and that as events unfolded it would be made clear to me what I had to do. I don't think Elisabeth was too pleased – she had had a lot of clerical family life – but I knew that I could not face myself if I took up some secular vocation and turned my back on God's plan for my life.

And so the die was cast, although I would still have to pass the church's selection board when I got home. I wrote to Kenneth Riches (later Bishop of Lincoln), then Chaplain of Sidney Sussex College Cambridge, and Ordination Secretary, to register my name. I let it be known among my fellow officers what I had done. Of course this became the joke of the mess. They knew I was a practising Christian, but I fear they could not reconcile my future vocation with my present reality! I remember on one occasion having more drink at a regimental party than was good for me, and realising that this would have to stop. I have to say, alas, that I was not particularly inspired or encouraged by our army chaplains. We started off in Britain with a nice enough man who at least was on the men's wavelength. We had another who was subsequently the first parson to be prosecuted under the clergy discipline measure after the war for his pastoral ill practice. Then we had a gloomy and rather depressed priest who subsequently became a South African bishop. My church attendance in the field consisted of communicating at the Eucharist when it could be celebrated, usually in the open air, and sometimes I and the celebrant were the only people present. Myself and Bill Davidson were the only two ordinands in the division. Bill was a Staff Captain at Div. HQ RA, and subsequently a Cambridge cricket Blue (wicket keeper) and Vicar of St Stephen's, Rochester Row. We two were always wheeled out whenever it was decided that it was time some high-up prelate should visit the division.

Suddenly, in March 1944, 2 Division had to be mobilised and rushed across India in order to meet a threat from the Japanese to the whole Indian continent which came within an ace of succeeding. We were taken by train on 24th April across India again, to disembark this time at the railhead in Dimapur in Manipur State not far from the Burmese border. When the British had retreated from Burma the previous year, they established themselves in Imphal on the Manipur Road, some eighty miles south. The Japanese in a daring action across the jungle isolated the troops at Imphal and attacked Kohima some fifty miles further north on the way to Dimapur. When we arrived no one quite knew where the Japs were: we had to make the last part of the journey sitting in railway carriages with rifles at the alert, and with officers holding their revolvers. In fact a scratch garrison had, with enormous courage, held them up at Kohima, and continued to do so until 2 Division came to relieve them. When we disembarked at Dimapur the town was in disarray with evident signs of panic. Had the Japanese taken this town, with all its vast stores (and they would have done so if we had tried to relieve the Kohima garrison only a few days later), they would have debouched into the plains of India, and with Sandra Bose of the Indian National Army, they would easily have raised the whole continent in revolt, involved as it was already in the 'Quit India' campaign. Few people realise just how close the Japanese got to conquering India.

The battle of Kohima was one of the fiercest battles of the Second World War. XIV Army (of which we were a part) was rightly known as the 'Forgotten Army' and this dreadful battle was hardly known in Britain. The marvellous victory which the British and Indian troops won at such great cost was barely mentioned in the British media because it coincided with the landing of British troops in France at the opening of the Second Front. It was exactly the same fifty years later when there were nationwide commemorations. It is still unknown.

With no battle casualties so far among our officers, and the successful policy of preventing them being posted to Indian divisions, there was little prospect of promotion. I continued as intelligence and survey officer. The 'meteor telegram' gave information about wind speed and temperature which affected both the range and direction of the shells that were fired. It is almost unbelievable, but our meteor telegram came from Delhi a thousand miles away; and so it was useless. On a leave I had met someone from the Indian meteorological office, and with his encouragement I decided to make our own meteor telegram. I got REME (Royal Regiment of Electrical and Mechanical Engineers) to make me an efficient anemometer to measure wind speed, and I got hold of oxygen and balloons. Knowing their rate of ascent, I could measure wind speed. I gather that these curious objects in the sky attracted attention in Japanese intelligence reports.

I was not involved in the first part of the battle of Kohima. When we relieved the West Dorsets on Kohima ridge, scenes of very fierce fighting took place against Japanese strongholds, and our gunner observation posts were in the thick of the battle. The position looked impregnable. Kohima was a small town on a ridge 5,000 feet high, surrounded by towering jungle-clad hills up to 10,000 feet. Through them passed the all-important road from Dimapur to Imphal on which all our transport had to go, with precipitous drops below of more than 1,000 feet over the *khud*. Little progress was made, with the Japanese dug into immense bunkers and displaying heroic qualities of resistance. We were greatly helped by the RAF both here and later. (They dropped not only our rations, but also my airmail *Times* and our precious mail: Elisabeth was a wonderful correspondent.) Everything floated down on us. I remember on one occasion the *Journal of Roman Studies* dropping from the skies. I'm afraid we tended to order goodies from the Army and Navy Stores in London which would shower down upon us to feast on. We were greatly helped in the steep jungle hills when we were off the road by the Nagas, the local hill tribesmen, rather like Gurkhas. They were very friendly, partly because of their relationship with District Commissioner Pawsey. They acted as our carriers, and would bear on their backs impossible loads up steep gradients at a half-run, singing cheerful songs. Not long converted to Christianity by an heroic Scottish missionary lady, they still had skulls hanging on trees outside their hill-top villages.

It was decided to attempt a three-pronged attack, one brigade down across the jungle to the north, one brigade along virgin jungle skirting the 10,000-foot Mount Pulubadze, and a third more frontal. Our new Commanding Officer, Col. James, had only recently joined us. He went with the Pulubadze brigade, and as intelligence officer I went with him. The monsoon rain was pouring down most of the time. The mountainside was so steep that at times ropes had to be put in position to prevent us slipping down. A way had to be cut through thick virgin bamboo. Hundreds of us had to go along this manmade path in such a way that the enemy would be ignorant of our encircling movement. We only had ghastly American 'K' rations, we were not allowed to light fires, and we were allowed one water bottle a day for all purposes.

After three days of this the troops were exhausted, and it was decided to rest for twenty-four hours in what we called 'Death Valley' because everything was putrid and stank. The brigade relied on the gunners' wireless; and at that point it was found that our wireless had gone wrong. We could not tell the division where we were; so I was sent back with the message. It was eerie retracing my steps along this newly-made jungle path by night, never knowing what one would meet at each step. I passed one Naga village, and I did not know whether the Japs were in occupation. However, I was reassured when I heard from one closed hut the tune of 'Onward Christian Soldiers'. The Nagas were obviously having some hymn singing. When I had delivered my message, I found that wireless communication had been restored; so I made my way back to Death Valley, where the troops were just beginning to move down to do battle.

And a very bloody battle it was. At one time we were pinned to the ground by snipers in heavily wooded country. A shot nicked through the sleeve of my pullover, and found its mark in my colonel lying next to me. Alas, he subsequently died. As we made our way eventually into the open, it was a horrid sight. There were casualties all around including soldiers lying about with their heads blown open. The three-pronged attack had achieved only modest success.

To quote a recent history of the battle, 'after thirty-four days and nights of close and bloody fighting, after hunger, thirst, discomfort, after appalling casualties, the enemy still held the bastions of their position. No bombs, shells, mortars, flame throwers or grenades seemed to shift them.' Eventually, however, the bunkers were slowly overcome by anti-tank guns manhandled to fire at point blank range. The Japanese, whose situation was far worse than ours, without food supplies or reserves, were forced to give way, but not without great difficulty.

At last, on 7th June, the road was cleared to Imphal, after nearly two months of fighting since Kohima came under threat on 4th April. Indian, Gurkha and British casualties amounted to 4,000 killed and wounded against known Japanese casualties of 7,000. The District Commissioner's bungalow in Kohima and his tennis court, which were the focus of the battle, were as bad as any First World War battlefield. There is a British cemetery at Kohima with 1,200 graves and the following moving inscription:

> When you go home,
> Tell them of us, and say,
> 'For your tomorrow,
> We gave our today.'

That is why I have told the story of Kohima in some detail.

It is ironical that a few days after this stunning victory our divisional General Grover, known as 'God' and universally respected by the troops, was summarily sacked because brasshats who lived far behind the lines had little idea of the impossible terrain, the ghastly monsoon conditions and the ferocity of the Japanese resistance, and had wanted a swifter victory with fewer casualties. But it is even more ironical that General Sato, commanding the gallant Japanese forces, was sacked a day later by his army commander with whom he too had violently disagreed and whose impossible commands he finally disobeyed.

Nearly fifty years later, a Roman Catholic cathedral has been built in the reconstituted Kohima, now a thriving town of 80,000 souls. At its consecration in 1991 there were present both Japanese and British veterans. During the Consecration Mass, at the 'Peace' some British in a spontaneous movement walked over and shook the Japanese by the hand, in a symbolic gesture of reconciliation. It had taken a long time. To us during the war the Japanese seemed hardly human in their endurance and courage, their refusal to take prisoners and at times their barbarity. It was not until later in the campaign, when we camped for the night in an overrun army post office, and I saw all the mail from families to their loved ones, with pictures of their children and signs of endearment, that I really understood that they were as human as we were; but it was a long time later, when I undertook a lecture tour for the Episcopal Church in Japan in 1991, that I was able to make friends with them.

Shortly after breaking through to the 'Imphal Box' I got word that my eldest brother Denzil was there, recently flown in as a signals officer. My surname was so extraordinary that anyone who shared it with me would soon be known! I was glad to meet up with him, because his wife at home had recently died of septicaemia leaving a young daughter; and there he was thousands of miles away. I think the meeting cheered him up.

Relentlessly the pursuit of the Japanese continued. They were as gallant in defeat as in attack. We found lorries with their drivers starved to death in the driving seat. At this time I was at last removed from regimental headquarters, promoted to Captain and put in charge of a troop of guns. This meant that I went forward with the infantry to man observation posts from which I could direct gunfire. I was often apprehensive, but I think that the only time I was really frightened was when I was temporarily seconded to work with the Nepalese State Forces. We were being mortared in the open, and I was in my carrier with the driver and signaller. The battle continued. Nothing would stop the Nepalese officers having the officers' mess kit spread out when darkness fell, despite the Japanese all round us; and of course a splendid curry meal was served on the battlefield!

It was around that time that some of my friends were killed: Colin Richardson, the brilliant son of my prep. school headmaster, who had joined the regiment shortly before myself; John Beamish (brother of the MP Tufton Beamish) and 'Goodie' or Captain Goodchild, with whom I had often been away on leave, and who inexplicably killed himself, no one knew why. Who does know what goes on in another's head? I used to visit his parents after the war in Great Yeldham where they had farmed for generations – and he was the only son. 'Goodie' had been in the Essex Yeomanry originally, and then transferred to the Royal Bucks Yeomanry. He was a quintessential yeoman himself.

It would be tedious for me to continue the story of our advance, down the Kabaw valley full of teak forests, over the Chindwin river, on towards Mandalay, and finally down south to Myingyan. There was fierce fighting some of the way, but nothing like the determined opposition we had met in the Kohima area. It was difficult crossing the Irrawaddy, which is a huge river, and it seemed rather like crossing the Channel; and we had no idea what kind of reception we would meet on the far bank. Part of the regiment met opposition, but my transport was fortunate: we had none. I continued with the infantry, firing at targets. I remember to my shame enjoying some of my shoots when I caught Japanese in the open and brought down salvos upon them. I enjoyed it when I hit my targets, especially if there were Japanese there. It has taken me a long time to get over my guilt about this. It is perfectly proper to enjoy efficiency as a gunner officer. It seems to me that it is immoral to enjoy killing other human beings. I fear that war inevitably desensitises those who fight in it, especially in close combat. Some people say that for this reason it is always wrong to fight; but I do not agree. The consequences of not fighting may be worse than the consequences of fighting. But it is always a second best, always should be the last resort, always the minimum force is required, and it always should be in defence, and non-combatants should be always respected – and one should always be assured of a reasonable chance of winning. But one should surely never enjoy killing other human beings. I have repented at leisure.

At Myingyan we were flown out to Calcutta. This was because we were the only British division in Burma, and the powers that be wanted the British division to enter triumphantly into Rangoon from the sea. But events moved too fast for them; Rangoon fell without a shot being fired. So we were left around a 'tank' (artificial small lake) just outside Calcutta, just before the monsoon broke. I have never known anything so humid in all my life. If we changed our clothing, it was soaking wet with sweat within the hour. Thankfully we went from the environs of Calcutta to a camp in Secunderabad, the British cantonment town adjacent to the Indian Hyderabad which was out of bounds to the British troops because of anti-British feeling, although I managed to get a peek at the very Indian sights in that city.

It was there that the news broke of the nuclear bombs over Hiroshima and Nagasaki. I was appalled, horrified, disgusted. Should I resign my commission? It was something that I seriously considered; but I came to the conclusion that it would betray my own men placed under my command. I was there to support and encourage them. As a matter of fact, I was possibly wrong. When I went out to Japan in 1991, I said to an Anglican Japanese chaplain how ashamed I was about the Allies using nuclear weapons. He told me that, on the contrary, they shortened the war and reduced future casualties. He said that his fellow countrymen would never have given up, that there would have been a contested invasion and very bloody fighting in Japan with enormous casualties on both sides. I said that the bombs could have been dropped out to sea; but he said that notice was only taken of them because these bombs were dropped on populated Japanese cities. Was he right? I am still rather ashamed of what we did.

We celebrated VJ Day when the Japanese had surrendered after the nuclear attack; and now we were waiting for repatriation. It looked as though we had survived the war after all! People relaxed. But what were the troops to be given to do during this waiting period? The army decided on education, and various courses were devised, some to help people to adapt themselves again to 'civvy street'. The officers could take things easy, except for me! I was made Regimental Education Officer, and I had to supervise all this. Still it gave me something to do. We had Field Marshal Wavell's son (who was later killed by the Mau Mau in Uganda) to help us. I shall never forget burly gunner sergeants, wearing simply khaki shorts in the heat, listening entranced as he explained the intricacies of the Peloponnesian War as expounded by Thucydides. Anyone who can grip army NCOs about Greek history as they wait in intense heat for repatriation must be a genius.

It was at this time that the General Election took place, and the troops abroad had voting rights. The political aspect was rather well covered by ABCA (the Army Bureau of Current Affairs), but when it came to voting, it had been decided that other ranks were not to be trusted to fill in their ballot forms correctly on their own, and officers had to oversee the process. So much for the secrecy of the ballot box! The regiment, like the nation as a whole, voted predominantly Labour, although I would guess most of the officers did not.

Eventually we were repatriated. We came home not the long way round, but via Aden, past Mount Sinai, and through the Suez Canal. The day I embarked on board ship, I received my Class B release, which my Oxford college had requested. This gave immediate release to certain classes of people, including students in the midst of their courses at the special request of their colleges. I was home, repatriated, sent on terminal leave, given a civvy suit and hat by way of recompense for all those years in the army, and in a fortnight I was married.

I was grateful for my time in the army. I went in as an immature, overgrown schoolboy. I came out as a man, not yet fully mature, but at least more mature than when I entered. I was glad that the war had been fought, both in Europe and in Asia, and that the evils of Nazidom and Japanese imperialism had been conquered. I was grateful for the providence which had enfolded and the grace which had upheld me, and for the Holy Spirit at work in the fellowship of officers and men which I had enjoyed. I was aware that great problems lay ahead in peace time. We had to have a better Britain for the returning troops and their families. And for me, I realised that a chapter of my life was over, and another about to begin.

Chapter Four

GETTING STARTED

The big item on the agenda when I got home was to get married; but first we had to get to know each other again. After our long separation did we really know each other well enough to share the rest of our lives together? What would Eliza think of all my little habits of which as yet she could know nothing? We had of course written to each other a lot. Elisabeth had sent me masses of things called aerograms, in which a page of her naturally small writing was microfilmed and an even smaller print of it arrived, which needed a magnifying glass to decipher; and I wrote as often as was possible. So we had been in touch in that way; but that was very different from being physically in touch. Both sets of parents had decided that it would be best for us to be married as soon as I got back, and had made arrangements with Elisabeth's approval. She had spent her last savings on her wedding dress, which I found greatly moving. It was lovely and so was she. As soon as we met, we knew we must go ahead as soon as possible, on 13th December 1945. It was extraordinary how quickly we picked up, but marriage was still a big step: the vows were *total*. It filled me with trepidation as well as with much joy.

The wedding would take place in St Albans Abbey, Elisabeth's parish church. I had to get my banns read – just in time. Dick Milford from Oxford agreed to tie the knot. My old friend Robin Barbour from Scotland was also back from the war and was my best man, and Eliza was given away by her eldest brother David, as her father, alas, had died. We were 'prepared for marriage' by Dean Thicknesse, a formidable character who had refused to hold a Thanksgiving Service in the Abbey because of the nuclear bomb. As part of what was called 'marriage preparation' (one hour!) he warned us not to engage in 'disgusting and degrading practices' which in those days obviously meant contraception, but today could mean *anything*. This seemed to me a bit rich, but I thought it best not to argue. I contented myself with glaring.

Before the wedding I had lunch with the family in 'The Abbey Tea Rooms'. Strangely enough, this was the building that later became 'Paton Books' of which I was to be a director and which Elisabeth's younger sister Catherine was to run. I was still technically in the army on leave and so I wore my uniform. Someone said that I was not fully dressed without a sword, and lent me one. I had never worn one before, and it wrecked the service for me. How on earth do you kneel down with that wretched scabbard sticking out? My father was in tears throughout; I knew it would hurt him, much as he loved Elisabeth, because I was marrying a Gentile.

It was a small family wedding, with a modest reception afterwards. My parents organised a large reception in a hotel after our honeymoon so that their side of the family could meet us. We had to tog up again in our wedding regalia, and, although it was meant very kindly, it was an ordeal. For our honeymoon we spent a fortnight in a private hotel in Cornwall. You could not go abroad in 1945 even if you wanted to; in any case, I had just come back from abroad. We could not go down to Cornwall the same day as the wedding so I had to find somewhere to stay in London. I couldn't find a spare hotel room anywhere, until at last in desperation I booked in at the Savoy. It was a strange way to start our marriage, but it served. When we arrived at the hotel in Cornwall, no one else was staying there. Of the couple who ran it, the lady looked after us well, but her husband would come in every hour to make up the fire and leer at us, just as he did when he called us in the morning. We hired a car for the week – a dreadful old crock which broke down as we made our way to the station en route for home. We phoned the garage and just left it where it stopped.

It was wonderful to *belong* to each other. It gave us great joy just to be together, and to learn more about one another. What a comfort marriage is, right from the start! It sounds trite to recall it now, but for me the sharing of our life was at one point summed up in a shared tube of toothpaste. I remember staring at it in the bathroom in wonder and delight! Mind you, I don't think marriage is of its nature indissoluble. But I do believe that the process of living and loving together produces indissolubility.

But where was home to be? We stayed at Elisabeth's old home with her mother until after Christmas, and I was due to start reading Theology at Oxford at the beginning of the Hilary Term, so after Christmas we went down there, staying with a great college friend of Elisabeth, Pam Mackenzie who was married to a Magdalen don.

Where would we live? Fortunately Elisabeth's godmother had an empty furnished house in north Oxford near the Woodstock Road roundabout, 3 Blandford Avenue, which she let us at a very modest rent. It looks just the same now as it did then. We were in luck. It was ridiculously large for a newly married couple; it had three bedrooms, and a large playroom as well as a sitting-room and dining-room, but it was there, and we took it. Its garden was mostly a tennis court, which we never used. Elisabeth is very ticklish, and I think we scandalised our very 'proper' next-door neighbours. I would bicycle into Oxford for lectures, and she would do the same for shopping. St John's College was clearly scared of this large influx of returning warriors as undergraduates, supposing that we would sit light to college regulations. So they made us all BAs on the basis of war service and a year's residence! The trouble was that you couldn't bicycle safely wearing a BA gown flapping behind you and getting entangled in the spokes!

We were rather poor. It was good that we were, because it is bad never to have tasted any form of poverty. My father had generously made us a 'marriage settlement' which guaranteed us a minimum income, but this disqualified us for a government grant. I had a £100 scholarship, but previously I had only been allowed £30 because of my father's income. The bursar quite unreasonably refused to increase this. However, the circumstances were entirely different. How could I, a married man, ask my Jewish father for help so that I could read Christian theology instead of earning my living? But our poverty was only comparative (we still had Esmeralda), and we made do – herrings were only 1d each. In the second year, when Teresa had been born, we took in undergraduates as lodgers.

Life was now utterly different from what it had been in the army. Eliza and I were on our own. Instead of obeying orders, I could make my own timetable, and we could plan our day together. Far from concentrating on killing, we were actually intent on procreating. Above all, so far as I was concerned, instead of an almost entirely male existence, I now spent most of my days and all my nights in the company of the woman I loved.

Looking back now, I do not remember this sea-change in life as particularly traumatic. It was, rather, a blessed release; marvellous. I have always managed to sink myself in the present moment rather than look back in nostalgia to the past, or daydream about the future. This certainly prevents excessive worry, but it is not always a good thing. However, it stood me in good stead now. I certainly sank myself in the present, and the past seemed to belong to another world.

I remember that at that stage we were both very shy in company. There were plenty of other students returning from the war, but few were married. Except when I had to work in a library or attend the occasional lecture, I worked at home. Elisabeth welcomed the break from almoning, and enjoyed exercising her skills in the house, which even at that stage were marked. So we were fortunate in that we saw more of each other than most newly marrieds. There was still a lot of catching up to do. Eliza's pregnancy gave us both much pleasure, and fortunately she kept very fit.

I returned to Oxford to read Theology. I worked hard, as did all of the ex-servicemen. Most important was my tutor in Theology. Who would he be? I was sent to see H. E. W. Turner at Lincoln (later Professor at Durham, and a future colleague of mine on the Doctrine Commission). At that time he was known for his love of the contemporary reference rather than for his profundity (he liked war jargon: 'The Apostles were the right markers of the New Israel'). I did not think he was the man for me. Fortunately after a fortnight Geoffrey Lampe appeared at St John's, released from running an army religious centre in Germany. A large man in every sense, and apparently vague, he had been awarded the MC for wandering unconcerned across a minefield to rescue a wounded man. In fact his mind was entirely other than vague. He had an enormous influence on me. He started me off by getting me to read the entire Bible with a commentary, and he supervised me in every part of the syllabus except for the philosophy of religion, which I elected to do as a special subject. I really should have been reading Ancient Philosophy in 'Greats', but at the age of twenty-five I could not face two years more of Classics before starting on Theology, with theological college still further ahead.

Geoffrey Lampe was very patient with me. He seemed to have encyclopaedic knowledge, despite the fact that he had been away at the wars. His service in Germany as an army chaplain resulted in his being particularly conversant with German theology. He too was recently married, and our children came about the same time. He was a formidable walker, stepping out as an undergraduate all the way from his home in Bath to Oxford; and I learnt to dread his invitation to spend a day with him in the country, which seldom meant less than a fifteen-mile trek. His 'short cuts' across ploughed fields are never to be forgotten; I always used to clear my diary so that I could spend the next day in bed. Later he and his wife Elisabeth became enamoured of a caravan, which they intrepidly conveyed by horse power to Aberdaron, where we used to visit them when holidaying nearby.

At that time he was concerned mostly with scriptural theology and the early Fathers, and he made his reputation with his writing on primitive Christian initiation in *The Seal of the Spirit*, a large part of which he wrote on a seaside holiday with a typewriter on his knee on the beach. He later edited the *Dictionary of Patristic Theology*, an enormous undertaking. I remained a friend of his and Elisabeth until they both died of cancer in short succession. Beginning as a moderate evangelical, as he grew older he became more radical, questioning traditional doctrine about the Resurrection and presenting the doctrine of Christ in terms of Spirit rather than metaphysics. He became Professor of Theology in Birmingham, where I once acted as his external examiner; and he was also a very popular Vice Principal of the university. Then he became Regius Professor of Theology in Cambridge and I persuaded Gonville and Caius College, of which I was then Dean, to snap him up as a professorial fellow. He was a reconciling presence in the college, and acted as Dean during the year's interregnum after I left. He was a courageous man, never frightened to speak his mind; a man of huge knowledge as well as wide sympathies, although perhaps not as incisive as some. I was his first pupil, and I count myself most fortunate to have begun my studies under him.

As for Oxford lecturers, I listened with appreciation to Professor 'Jahwe' Simpson, who not only lectured on the Old Testament prophets but looked like one. His nickname derived from the fact that he was believed to have lectured for a whole term on Jahwe, one of the Hebrew names for God. The doyen of the New Testament scholars was Robert Henry Lightfoot. Elisabeth's brother Bill, who had been a scholar of New College, grew very fond of him as an undergraduate; but some students dowsed him in the college fountain, and I don't think he had ever fully recovered. He was a hypochondriac, and when we first visited him he was lying in bed wrapped in a shawl. He introduced form criticism from the Germans into British New Testament criticism, and he was a character. I remember too the great Austin Farrer lecturing in Trinity College on the philosophy of religion. I can see him now gazing hopefully out of the window at the college clock, and when it reached five minutes to twelve he literally ran out of the room. I later asked Farrer, when he preached for me at Caius, how he managed to be so eloquent. 'Poof', he replied. 'It's inherited. My father was a Congregationalist minister.'

I remember turning up to listen to Thornton-Duesbury on St Paul's Epistle to the Colossians. I was the only person present. He gave his lecture, but next week he simply didn't turn up. (The same thing later happened in Cambridge when Dr Katz lectured on the Septuagint; but he continued his course, giving it formally as though there was a full lecture room. Having a son called Tom, he later sensibly changed his name.) Professor Cross was at that time editing the classic *Oxford Dictionary of the Christian Church*: while I was there he published the thesis that the First Epistle of Peter is really a baptismal liturgy. Dr Lowe was Master of Christ Church, and so, although learned in the Fathers, he did not lecture. When he was Vice Chancellor, he descended on Christ Church meadows by helicopter, while undergraduates assembled below and sang 'Lo, he comes with clouds descending'.

I enjoyed listening to the Baptist Dr Payne, later Chairman of the World Council of Churches. Through him I learnt about St Augustine, and the difference between *non posse peccare* and *posse non peccare* ('not able to sin' and 'able not to sin'). It was customary to attend at least one lecture by Claude Jenkins, Professor of Ecclesiastical History. He was known to have lectured for a whole term on a single year's history. He was and looked a great eccentric: he lived on his own in Christ Church, and was well known for putting the toast into his pocket when sitting on high table in hall. I also used to listen to Professor Leonard Hodgson, the Regius Professor, who lectured on Christian doctrine: it had nothing to do with the syllabus, but it was the best course of lectures in the faculty.

I was tutored in the philosophy of religion by Dennis Nineham of Queens'. He had scarcely left his college between being a student and being a don. He was a slavedriver (I remember once he told me, for a week's work: 'Read Kant', and I was expected to produce my weekly essay on his philosophy). But it was well worth it. He had an incisiveness and a refusal to be put off with less than a direct answer that made a lasting impression on me. He and Ruth have remained friends, and I am godson to his son Hugh. They used to attend Great St Mary's when I was Vicar there and he was Regius Professor; but I don't think that our churchmanship was really high enough for him. Although a radical, who held a more sceptical view of the Gospels than most, he held a very high doctrine of the Church.

I became quite fascinated by theology, a fascination that has never left me. It was wonderful to make sense of the Bible at last, rather than to regard it as a book of oracles. I was confirmed in my conviction that the New Testament fulfilled that to which my Old Testament upbringing pointed. I was glad that I was forced to think hard about the fundamentals of faith by taking the philosophy of religion as a special subject. For the same reason I entered an essay for the Ellerton Prize. Although I did not get it, I was given a grant from the fund. But the Oxford course of theology (for which it was not necessary to know anything after AD 361) was not really theology, but an introduction to theology (and a very good one too), giving one the necessary tools to do the real subject later. Few people ever did, except in the superficial way that doctrine has to be taught at a theological college, in competition with other subjects.

I worked hard but I did not work all the time. I enjoyed Elisabeth inducting me into the world of English literature, which she thought I had been shockingly taught at school. And before baby Teresa arrived, we could get out in the evenings.

We decided that it would be good to have a change from Oxford when it came to joining a theological college. But I was so fascinated by theology that I felt I must be in a university city, so I applied to Westcott House in Cambridge. Billy Greer (whom I had met when he was lecturing at a SCM conference) was Principal. He was then unmarried. (When he became Bishop of Manchester he did marry.) He accepted me but advised me that my wife should live at home. I looked at him, and of course took no notice. What on earth would Elisabeth be doing living in St Albans with her mother when I was in Cambridge? Those whom God joined together theological colleges tried to put asunder!

We were able to visit people during the vacations. But it was not much fun driving in the winter. Cars in those days had no heating; we used to travel in Esmeralda huddled in rugs and comforted by hot water bottles. Then Elisabeth became pregnant, and Teresa was born in Addenbrookes Hospital during the great freeze of 1947. Of course in those days fathers were not allowed near their wives for the birth itself. When I visited her in the Radcliffe Hospital, I used to take textbooks into the waiting room to read. It was the only warm place I could find in Oxford.

My parents had sold their house in Aberdeenshire before the war, and had bought a delectable cottage called 'Tuck Mill' in Eaton Bishop, some five miles west of Hereford on the Wye. It was tucked away in the middle of nowhere, near the village of Clehonger where the Ridleys made their cider. It had a stretch of the river Wye, where I used (vainly) to fish. Above it was a wood, where nearby Belmont Abbey had a meditation hut overlooking the river. I would sometimes be able to go there with my friends. After the war my parents sold it and bought 'Fernie', a fairly large house in the country not far from Ledbury. My father, with his entrepreneurial spirit, wanted to cultivate every inch of the land, and even planted gooseberry bushes in the hedges! He also kept pigs, somewhat strange for the President of the Synagogue, but as he never ate them, he claimed it was all right. (I believe Israelis do the same thing.) We took Teresa there as a baby, a somewhat hazardous expedition, as she got ill and the local doctor was a clot. My parents at one point decided to entertain the locals. Flour was rationed at the time, so my father brought down from the East End a vast and tempting array of Passover gateaux (known there as 'gottas') which looked like the last word in French confectionery, but which were made with potato flour and tasted frightful. They were mostly uneaten, and masses of nibbled slices remained on people's plates. I was required to take the uneaten 'gottas' to the local hospital, and I always wondered whether they ended up in the hospital dustbin.

It was at Fernie that I realised that something was very seriously wrong with my mother. Later in London she removed herself to the Royal Palace Hotel in Kensington, and seemed to type day and night. The gist of her letters to me was that I must not disgrace the name of Sebag-Montefiore by becoming a Christian priest. Elisabeth's mother had been a Macdonald before marrying William Paton. My mother was insisting that I change my name to Montefiore-Macdonald. It was then that I realised that she was going round the bend. I humoured her by altering my name by deed poll to simple Montefiore, which I did not mind doing as my full name would be a bit of a mouthful for a parish priest.

Elisabeth's brother Christopher at that time was a District Commissioner in Ghana, having been specially asked to stay on after independence. (Later he was in charge of the International Students Hostel in London.) He asked Elisabeth to be kind to a friend of his called Busia who was doing some research in Oxford. We got to know them: he and his wife were a charming couple. She used to come and do some 'bottling' in our kitchen in the days before fruit and vegetables could be frozen. We were somewhat electrified later when we read that he had become President of Ghana.

The time was coming round for me to take the final examination, or 'Schools'. All of two years' work was concentrated into a week's written examination. Teresa was teething, and bellowing at night. Elisabeth rigged up a bed in the sitting-room and insisted that I slept there during Schools. Happily I did triumphantly well this time, the only First awarded, and when I got my marks unofficially later, I was astounded. Of course I had concentrated on work, and eschewed such activities as the Oxford Union, or theatricals, and I did not go much into college. Naturally what spare time I had I spent at home, as I was a married man with a family.

And then the move to Cambridge. Where would we live there? By putting together all my savings, I had managed to buy a small semi-detached house on the very outskirts. 12 Chalk Grove, off Queen Edith's Way, is now in the centre of a large housing estate. It was then the last house in Cambridge: our road was unfinished and one side of our house was beside a cornfield. Ingram Cleasby and my brother-in-law Michael (also at Oxford) helped me to decorate it before Elisabeth and baby Teresa moved in. Rationing made life still difficult, although not as bad as our last year in Oxford, when even potatoes were rationed. A butcher had his home in the road, and he used to deliver our pathetic weekly joint, and if we were lucky, an exiguous amount of sausage meat. Petrol was still rationed, and I rather envied the scientist neighbour who had converted his car to gas, and drove about with a great rubber reservoir on its roof, which I nursed a hidden desire to puncture. I would bicycle to Westcott House, some two and a half miles away, to be there in time for Matins at 7.30 am.

The ethos of Westcott House was very liberal. There were no rules except that one had to be in chapel for compline on Friday night, when there was an address, and then students were supposed to go to bed in silence. Even on Quiet Days (the euphemism used for retreats), those who found it hard to keep silent were allowed to go to the bathrooms and chat. When the front door was locked, the back door remained open. One was expected to attend either matins or Holy Communion (or both) every morning and only to have one 'morning in' each week. When I first got there I used to praise this kind of freedom compared with what we understood to be the case in other theological colleges. After a while I was not so sure. If there were no rules, there were certainly moral expectations, and failure to meet them resulted in just the same kind of atmosphere of silent but moral disapproval which had been such an unpleasant feature of my childhood. Mum and Dad never said anything, but they exuded disapproval; and now it seemed the same, as it were, with Big Daddy.

When I arrived at Westcott House, there was no Principal. Billy Greer had gone off to be Bishop of Manchester, and Ken Carey, the newly appointed Principal, had not yet arrived. The Vice Principal was in charge. Geoffrey Styler was an excellent New Testament scholar (although he has never actually published anything); but he was then rather a lonely man, and used to play the piano a lot. The next term Kenneth Carey arrived. He had been Vicar of Haltwhistle (and we would hear quite a bit about his pastoral experiences there) and then one of CACTM secretaries. CACTM was part of the Anglican *curia*. It kept changing its name and acronyms. CACTM was the Church's Advisory Council for Training for the Ministry, succeeded by ACCM. I managed to get this accepted rather than the intended CACYM which sounded ridiculous. It stood for the 'Advisory Council for the Church's Ministry', which has now become ABM (Advisory Board for Ministry). The recurrence of 'advisory' throughout is worth noting. In fact bishops can ordain whom they like: it is about the only untrammelled power left to them. But no grant is available to an ordinand unless he or she has been to a Selection Conference. Technically they do not even have to have been recommended for training at such a conference; but they must have attended one. Later on I only once went ahead with the training of an ordinand despite a negative response from such a conference, and I do not regret having done so.

Ken Carey had got only a Third in Theology. There were those who said that a person with such a low-class degree should never have been appointed Principal of a theological college. They have a point, but there should be exceptions to every rule. Ken, who was very sensitive to criticism, had an inferiority complex about his intellectual capacity. This was rather ridiculous, because he had quite a good brain, a good theological judgement and he was also a shrewd judge of people, all of which made him a good Principal. I learnt a great deal through him, and I am very grateful to him in many ways, although I never became one of his inner circle, nor like others was I reliant on him as a 'confessor' or as a spiritual adviser. There were some forty-three students at the college, and this meant that the staff could get to know each one personally.

Unfortunately theological colleges after the war were not geared to married men; and quite a few of us were married. There were no married quarters. No concessions at first were made on account of marriage. Elisabeth with the baby would come to Communion on Sunday mornings. The noises made by the baby did not endear us to the Principal. After the service, Elisabeth would go two and a half miles home to make her own breakfast, while I went into hall to eat mine. For my first year I had to live in college during term (and there was a fourth term during the Long Vacation in those days). If I was lucky I would get home after lunch for two or three hours, so long as I was back in the house by 5 pm. I was allowed one night at home a week, otherwise Elisabeth had to live alone in the last house in Cambridge with no arrangements whatsoever made for her convenience, and almost no preparation for her life as a vicar's wife. She told my second daughter Janet (like her, an English scholar) that she used to read Coleridge's 'Dejection: An Ode'. She was quite desperately lonely, and she used to say it was quite an event in the day when the postman came. I found this terrible to bear, but for her it was far worse.

We were told it would get us used to the frustrations of clerical life. In fact the policy was a mixture of insensitivity, traditionalism and a feeling that marriage is of secondary importance to ordination. It isn't. If a married man is to be ordained, his marriage is part of his vocation quite as much as his ordination, and he should be trained as a whole person and not as a temporary celibate who is allowed to resume his married obligations to his family during the vacation. The tradition died very hard. Years and years later, when I was a don, I was invited back to Westcott House under another Principal together with Elisabeth to talk about marriage. I was invited to dine with the Principal and students in hall. I was asked 'You won't mind, will you, if your wife has supper with the housekeeper?' I preferred to make no comment: I simply said that it would be inconvenient for either of us to dine.

The Principal only felt up to lecturing on prayer and pastoralia. I certainly needed help with my prayers, but we were not encouraged to read the mystics and other primary sources, and we were recommended such books as Bede Frost's *Art of Mental Prayer*. As for pastoralia, it is hard to instruct young men about how to be a curate when many of them knew little about parish life. This training would come after ordination to the diaconate. I can remember little about the Principal's lectures, except that on one occasion he brought in a doll to show us how to hold the baby for baptism. We had to visit once a week in an old people's home in Chesterton, and this was more eye-opening to us than it was helpful to the inmates: poor darlings, most of them would be sitting in the dayroom in silence, incapable of speech or of listening to others speak. It was very good for us, in the prime of life, to see what life was like for them.

We also used to take the service on a Sunday evening in the Leper Chapel: this was an ancient building which lepers once attended, and a few people (not lepers) still did attend it. This was where I preached my first sermon. I blush to remember it now. I took enormous trouble over preparing a written text on the subject of the Trinity. Alas, my theology fell if not on deaf ears, at any rate on four ears which were very hard of hearing so far as theology is concerned. Two old ladies listened bemused to my discourse. I was very properly humbled by the occasion. We also had a weekly sermon class at the House. One of us in turn would prepare an actual sermon (which was never preached) and the others would criticise. This was a useful occasion; but it was important to remember that people had done their best, and harsh criticism could wound. I fear that this was not on every occasion remembered.

Geoffrey Styler soon left to became a don at Corpus Christi College, Cambridge. Alan Webster moved up from Chaplain to Vice Principal, and Harry Williams arrived as Chaplain. Alan was a church historian at root: he was a great comfort to us all, with a sense of humour and an earthiness about him which made him very approachable. Harry Williams was not yet the radical don who set the theological world by the ears with *The True Wilderness*: he was at that time the ex-curate of All Saints, Margaret Street, the high-church member of staff who had spent hours in the Confessional in London, and whose views were (if you can credit it) very conservative and orthodox. These two did all the supervision for the forty-three students in the house. Students had to satisfy the General Ordinands Examiners about their proficiency in the Old Testament, New Testament, the whole of Christian doctrine, early and modern Church history, ethics and liturgy. This meant a great deal of study for a two-year course, with many 'extras' in connection with spiritual formation and future pastoral work. As a result it was inevitably somewhat superficial – a kind of 'Tell me ten facts about the Holy Spirit before breakfast.' As I had read the Oxford School of Theology I was excused the biblical papers and the paper on early Church history. As a result I was able to read widely, and I laid the foundation of my knowledge of Christian doctrine in those two years, as well as deepening my knowledge about the New Testament.

We had occasional lectures in Westcott House. I remember being inspired by what Mervyn Stockwood was doing in Bristol together with his neighbouring Methodist minister. I remember too the learned Dr Telfer, Master of Selwyn College, coming to give us a lecture. He was a grave cadaverous-looking man who lived with his two sisters and their dog Whisky in the Selwyn College Master's Lodge. His lecture was about 'the process of nidification', although I have now forgotten exactly how birds' nests can illuminate the Christian faith! He also told us a story about how he had taken his youth club up a mountainside when he was young (it was hard to imagine that he ever had been young). They went up a valley with a stream, and when they got to the top they found a dead sheep lying in the stream, so that the water was polluted all the way down. This was to illustrate the need to believe in the Virginal Conception of Jesus: if one did not, the whole of the rest of Christian doctrine, according to Dr Telfer, would be polluted. Few of us were convinced.

We were able to attend lectures in the university. Charles Raven was in his last year as Regius Professor, and I remember his lectures not so much for their content as for their manner. A tall striking figure in a doctor's gown, he would stride up and down the largest lecture theatre in the Divinity School, while pearls of wisdom would drop from his mouth, with his handsome face from time to time suffused with a smile as he meditated aloud on the glories of divine grace. Later on I got to know him quite well – in fact I actually buried him when he died – and he told me that he had had to give up conducting missions because he found that he hypnotised people into belief. I am not surprised. Raven was also Master of Christ's College. He had lost an earlier election there, a story which forms the basis of C. P. Snow's *The Masters*. He was also at this time Vice Chancellor of the university. Some rowdy ex-warrior students had, on Guy Fawkes night, broken some stained-glass windows in the Senate House. Raven was eloquent in their denunciation. I remember him at this period preaching in Great St Mary's at a student service, his face contorted as he confessed: 'I need to be broken.' As a liberal theologian, he could be a powerful opponent with quite a temper. He was a scientist and a botanist of distinction, knowing the habitats of many rare wild species. In some ways he was prophetic, for example in his championing of women's ordination before most people had even thought of it.

Professor C. H. Dodd was in his prime. He lectured on the fourth Gospel. Although somewhat blown upon nowadays, as fashions in New Testament criticism have changed, he was in fact one of its great masters, as great or greater than Lightfoot had been in Oxford. He was a small man. I can see him now ascending the rostrum in his gown, and snapping open his Greek New Testament, always precisely at the right page. Norman Sykes was Dixie Professor of Ecclesiastical History; a formidable Yorkshire man, his lectures were seasoned with a wry sense of humour. I can remember Bob Runcie taking him off perfectly as he wiped his spectacles on his surplice, while Simon Phipps was brilliant at mimicking Raven, sweeping his gown and telling us of some 'profoundly moving occasion' (these happened to him frequently). Charlie Moule had not yet been elected to a professorship, but already his lectures were noteworthy. These are the theological lecturers I most remember. Like many others, we all attended Noel Annan, who used to lecture on eminent Victorians on Saturday morning. This was a quite a social occasion as well as a theatrical performance.

Westcott House at that time held a distinguished group of students, although when I look at the house photograph forty-five years later, our faces seem as yet immature and unformed. There was Bill Vanstone, who had got a double First in Oxford and then a starred First in Theology Part III during his first year with us, and who elected, like his father, to be a parish priest all his life in Chester diocese, and who later wrote that Christian classic *The Stature of Waiting*. There was Bob Runcie, who in the house play very appropriately played the part of Emperor in Bernard Shaw's *Androcles and the Lion* before later becoming Archbishop. Simon Phipps, later to be Bishop of Lincoln, had been President of the Footlights, the famous Cambridge revue society which lay behind 'That Was The Week That Was'. He was also a friend of Princess Margaret. Once when she visited him in the House a student was so astonished when he saw her entering that he dropped his scuttle full of coal and ran. Simon was once invited by King George VI to Sandringham for the weekend. This would have entailed missing Friday night compline. The Principal, agonising over the problem, in the end refused Simon permission. Word came from royal circles: 'Tell your Principal who's head of the Church of England.' Simon went. With all these distinguished people in the House, the Principal feared that there was becoming too much of a gap between rich and poor, and sherry, which had previously flowed freely, was no longer permitted. The last bottle was ceremonially placed in the House museum, alongside Westcott's Bible and other sacred relics. I gather the veto has been lifted.

Among others at Westcott at this time were Kenneth Woollcombe, later to become Bishop of Oxford, Pat Rodger to become Bishop of Manchester, and Vic Whitsey to become Bishop of Chester, all considerable characters even at that stage. There was also the future Canon Frank Wright, well known for his religious television and his pastoral books, and Barry Till who became Dean of Jesus College, and then Dean of Hong Kong. I was overjoyed to find that John Hoskyns, born within hours of myself, and my friend from our days together at School House, Rugby, was there too. He had called his home Hobbitt House, and he had a very old Austin Seven. When the time came for him to leave home to be ordained, its engine fell out en route. He sold the car to a garage for a fiver, and managed to arrive on time for the bishop's hands to be laid on him correctly.

There were many others, and we all formed quite a close community, but I was not really happy there. Perhaps it was because we had to change too much too quickly, and spiritual growth is always painful. Perhaps it was because we heard too much about B. K. Cunningham, a former Principal, who was certainly a great man, but who belonged to a former age, and who put on a dinner jacket every night for dinner. Perhaps it was because there was just a little too much forced laughter about the place, and too much emphasis on 'the House spirit'. (The head student was somewhat ludicrously called the Sheriff, and he was assisted by the 'Bailiff of the Flatiron'.) Perhaps it was because of the lip service which was paid to our wives and to our married lives. Mostly I think it was because the whole atmosphere of the House was ecclesiastical, and I was not a very ecclesiastical person. I had been converted by a vision of Jesus, not a vision of the Church.

Although I realised that following Jesus involved the Church, it was not to me a very attractive institution. The forces of reform had hardly begun. Fisher was Archbishop of Canterbury, and his interests centred on canon law reform, which was hardly likely to turn one on. The Church of England at that time had no relations with Rome. It also had very little to do with the Free Churches. As a matter of fact the Cambridge theological colleges, later to became a federation, did have a corporate service once a year. (Dr Newton Flew, Principal of Wesley House, commented to our Principal: 'You Anglicans always pray with your eyes open' to which he appositely replied: 'How do *you* know, Dr Flew?') In my student days there was no hint of any loosening up of traditional theology, and we were still committed to Cranmer's monotonous diet of gloom and confession in the beautiful cadencies of the 1622 Prayer Book. All this contributed to my unhappiness at Westcott. I was, however, still a very shy person, and perhaps at that stage I would not have been happy anywhere. At any rate I was glad that my time there was coming to an end.

It was while I was at Westcott House that the opening session of the World Council of Churches took place, and we felt (mistakenly, I fear) that this heralded a new chapter in the history of the Church. Students could not attend the World Council itself at Utrecht, but I did attend a special meeting for theological students at Woudschoten nearby, to which some of the more distinguished delegates came to tell us about it. It was quite an experience, quite apart from the novelty (to me then) of having cheese for breakfast. To meet Christian students from so many nations, united in so much of what they believed, made a very deep impression on me which has lasted over the decades; and to sing the same hymn to the same tune in different languages gave us a feeling of unity in diversity that is unforgettable.

While playing hockey I had done something to my back. My doctor advised applying Ellerman's lotion, but it simply got worse. First I could not kneel in chapel, later I was unable to move from my bed. I had to have a ruptured disc removed in a laminectomy at Addenbrookes Hospital. People complain about the NHS nowadays as though its problems were new, but even in 1949 I was told by the orthopaedic consultant that he would not be able to operate on the NHS for six months (and I was unable even to move in bed). But of course he could do it straight away if I paid him and went into the paybed ward. I had little option. This bad back made me miss a whole term at Westcott House, and in those days laminectomy was a somewhat difficult operation. But it did mean that Elisabeth and I got away to Cambus O'May in Aberdeenshire, some five miles from where my parents had had their holiday house, for a wonderful completion of my convalescence. That holiday stands out over the years as the happiest we ever had; yes, better even than our honeymoon.

Chapter Five

THE FIRST FIVE YEARS

The question arose during the later part of my time at Westcott House: Where should I go for the next stage in my life? Where would I 'serve my title'? It seemed to be *de rigueur* to go north, otherwise one was regarded as having it soft. I was friendly with the Franciscans, whom we had known from Rugby days, when some of us used to spend a few days at their mother house at Cerne Abbas. The Brown Brothers were a great encouragement to many of us younger Christians. In Oxford Fr Algy Robertson, who used to walk around with a hot water bottle under his habit, knew many undergraduates.

Fr Dennis Marsh, who was Teresa's godfather, suggested that I went to St George's, Jesmond, in Newcastle upon Tyne, where John Ramsbotham was the Vicar. I went to look over the place. It was a huge church, with a tower built on the model of St Mark's campanile in Venice. I asked what the hoops were at the back of each pew; and I was told they were for the top hats. When the church was built Sundays had been a fashion parade, but now the large houses in the parish were mostly divided into flats. I agreed to become the next curate. Unfortunately no one thought fit to tell me that the Vicar would shortly become Bishop of Jarrow. I only discovered through the Principal's grapevine. I was shattered. All this talk about the importance of a training vicar for one's first curacy, and then no one tells me that I won't have a vicar at all. I very nearly threw the whole thing up. If this was how they behaved *before* ordination, how in heaven's name were they going to behave *after* ordination? However, my sense of vocation prevailed, and we went up north. I had no idea what it would be like. For God's sake, what next?

We knew we were among friends when the porter at Newcastle Station lifted Teresa in his arms from the carriage and said: 'Come along now, my love.' The curate's house really belonged to the

Vicar's wife. It was a poky little place, and the bathroom window looked out on to the railway track, so that smuts from the steam engines accumulated as soon as they were cleaned. How we lived on our pittance I can't think: about £200 a year, I seem to remember. I had to go straight on up to Riding Mill, the diocesan retreat house in exquisite country in the upper Tyne. Elisabeth was left alone in this strange house; and the main electricity fuse went. It must have been awful with a small child. However, in time it was repaired. In fact the electrical fittings had been carried out by a member of the congregation, and Teresa would have been electrocuted had she not had on rubber-heeled shoes, for an electric point in the kitchen had been connected up wrongly and was 'live'.

Fortunately our next-door neighbour was a keen parishioner; in fact she was 'Brown Owl'. She was a great comfort to us. She had given over her whole life to looking after her old father. I expect there have been many like her; but somehow this sacrifice deeply touched me. She went about the house singing *fortissimo* in a piercing voice. Her father was deaf so he couldn't hear, but it penetrated through the walls to us. We grew very fond of her, and she became godmother to our second daughter. She was always late for everything. I remember saying she was bound to be late for her own funeral: she was! The hearse arrived at the church a quarter of an hour late.

The Vicar and his wife were preparing to move to Durham to his new job. He did his best to initiate me into some of the things that happen in a parish, but he was not administratively minded, and there were no parish records. He was a very nice man and a good priest; and he went on from being Bishop of Jarrow to being the Bishop of Blackburn diocese; but this was really beyond his competence, and he had a stroke and retired back to Newcastle diocese, to Hexham, where he was much loved. His son, who by that time was General Sir David Ramsbotham, flew me up to Hexham after my retirement so that I could preach at his father's funeral service.

Soon I was left on my own, but luckily there was a dear old Archdeacon Ritchie who had a large house just by the church, and he was at hand for the more difficult crises. He was a man of limited intelligence ('justification through faith' meant for him that one was justified in believing the Christian faith) but he was rather holy. There was a daily Eucharist, which caused some difficulty, as I was still in deacon's orders. However, the local clergy were very helpful, and took turns. I remember that Jim Bate, then Vicar of Jesmond Parish Church (so low-church that it doesn't even have a patron saint) said he didn't mind wearing vestments provided I put them on him. Very different from the tradition at that church now, with David Holloway as Vicar. The Bishop, who very rightly had a bad conscience about landing me in this situation, celebrated once a week, and then came on to our humble abode for breakfast afterwards. I remember one occasion when Teresa took it upon herself to upset the teapot. 'Now is the time to think of eternity,' he said, as he withdrew from the table until mopping up had been completed.

The Bishop was Noel Hudson. Formerly he had been a missionary in Borneo, and then in charge of the Society for the Propagation of the Gospel. Earlier still he had been the youngest Brigadier in the First World War, with a DSO and bar. (He used to refer to his two honorary DDs as 'DD and bar'.) He was an awful snob in a very endearing kind of way, as he wore his snobbery on his sleeve. He had a mantelpiece full of what he called 'my snob photographs' and he was not backward in referring to 'my sister-in-law, the Duchess of Richmond and Gordon'. He got on very well with the nobs, and also with the farm workers in the diocese. Later he was translated to Ely diocese, when I was living in Cambridge; and he was scared stiff there of what he called 'these professor fellers', and rather took to the bottle. He was a very godly man, and I grew to love him, and I greatly respected his advice. He did, however, drive very fast and smoked incessantly, tending to light a new cigarette from a smoked-out one, usually when rounding a corner. I remember he once called at the house. 'Hugh,' he said, 'come for a jolly.' The jolly consisted of going in his car to Berwick-upon-Tweed, the furthest point in the diocese, for a confirmation, and acting as his chaplain. After a hair-raising drive, we arrived just as the open-air street tea party had come to an end, the company having despairingly started tea in default of our arrival.

Almost as soon as I arrived at Jesmond, it was discovered that the tall tower, modelled on the Venice campanile, was in danger of collapse. I had to organise a huge thermometer outside the church and start an appeal. This was my introduction to parish life! Still, I suppose it was good training. I decided, in default of any church records, that I would make a personal visitation of every house in the parish. Every afternoon I would go visiting, knocking on doors, finding out about the inhabitants, and introducing myself to them. Only a few stood their ground on the doorstep and refused me entrance. I found it fascinating. Few of them of course actually attended church, but most of them in those days (1950) seemed to feel rather guilty that they didn't. Naturally they all complained that 'the Vicar never calls' without asking themselves how he would be able to visit 7,000 people every few months, or why they had never made themselves known to him. I learnt a lot about people from this visitation, which I almost finished before I left the parish.

There was a very good youth organisation called AYPA (Anglican Young People's Assocation); but there was a dreadful tradition of the curate taking the young people out on a 'hike and bike' in the lovely countryside on the Whitsun bank holiday. I remember one ghastly occasion when I took a bunch of boys and girls away out to the beautiful moors nearby. The only trouble was that it began to snow hard. What could I do? Well, what I did was to take them into a pub to shelter from the blast. I never heard the end of it when I got back. And then there was the Mothers' Union. They asked me if they could all go to a matinée. Of course I agreed. But it happened to be in Lent, and once again I was hauled over the coals by the parochial church council, whose vice chairman was a nice chap, but seemed to regard himself as acting Vicar during the interregnum. How things have changed since then!

As I went visiting around the parish, I found that there were a large number of young married couples living in flats in what had been big family houses before the war. These couples were really rather lonely. They didn't belong to the church and they didn't know each other, and many of them had no roots in Newcastle. I decided that the church could help them by having a 'Marrieds Club'. This seemed to be a very popular idea, and dances were to be arranged in the parish hall along with other activities. The time came for its inauguration. It was the first time that I had tried an initiative of this kind in the church. What would happen? Would people turn up for the first night? I was all agog; and then that day I went down with a roaring flu. I had to take to my bed, and Elisabeth had to do it on my behalf, while I stayed at home babysitting. Needless to say, Elisabeth coped wonderfully, and the Club was an enormous success, and continued for some twenty years.

Holidays were fun in Northumberland. Esmeralda was still alive (although she was beginning to fail in old age) and so we could explore that beautiful countryside, fortunately ignored by tourists who seemed to think that they must go on up to Scotland. I remember sketching Bamburgh Castle: I had it framed, and it is hanging up in the house now. I remember us staying at the Salmon Inn in Holystone, in the Cheviots, where St Paulinus is said to have baptised 3,000 people in a day (there is a lake there ideal for the purpose). There was a holiday with another young family, if I remember right, by Seaton Sluice, a not very elegant name for a nice seaside village. It was one of those places where you could leave young children in the bedroom at night, and they told you when and if crying was reported. What sticks in my memory was the perpetual diet of mince for lunch.

Newcastle was a happy diocese, helped by the breeziness of the Bishop, who himself had once been an incumbent there. Almost all the parishes in the city had adopted the parish Communion. We take it for granted today, but then it was comparatively rare. Most of the parishes were moderate catholic, with of course a scattering of extremes at both ends of the spectrum. The next-door parish in Gosforth had a vicar I admired tremendously, and he told me that he needed a curate (he certainly did: he had hundreds of communicants) but since he came from an obscure theological college, he despaired of getting one. I wrote and suggested it to Bob Runcie, whom the Principal intended to send to the prestigious parish of Hexham Abbey. At any rate Bob (who was ordained a year after me) went to Gosforth, and it was nice to have him near me.

My vicar of six weeks had four children, and the patrons appointed a new vicar who had five. That was really all that they had in common, if it could be so called. The interregnum had come at last to an end. The new vicar came from the vicinity, and had once been a Methodist; and he embraced High Anglicanism with all the zeal of a convert. The time came for me to be priested, and away I went for retreat to Riding Mill. It was an Advent ordination, and what appalled me was the prospect of me, nearly tone deaf as I was, having to sing the Christmas Proper Preface on my return. Although we were supposed to be in strict silence, I persuaded Bob Runcie to go out in the woods with me so that I could practise the Preface *fortissimo* under his guidance. It was just unfortunate that the Bishop had decided to take a walk in the same direction.

After my ordination my vicar put up a notice at the door of the church 'Now you can call him Father Hugh'. If there was one thing that in those days annoyed a middle-of-the-road Anglican congregation as much as incense, it was being told to call a clergyman 'Father'. Personally I didn't mind much what they called me, although I preferred just my Christian name. I can never understand why Christians don't naturally call one another by their Christian name: I thought that was what we have them for. I think the right phrase to use is that there was 'a father and mother' of a row. Like all church rows, it blew over.

Then I suddenly received a letter from the Principal of Westcott House asking me to go on the staff there. It meant leaving St George's, Jesmond, in under two years, whereas a curate is expected to stay three years. But there had been a change of vicar, and when I consulted the Bishop he reluctantly said that I was entirely free to go. So I went. Perhaps it was a strange decision, seeing that I had not been all that happy there. I have often asked myself why I did it. I think it was because of Cambridge and Cambridge theology: I was fascinated by theology.

Earlier in my curacy I had been invited to two Oxbridge colleges, but had failed to win a job at either. At Lincoln College, Oxford, Hughie Turner was off to a chair at Durham University, and I was asked to go and meet the Fellows with a view to taking his job. I sat next to the Rector at dinner, and I was slightly taken aback when he said to me: 'The person sitting opposite to you is your rival for the job.' His name was Green and he was an historian from Sherborne School. The college decided it did not want another theologian as Fellow and Chaplain and he got the job. He subsequently became Rector of the College. I didn't mind that: I did mind that the college never offered to pay me my travelling expenses.

Then there was a strange episode at Trinity College, Cambridge. The Dean was John Burnaby, a great expert on St Augustine, but only recently ordained. He was a melancholy-looking person, and always saw difficulties ahead. I remember once later on, during a university mission, Burnaby was to chair a study group after the mission address. I heard him say: 'Come on, hurry up: the sooner we begin, the sooner we end', which hardly showed great enthusiasm. At this time he was leaving the deanery at Trinity College to become Regius Professor of Divinity at Cambridge, and was concerned with the appointment of his successor. So down I went to Cambridge, and sat next to him at dinner. After dinner he said: 'Well, Montefiore, I knew you wouldn't do, but I really wanted a foil for Harry Williams.' As a matter of fact, it was a lucky escape. The college was too large for me. I would have loathed going there as Dean.

So now Harry Williams was leaving Westcott House, and I was to take his place. Down we went to Cambridge again. It was all just a little awkward, since I had not been away two years, and that meant that there were some people still there who had been my fellow students. Others had come since I had left, among whom were Stanley Booth-Clibborn (later Bishop of Manchester) and Michael Hare-Duke (later Bishop of St Andrew's). I had to teach New Testament Studies and Doctrine. This meant a tremendous amount of work. I had to get together a course of lectures on the whole of the New Testament, and I had to arrange seminars of four or five people who would come to me weekly, one of whom would read me an essay, and the others would hand in an essay for me to comment on. This was in preparation for the three New Testament papers in the General Ordinands Examination. Teaching was complicated by a local variant, called the Cambridge Ordination Course. And I also had to arrange seminars in the same way on Christian Doctrine, which was divided into two parts, one of which had to be taken each year. I still had a lot of reading to do, and there was very little time in which to do it, as seminars and lectures took up most of the morning and evening hours set apart for work.

Soon Alan Webster departed. He had married while he was Vice Principal, and he and Margaret now had a baby daughter. They had a small flat in Westcott House, and I fear that baby noises and other domesticity were too much for our bachelor Principal, dearly as he loved them. At any rate they came and lived with us in our house for a bit, and then went off to Barnard Castle, where Alan had a most successful incumbency. (He later became Dean of Norwich, and then Dean of St Paul's in London.) Who was to succeed Alan? Ken Carey consulted me, and we both agreed that Bob Runcie was the man, and he also came down from Newcastle to join the staff. I continued to teach the New Testament and Doctrine, while Bob took the Old Testament, Church History and Christian Ethics. Bob was very self-assured and then as now a brilliant conversationalist, while I was still shy, sensitive and somewhat introverted. Although I was Vice Principal and he was Chaplain, I felt somewhat eclipsed, although Bob was somewhat handicapped in that he had read Greats and not Theology at Oxford, and did not seem really interested in theology so much as in history. He was the traditionalist on the staff.

I was allowed to join the theology faculty's senior New Testament seminar, which I attended for the rest of my time in Cambridge. Professor C. H. Dodd chaired it brilliantly, and contributed the bulk of the papers; but there was a galaxy of stars there, or so it seemed to me as the most junior member. Wilfred Knox of Pembroke College was one of three brilliant brothers, the sons of Bishop Knox of Manchester. One was the famous Ronnie Knox, the Roman Catholic priest who translated the Bible (Knox's translation) and wrote *Essays in Satire*, including his famous essay on 'The New Sin'. Another was editor of *Punch*. Wilfred was a staunch Anglican: he was also a wonderful scholar, not only in the New Testament but in classical literature as a whole. I can remember him saying: 'I think there's some reference to this in Josephus' and then he would go up the ladder in the Divinity School senior library (where the seminar was held), pull a dusty old book off the top shelf, open it, turn a page or two, and say: 'Yes, here it is . . .' Another was David Daube, who was a Fellow of Caius. He was a lawyer (he left Cambridge to become Professor of Civil Law at Oxford, and later went to the University of California at Berkeley). He was also most knowledgeable not only in rabbinics, but also in the New Testament. I remember one paper he read about the Aphikomin, the large Matzah (unleavened bread) which is used by the person presiding at the Passover meal. He suggested that it was not a Hebrew word in origin, but the Greek 'aphikomenos', 'he who is to come', referring to the Messiah. I found this kind of scholarship absolutely fascinating.

I remember once preaching at St Edward's Church in Cambridge, and as I was in difficulties for a theme, I betook myself to Dodd's *Parables of the Kingdom* and got my subject from there. You can imagine my horror when on ascending the pulpit I saw sitting straight in front of me Professor C. H. Dodd himself! I had not known that he habitually worshipped there, although he was a Congregationalist. Professor Dodd was always most kind to me. I remember reading a paper about the quotation from Isaiah in the Gospel concerning 'Galilee of the nations' and the beginning of signs (according to the Fourth Gospel) in Cana of Galilee. I had the paper published in the *Journal of Theological Studies*, and Dodd included a reference to it in his forthcoming 'Interpretation of the Fourth Gospel'.

I mention this in some detail because this small triumph was a factor which sparked my ambition to become a real New Testament scholar. I had already started reviewing (anonymously) for the *Church Times* when I was in Newcastle. Here in Cambridge I was invited to do a long review article for *Theology* on the new *Catholic Commentary on Holy Scripture*. The Roman Catholics were just beginning to embrace the higher criticism of the Bible and this was their first fruits. This also sparked my interest and made me wish to become a really professional scholar, as well as to continue as a priest and a pastor.

I remember at this time going to a meeting in Clare College senior common room. It was the inaugural meeting of SNTS (Societas Novi Testamenti Studiorum), the prestigious New Testament society which now has hundreds of members. No one could have guessed from that meeting how prestigious it would become. There were only about twelve people present. Dodd presided, Charlie Moule was there, and so was the great German New Testament scholar, Rudolf Bultmann. I remember his face: it had the kind of look that said: 'Nothing can ever surprise or shock me.' (However, he could surprise and shock others.) It was the only time that I ever saw the great man.

At this time the Church of England was going mad about South

India. This improbable state of affairs had come about because of a plan to unite the Churches in India. The Lutherans and the Roman Catholics had not been able to come into the scheme, but the other Churches had reached agreement to enter into union. All future ordinations would be conducted by bishops who themselves would have been consecrated within the apostolic succession; but the ministry of the remaining non-episcopally ordained ministers would be fully accepted within the new Church without their episcopal ordination. This raised the hackles of the Anglo-Catholics, who felt that this would be betraying the essence of Catholicism. I could not see it myself, since there are bound to be some anomalies at the beginning of a reunion scheme, as disunion itself is an anomaly. Looking back at the controversy now, it all seems very strange; but there are points of comparison with the controversy over the ordination of women to the priesthood. We were told that masses would leave the Church of England if it gave its blessing to the Church of South India; but in the event only a very few left, though of course there was then no financial compensation offered to those who did leave. Even so, we did not recognise those presbyters of the CSI who had not been episcopally ordained, and we gave them no welcome in the Church of England.

At Westcott House we began the custom of taking students on parish visits so that they would be able to know a little about parish life before ordination. In some theological colleges students are taken on 'missions', but that was not our style. During the time that I was on the staff, I led two such visits. One was to the somewhat rural parish of Madron in Cornwall. I cannot remember much about it except that the daffodils were out (it was the spring vacation), and there was a considerable trade in flowers which were despatched wholesale to London. The Vicar was Michael Hocking who wrote books on pastoral theology; and it was good to see that he practised what he preached. The other visit was very different: to George Reindorp, who was then Vicar of St Stephen's, Rochester Row. In his own graphic phrase, there was grass growing in the aisles when he arrived there, and now the church was brimming with life – and with people. All the organisations worked like clockwork, all the services were taken with the utmost efficiency, and there was popular preaching of the highest order. There was a vast staff. I will always remember a staff meeting which we all attended. 'What is your stipend, and what are your expenses?' George asked his staff. The poor deaconess did not know her details, collapsed in a flood of tears, and had to leave the room.

George Reindorp was a great character in the Church of England.

The trio of George, Mervyn Stockwood (Bishop of Southwark) and Gerald Ellison (Bishop of London) were all students at Westcott House together – they must have been a handful for B. K. Cunningham, the then Principal. George later became Provost of Southwark where he woke things up, and then Bishop of Guildford, where he was in his element. He was then despatched to Salisbury to clear up the chaos left by that saintly man Joe Fison (more about him later: I was his successor at Great St Mary's, Cambridge). George was a marvellous radio preacher as well as an outstanding parish priest. I remember him once preaching: 'Every communion we pray: "O Lord, we offer thee our souls and bodies to be a living sacrifice . . ." and then 6d in the collection'. I used to invite him to preach at Great St Mary's. On one occasion he arrived on a Saturday evening when my back was in spasm and I could only lie full length on a garden chair. 'Never mind,' cried George, 'I will take all tomorrow's services for you.' And he did, with gusto – and enjoyed it.

I was getting very fed up with my life as a member of staff at Westcott House. I was overworking, and I never seemed to see my family. We couldn't even have decent summer holidays because of the Long Vacation term. Elisabeth had no sort of role at the college. This time we did not live so far out of Cambridge: we had a house in Chesterton, about a mile away. Chesterton had its own village life, and in the vacations we used to go to Chesterton Parish Church, but the vicar used to shout at God very loudly, so the congregation was not large; and he told me that he kept on the parish communion 'for purely financial reasons'. Elisabeth was fairly well marooned out in Chesterton with three young children. Her back was beginning to pack up partly as a result of childbirth, but also I am sure because of the strain. Two of the children went to a pre-prep. school at the end of the road, but she had to bear the whole brunt of the family, without much relaxation or leisure. I remember one Christmas when she was laid up in bed, and I had to take services and produce the turkey and plum pudding – after a fashion. I never heard her complain, but it must have been awful. During term time I found that we were not even talking to each other, except in bed at night, which was almost the only time in the twenty-four hours I was with her. I felt that this situation was endangering our marriage.

I did the one thing that no clergyman in the Church of England should ever do. I handed in my notice at Westcott House, without having any idea what other post I might be offered. This is a lunatic thing to do, and it has been some people's undoing. (My brother-in-law, David Paton, announced that he was going to leave MECCA in Church House Westminster [Missionary and Ecumenical Council Church Assembly], and he was unemployed until the Archbishop's Adviser on Appointments told the Prime Minister's patronage secretary *he* would resign if something wasn't found for him at once.) The fact that I was driven to this mad step shows the depth of our misery. The Principal of Westcott House never forgave me for resigning – at least I presume he didn't, because I was in Cambridge for another nine years, and he never once invited me back to Westcott House.

I did indeed pray: 'Oh God, what next?'

Chapter Six

FELLOW AND DEAN

Charles Raven was an old Caian, and when he heard that I was, as it were, on the market, he told Gonville and Caius College which was looking for a Dean, after the departure of Eric Heaton to a residentiary canonry at Salisbury. (Eric subsequently became Dean of Durham, and then a highly successful Dean of Christ Church, Oxford.) I was summoned. It was the strangest kind of interview, in the Master's study. The Master, Sir James Chadwick, OM, was a world-famous scientist who had discovered the neutron which made possible the atom bomb, and he had been the chief British representative in the making of the bomb at the Manhattan Project during the second world war. It is said that he was so shaken by its use that he never again entered the Cavendish Laboratory in Cambridge. I found him very likeable, but he was a tired man who kept smelling-salts on his desk, and he had a habit of closing his eyes when one went to see him, presumably in the hope that when he opened them, you (and the problem you brought) would have gone away.

The others present were Stanley Dennison, the Senior Tutor, an economist, and 'Paddy' Hadley the chapel precentor (and incidentally Professor of Music) and Francis Bennett, President of the Senior Combination Room (the senior don). The Master opened the batting by asking me, in default of any other question he could think of, how many candles I liked on the altar! I said it was a matter fairly indifferent to me, but I was used to two, for purposes of decoration, not illumination. After that, the Master could think of nothing further to ask and sank back exhausted; and a long silence ensued. This was finally broken by Paddy Hadley, who asked me what I had done in the last war. When he discovered I had been in the army, he chirped up, and a spirited conversation ensued on army topics. That was all! I was later asked to go back to see the

Master about terms of employment, such as rooms and pay, about which he was meticulous. It was rather sad to see that great brain being turned on to the smallest details of college administration. Whether or not this was a satisfactory method of filling a major college office, ranking only after the Master and Bursar, it was certainly very satisfactory for me.

So I went to Caius as Fellow and Dean. It was a liberation. I seemed to be in the real world again. My actual duties were slight: according to the college statutes the Dean 'shall preserve moral and spiritual discipline among members of the College *in statu pupillari*, and shall be in residence at those times of the year when the Chapel is open for daily service'. I had to take morning prayers (often just me and the lesson reader) and evensong; and I had to read the grace before the first hall dinner. And of course there were the Sunday services of Eucharist and evensong with sermon usually by a visiting preacher. Those were my formal duties, apart from directing studies in theology and supervising pupils who were reading it. But of course there was the pastoral care of the whole college, a huge undertaking when you consider that there were only three eight-week terms in which to do it. There were some sixty fellows to get to know, and some 350 undergraduates, the research students, and of course all the college servants.

I decided that, apart from the leaders among the undergraduates, I had best concentrate on the freshmen, as they would be there for three years. Fortunately I had to interview them all on their arrival for a quarter of an hour each; and there were 120 of them. This gave me an opportunity to get to know something about them. I had pored over their files previously, as a lot of them had to share rooms, and I was responsible for pairing them off. According to my diary, I said to one in connection with the choir 'So you're a great singer, are you?' He misheard me and replied 'Well, not a *great* sinner, sir.' I remember one occasion when I was afflicted with gastric flu. I determined to go ahead with the interviews – at home. I moved into the spare bedroom. I had heard that champagne was good for this particular affliction; the sweetness gave energy, the fizz cheered up the tummy, and the alcohol cheered up the person. Those young men, newly arrived from school, were somewhat taken aback to be summoned to meet the Dean in his pyjamas, lying in bed with a large bottle of champagne beside him. But it served.

The freshmen who had done National Service were far more mature than the others. Those straight from school were very shy: some of them had never been away from home before. The college was very generous to me about an entertaining allowance;

and I soon discovered that if they were holding a knife and fork, they soon relaxed, partly because otherwise they did not know what to do with their hands. Some of them answered my invitation to a meal very naively, beginning 'Dear Mr Dean' and ending 'with love from . . .'. I decided to entertain all of them in groups of four or five during their first term. This meant that I put on at least a stone in the Michaelmas term, with the result that the following Lent term was indeed a penance. I soon discovered that they had no idea when to leave: I used to invent a permanent engagement at 2.30 pm every day.

I would lunch in college most days, and also have dinner in hall straight after evensong in chapel. This meant that I said goodbye to the family for most of term, but there were the vacations and above all three months in the Long Vacation when I could be at home. I found the company in the senior common room absolutely riveting. There were no fewer than thirteen FRS's among the Fellows, and it is from my conversations with them that my fascination with the natural sciences began. There were experts in almost every subject (including Tibetan). After hall there would be coffee, dessert and wine in the senior common room, and conversation then on some evenings could be brilliant. I was in a different world from anything that I had met before, and I lapped it up. Religion frequently cropped up in conversation, and I found among the dons at that time that there were many of them who practised their faith (whether Christian or Jewish), although naturally they tended to go to their parish church rather than come in to college on a Sunday. In fact I was the only who had to be there both on weekdays and on Sundays.

I will always remember biking in one Sunday morning, and seeing something on the senate house roof (adjacent to the college). I could hardly believe my eyes: it was a car. As a result of a bet in a pub, a major scholar in engineering in Caius had masterminded the hoisting of a motorcar on to the roof. It was all very carefully worked out, with safety factors diligently calculated. The car had been left on a Saturday night in the lane nearby, and during the night he and his friends had brilliantly carried out the feat. I gather that he was so worried by the safety factors involved in the particular way in which the fire brigade tried to take it down again that he very nearly gave himself up. Fortunately he did not, and he was never found out. It was the kind of jape in which undergraduates rejoiced. I think that the dons were really rather pleased about it. The older ones remembered that long ago a gun had been stolen from Jesus College and erected in a Caius court pointing at the Master's Lodge.

Later on when I was a tutor I was involved in another such jape when the first motorway, the M1, was opened. Some students thought it would be fun to steal one of those huge motorway signs, and to hang it over the road outside Caius between the buildings on either side. On this occasion they were caught, fortunately before the sign was actually erected, because it could have collapsed on the street below with fatal results. As their tutor I had to appear with them in court. Fortunately I had got hold of a good lawyer. He informed the magistrate that in order to prove a theft, it was necessary to show that the person involved had an intention permanently to deprive its owner. Since these students had intended publicly to display the sign, it was ridiculous to suppose that they intended permanently to deprive the motorway authority. With great reluctance the beak dismissed the case, first summoning me, and asking me if I would speak to the students about what they had done. I said that of course I would, and invited them all to sherry on our return from court.

Caius had many medical students, as befits a college to which Harvey (who discovered the circulation of the blood) had belonged; and though they said dissection of a body was not smelly, I noticed that they tended to start smoking a pipe when they began dissecting. We never had many theological students in Caius, and so, when invited, I also took on the direction of studies in Theology for Sidney Sussex and St Catherine's Colleges. The latter had so many theological students that after a few years I had to give it up. But I used to take in quite a number of students from other colleges for New Testament teaching. I had to do quite a bit of reading to keep up with my subject. I enjoyed supervising, and I found that learning was a two-way process; I could usually pick up something from them, and I hope they learnt from me.

Supervision is a very extravagant way of teaching, but there is nothing quite like it, as it involves person-to-person contact between supervisor and supervisee. One or two people would come to one's rooms weekly, one of them would read aloud an essay, I would then comment, and conversation ensued; and I would write comments on the other unread essay. It was always interesting to try to spot passages copied out from books I had suggested that they read. (There is a charming story of a student who had paid another student to write his weekly essay, and not being very conversant with his subject, read out 'Bophocles' instead of Sophocles. When his tutor expostulated, he responded 'That's what it says here, sir'.) In this mode of teaching, students could pick up not merely facts, but the spirit of the subject and how to approach it.

I only supervised the New Testament (and took in pupils from other colleges on that subject) and in turn sent mine to other supervisors for the other subjects in the Tripos. Unfortunately Geoffrey Lampe, although a Fellow of the college, was not allowed as a professor to teach undergraduates. But I was fortunate in that the college had a Bye-Fellowship in Theology, and this gave me some distinguished colleagues who would share in the teaching; Raphael Loewe, the rabbinics scholar; William Frend, later Professor of Ecclesiastical History at Glasgow (he claimed to teach 'from Adam to the present day'); and John Hick, the distinguished philosopher of religion. As a result I had time to start writing some learned articles for theological journals, of which I wrote a good many. I got hold of an idea, and I enjoyed the research needed to see how it worked out if it did, and what earlier authors had said about it.

After a couple of years I put in for an assistant lectureship in the New Testament in the Theological Faculty, and to my surprise I got it. Subsequently I became a full lecturer, with tenure, and was on the faculty board, and had to examine for the Tripos, etc. (One examiner told me a charming story: one examinee answered thus: 'The Pharisees were a mean and beastly lot. When Jesus asked for a penny, they said: "Whose subscription is this?"' I suppose he was failed.) In one way I was sorry I had the lectureship and not Roland Walls, Dean of Corpus Christi College, because I thought he had better ideas than I had. He was an utterly lovable and brilliant man, but very chaotic, and wrote his ideas on the back of an envelope which he would subsequently lose. (He later opened a house in Sheffield on the same basis as the 'little brothers of Charles de Foucould', and went on to become a lecturer in Edinburgh University, and joined an ecumenical religious community there. After praying in vain for a Roman Catholic member of the community, he realised the only way to get one was for himself to become a Roman Catholic, which he did.) As a lecturer I had my lectures to prepare, and I remember almost the whole of one Long Vacation being taken up with writing a long course of lectures on the Gospels. There was no time to do anything like that during Full Term.

Although the Principal never asked me back to Westcott House, I was elected a member of its council when I left. I am amused to find this entry in my diary: 'Meeting of W. H. Council this afternoon to discuss new building plans. The Chairman opened with the following remark. "As this is an extraordinary meeting of the Council, there will be no need to begin it with prayers."' It seems tactful not to reveal the identity of the chairman.

It was around this time that the marriage of a great friend of mine began to break up. His wife began to act strangely and promiscuously. She was in no state to look after their children, one of whom she even fed with sherry as a babe in arms. She then took up with a former admirer and lived with him. This was the first and last time that I tried to bring together a married couple who had fallen out. His wife did not take kindly to my endeavours: on the contrary she responded fiercely. I was very taken aback when her lover challenged me to a duel. It became a family joke: 'Daddy, when are you going to fight your duel?' I was not going to fight any duel, and I refused to take the challenge seriously. I had forgotten all about the episode until I learnt the other day that it *had* been intended seriously. The man concerned had rung up various South American embassies to find out whether duels were legal in their country. (No doubt the embassy officials were somewhat surprised at such an enquiry.) I gather he did at last find somewhere where duels could take place – I believe it was Chile. How he thought I would go there to fight a duel with him, I have no idea. My friend married again very happily – indeed it is hard to see how his infant children could have been brought up had he not done so – but of course this ended his career in the Church of England. Thereafter I have taken up the cudgels in favour of remarriage in church; not very successfully, I fear, for the question has not been settled forty years on.

When I went to Caius we moved house. On the corner of the Backs and Sidgwick Avenue there was a large house called 'Springfield'. It belonged to Caius, and had been a college hostel. The Master gave the casting vote to turn it into two flats for Fellows. (It has since been returned to a hostel.) I got the downstairs flat, with lovely large rooms, and we invited a friend to advise on their decoration. There was also a large garden. The college asparagus bed had been in that part of the garden that did not belong to us, and this was a great trial, especially as the occupants of the other flat did not seem to care for them. It was not unknown for a daughter to slip out of the kitchen window early in the morning, and cut some.

It was lovely to live so close to the centre of Cambridge, and to be on Backs seems a very privileged position. However, there were debits as well. Before the new Cambridge relief roads were built, it was on the direct route to the container port of Felixstowe, and since there were traffic lights outside, the noise of low gears was very marked, and pollution actually killed the Russian vine by the hedge separating us from the road. Another disadvantage was that, unlike where we had lived previously, our children had no other children with whom to play. (The road of the house where we had been living was friendly: one of our daughters aged five had actually exchanged rings with a boy further up the road.) 'Finella', the house now next door to us, also belonged to Caius (it is now a college hostel) and stood in its own large grounds. It features in some of C. P. Snow's novels. We did not see much of the two families who lived there. One was a Fellow who was an explosives expert. On Guy Fawkes night he used to rig up splendid firework set pieces of naval battles, and would loose Montgolfier balloons. The wife of the other family was a ballet dancer, and half the young girls of Cambridge seemed to attend her classes.

'Springfield' features in that classic book about Victorian Cambridge. *A Cambridge Childhood* by Gwen Raverat. She had lived diagonally opposite us in what has now become Darwin College. We were once kindly invited to dinner when this college began. We were given trifle, in which salt had unfortunately been mistaken for sugar. Naturally we said nothing, nor did our hosts, although we all drank a lot of water.

Our house was overshadowed by trees. Once it had been the residence of the famous Victorian Professor Jebb and his wife. Lady Jebb's house was then the social centre of Cambridge. The spirit of Lady Jebb hung rather heavily over the house, we felt, and one of the children once claimed to have seen a shadowy Victorian figure around. All the same it was a great improvement over our previous house, and we were glad to rent it from Caius College.

The sale of our house had released funds which made it possible for us to buy a holiday home in central Wales. This was the old vicarage at Abergwesyn, in the wildest part, about six miles from Llanwrtyd Wells (known by the family as Polluted Wells) on a loop road which took in Beulah (sic) and about the same distance from Builth Wells (inevitably known as Filth Wells). We were on the old drovers' road which came down the Devil's Staircase (1 in 4 gradient) and then along the upper Gwesyn Valley. This forms now the longest wild open stretch of public road in Wales, all the way across to Tregaron: this was the way in which cattle were driven to London and the Midlands in the eighteenth and early nineteenth century. There is no inhabited house between the old vicarage and Tregaron, some fifteen miles away, except for Llanerch-yrfa at the bottom of the Staircase, where a family camped out in the summer; and it was equally deserted in other directions too. A lot of this country was common land, with wild horses roaming; and much of the rest was in due course planted with fir trees. We were lucky in that Thirza and Dai Jones at the post office in Abergwesyn cleaned and looked after the house while we were not there, until it became too much for them. In the last century Abergwesyn was quite a large village, but now the post office is all that is left with a few scattered farmhouses in the hamlet.

The family became much addicted to Theophilus Jones' *History of Brecknockshire* (1808), and this is how he described Abergwesyn:

> I am now travelling into the wildest, most uncultivated and uninhabitable parts of Brecknockshire, 'where the gilt chariot never mark'd the way'. And where no other carriage, unless it be the small wheel cart and sledge, can pass with safety; a few narrow glens, (where small inclosures, and one mansion house only excepted) intersect the dreary waste: man seems doomed to surrender these regions to the sheep.

Strangely enough there were two parishes here, one north and one south of the Gwesyn, each stretching for miles over the hills. There used to be two churches at Abergwesyn, but both now only have graveyards. St Michael's disappeared long ago. St David's was built by a rich Victorian lady who owned the whole area. (Mervyn Bourdillon, who inherited her estate, was very kind to us.) She insisted on building a church with Bath stone, which seeps up water; and the church had to be demolished in our time as a dangerous structure, and services were then held in the redundant schoolroom. Dai Jones was deacon of the chapel a little further down the valley; but we were an ecumenical village, and he acted as verger to our modest 'Church in Wales' services. He could not master the words of the hymns, but his voice could be heard singing 'Doh, ray, me, fah, so, lah, tee, doh' to whatever tune belonged to the hymn.

AberG, as we called it, soon became a great favourite with the family. There were marvellous walks from here, and a swim in the Gwesyn in hot weather; and soon electricity came up the valley, which transformed our visits, and the old paraffin lamps became museum pieces. It was a very Welsh part of Wales. We once attended a local sheepdog trials to find we were the only people not speaking Welsh. The local vicar, when carried away in his sermon, burst out in vehement Welsh.

We found a hidden valley where there were lizards! To get there we had to go to Soar y Mynydd, the 'Chapel in the Valley', where there had been an old schoolhouse in the middle of nowhere with a fascinating two-seater loo outside. The school had been kept going by the farm at the top of the hill with their six sons; but they had grown up and so it was closed by the time we arrived. Not long after we came, the whole valley below the school was due to be flooded in order to produce a huge artificial lake called Llyn Brianne for Swansea's water supply. I joined with the local schoolmaster in the defence. All the other defendants had some vested interest in the valley. When I was asked on whose behalf I was appearing, I said: 'On behalf of posterity'. This was thought to be someone's proper name until I explained the reasons for my objections. Of course we lost.

Our nearest neighbours at Abergwesyn were the Hopes, who rented a large farm around us. We had to take steps to 'beware of the bull' which was often in the fields opposite us. John Rhys Hope, a bachelor, was a marvellous repository of local folklore, which was extensive. His brother was parsimonious, and used to tie up the gates with string. His son Cledwyn was much beloved by our family, and he and his wife had a much treasured son who died, alas, of leukaemia. We later found out the Abergwesyn had one of the highest fall-outs from the disaster at Windscale (now known as Sellafield), and I have little doubt that their six-year-old Jeffrey was one of its victims. When we first came there were trout in the Gwesyn, but the stream soon became infertile, due both to acidity from the fir trees and acid rain from the skies.

The vicarage was quite extensive, with four bedrooms, lots of downstairs rooms, and a cellar which we made into a chapel with pews from the derelict church. (The rest went to a local pub.) There was a well in the back yard, but it had grown dirty through disuse and we never managed to use it. Water supply was always a problem. We could not persuade the nearby farm to share their supply (which came down from the hills over the river). I remember once Gerald Ellison, the Bishop of Chester (later Bishop of London), who had bought up the old wells at Llanwrtyd Wells as a holiday home (he had on tap the foul-tasting sulphurous water) brought Montgomery-Campbell, then Bishop of London, to see us. He was a great wag, and when Elisabeth told him that I was intending to take on some extra work, he said 'Forbid it absolutely, ma'am.' Unfortunately he asked to go to the loo. This caused consternation in the family because he was bound to pull the plug, which he did, thus perilously reducing our exiguous water reserves. It was all right in a wet year; but very bad in most years, which seemed to be dry ones. We even tried a water diviner to get better supplies, but we never really succeeded.

One year Maurice Wiles (a theology lecturer in Cambridge, later Regius Professor of Theology at Oxford) was convalescing after a nasty attack of meningitis. We suggested that he and Paddy his wife went to 'Delfryn' (the name of the old vicarage). He reported that there seemed to be mushrooms growing in the old vicarage study. When we came up we found this was virulent dry rot. Dry rot is endemic in these old Welsh houses. This one was specially well built with Canadian fir. We never really eliminated it from the building, despite some major surgery, but we did prevent the rampant kind from spreading.

The kitchen, when we bought the house, had an old bread oven. We installed a bath in the old larder just off the kitchen, and warmed up the latter with a Rayburn stove; but the house was deadly cold in the winter. Sometimes we went up there during the Christmas vacation, but it took fully three days to warm the place up. Fortunately there was a good supply of logs from the forestry nearby. The garden, such as it was, was a problem. Dai used to scythe the grass when we first went. Later on when the children had left home, I found it all rather an effort, and I seemed to spend most of my holiday putting it in order: the huge hedge by the road was a particular problem.

When I was made an Assistant Lecturer in Divinity the college no longer had to pay me so much, and it authorised the appointment of a chaplain so that I could be more on a par with other university lecturers. This made life much easier for me, and the two chaplains I had were wonderful people. But I loved the pastoral side of my work, and we shared our duties. During the Easter vacation, the chaplain would bring a reading party up to Abergwesyn, and so quite a number of undergraduates learnt to love that area.

One day I heard that there was a newcomer – a Mr Marlow – living in a cottage a few miles away on a forestry estate. I thought that I would regard myself as a local inhabitant and go and wish him well, especially as I was told that post addressed to Montefiore was being delivered there. 'Good God, cousin Hugh!' was his greeting when I knocked on the door. I found it was the head of the family, living there with a woman under an assumed name. On another occasion I was out with the girls in the snow during the Christmas vacation, and we had just got to the top of the Devil's Staircase, when to our amazement we saw a car making a vain attempt at ascent, faltering and finally coming to a standstill, without, thank God, slipping downhill. We went to see if we could help. Of all people it was Neil and Annabel, one of my nephews and his wife, away on a brief holiday. We rescued them, and brought them home for the night.

All holidays, however precious, come to an end, and we went back to 'Springfield' for the new term. I remember a don looking out of a window in the SCR and when he saw all the undergraduates there again, gloomily exclaiming 'They're here again: no more work for eight weeks!' There were always those who regarded teaching as an unfortunate interruption from their real work of research. Learned publications increased a person's standing. But in the old days, a don did not even bother with taking a PhD (said by some to stand for 'the phoney doctorate'). We had some of these among our senior dons. Sir James Chadwick was said to have been persuaded to take the PhD to make it respectable. Again, it was some time before the college elected a Fellow in English (Donald Davie was our first such don). This was because it had been thought that every educated Englishman was at home with English literature.

The Dean of King's, Ivor Ramsey, my next-door neighbour at Caius, was horribly teased by the dons of his college, most of them humanists and some of them anti-Christian. He could stand it no more, and one night threw himself down from the roof of King's College chapel, and killed himself. We were all in a state of shock about this, and it left Martin Hughes the Chaplain with a great load of responsibility. Suggestions were invited for his successor. I put forward the name of Alec Vidler, who at that time was Canon of Windsor (and incidentally editor of *Theology*). He was a really strong man, a member of the Order of the Good Shepherd, as well as being a very fine church historian, especially on catholic modernism. He was also a person of great character and charm, and also of some eccentricity (he wore a shawl and nightshirt in bed.) I was delighted when they elected him. He began as a fierce English brand of Barthian, preaching at his old church on the text: 'O generation of vipers, who has taught you to flee from the wrath to come?' He was a strong Anglo-Catholic in those days, and had been curate in one of the 'rebel' parishes of Birmingham. He proudly displayed on his mantelpiece a letter from Bishop Barnes of Birmingham telling him he was no longer welcome in his diocese. His views changed, however; and when he was at Cambridge he felt that the Church needed loosening up, and was much criticised for a TV broadcast in which he complained about 'all this church chattering'.

Alec became a great friend of the family, and always had lunch on great festivals with us. The girls were somewhat wary of his Christmas presents, as he was a Syndic of Cambridge University Press, and got all their books free, so that some of those he presented were hardly suited to their tender age. For example, one was *Forked Flame* (a study in D. H. Lawrence), another was Sherrington's *Man and His Nature* and a third was *Corpses* by an Indian writer describing massacres during the India-Pakistan war. When I asked Alec to act as sponsor in an insurance policy for my six-year-old daughter Catherine, he said he did not know her well enough, and to get to know her, he would have to take her out by herself to lunch at the Arts Theatre Restaurant, which he did! She also remembers that on other occasions he gave her a pot of honey (he was a keen apiarist). He retired back to his native Rye, where he became its last mayor, and lived in the wonderful Norman house where he had been born, near to his old college friend Malcolm Muggeridge.

There was considerable rapport among the Deans and Chaplains, and some of us formed a 'Deans' Cell', which included Simon Phipps, John Robinson, Bob Runcie, Murray Irvine (later Provost of Southwell), Charles Walker (who became a devoted Roman Catholic priest and Chaplain to West Indians, and lives near me now), Barry Till of Jesus College, and Roland Walls. We met once a term overnight at Hemingford Grey near Cambridge, where there was a Mirfield retreat house, run by a very 'holy' lady. I blotted my copy book when she asked if we wanted the Angelus, and I turned to the others and said 'Can't do any harm, can it?' And then my alb caught alight from the electric fire in the vestry. It was more of an hilarious talking shop than a retreat, but it did us all good to get away once during term, and to share with one another. At one stage we nearly all shared a watery grave, when we all but went over the weir in a boat.

John Robinson was then the most attended theological lecturer in Cambridge, and his advocacy of 'biblical theology' was becoming very popular. It may appear strange that at that time the future author of *Honest to God* should have in some ways seemed like a biblical fundamentalist, and that probably does not do him justice. But it seemed to some of us that you really could not solve the world's problems by looking up a word in a biblical concordance, and seeing all the uses of that word, and then applying them to today's situations. If that is a caricature of biblical theology, that is how it appeared to some of us.

I remember going with Howard Root (then Dean of Emmanuel College) to see Alec Vidler, and asking him if he would chair a group of us to think out a fresh approach to Christian belief. He graciously accepted, and one of us used to read a paper at our regular meetings. In the end Alec said 'I think there may be a book here' and summoned us all to Launde Abbey (the retreat house of Leicester diocese) to talk the matter through at greater length. I remember the occasion, because over the weekend Bishop R. R. Williams of Leicester, a staunch conservative and a somewhat Erastian figure whom John Robinson used to describe as 'the Leicester Permanent

Building Society', came out on Plough Sunday to bless the plough in this rural setting, which made something of a contrast to what we were about.

Around this time I began for a few months to keep a 'diary of a clerical don', and perhaps I could best illustrate my life at that time by quoting a few extracts:

> Lampes finally left by 11 am overnight, leaving behind a bottle of medicine. I had the car mended – gasket gone – so that at least I could drive in the afternoon. Had things to clear up in college. Left for Launde Abbey at 3 pm, feeling a terrible responsibility for driving the car as I felt I had the brains of the Church of England within – Joe Sanders, John Burnaby, Howard Root and Harry Williams. J. B. rather nervous – tendency to clutch with his hands and mutter 'The roads are rather slippery, aren't they?' Finally arrived at Launde Abbey for the conference; but as soon as I arrived, had to dump them there, and rush into Leicester to pick up Henry Chadwick, who was waiting at the station, having rung me up no less than twice in the morning to arrange a rendezvous.

Next day the conference got under way. 'We agree not to decide now about a new volume of Essays and Reviews but to meet again in a year's time with the rough draft of our essays. We allocate subjects to ourselves and I get Christology – thrilled at the subject and downcast at my inability to cope.' Thus was initiated the book Alec Vidler edited called *Soundings*, which caused widespread interest, and which really began the loosening up of theology in this country.

Donald Mackinnon had arrived from Oxford as the new Norris-Hulse Professor of Theology. He was one of those lovable eccentrics about whom many stories are told, and all of them true. Geoffrey Lampe, whose examination desk was immediately in front of Donald when they were undergraduates at Oxford, told me of the terrible groanings behind him, ending on one occasion with the scrunching up of all that Donald had written. Elisabeth used to remember when she was a student at Oxford joining a study group at which Donald was present when he was a young don at Keble. Donald lay under the table and bit the calves of those who made contributions with which he disagreed. I remember an occasion at a dinner party given by Alec Vidler when Donald spent the entire meal, apart from eating, sharpening a pencil with a bare razor blade. Donald had an encyclopaedic memory, and would quote from obscure foreign journals at will. He was a distinguished catholic Anglican layman

with no time for extreme Anglo-Catholicism. He had a very pen-
etrating mind and was much respected in the university, especially
by philosophers. He gave a lecture course on 'Evil' which was very
popular in the university, illustrating his points by such happenings
as the 'Brides in the Bath' murders. He was very helpful to me, for
example, by reading through my contribution to *Soundings*. He used
to turn up in my rooms in college, and stay talking for what seemed
hours, and suddenly I would look up, and he was gone.

During the vacations I could take a little time off. I find this rather
tetchy note in my diary.

> Went to London to have lunch with my mother (at her VAD
> club) and see 'Aladdin'. A typically Montefiore proceeding. S,
> with C and M (cousins) arrived late as D's chauffeur-gardener
> had got lost. The lunch was terrible frost to the grandchildren
> (who had come 120 miles for it). The best seats in the theatre,
> of course; so we were in the front row of the stalls where the
> children could hardly see the stage. And the panto was all legs
> and scenery and show, with no wit or humour. I was shocked at
> myself for being so angry with my mother who preferred to give
> the theatre tickets to Eliza as she thought I would lose them.

That was the way it was. Eliza always coped with her much better
than I did.

By this time I had been made a Tutor at Caius, so that in addition
to my duties as Dean of the college and university lecturer, I had
a quarter of the undergraduates (and also at that time the research
students too) to look after. As at that time twenty-one was the time
when one came of age, I was really *in loco parentis*. I would have to
sign permission for leave (absits) and suchlike, and consider terminal
reports from their supervisors and director of studies; and I was also
in charge of their discipline (having the power to 'gate' them, etc).
It was rather like a doctor's surgery: some pupils one only saw at
the beginning and end of term; others seemed to be always there.
Naturally much went on about which I knew nothing. Here is an
extract from my diary:

> Difficult moral situation. P mentioned in passing when I was
> giving him lunch that T is a lucky beggar to have a car up here,
> and that he will cadge a lift home from him. T is my pupil and
> has no permit for a car. Asked for help in hall from the fellows
> round me. As a result I've decided to send a copy of the college
> regulations to T, marking the passage about cars and then send

for him in a week's time to ask him if he has a car in Cambridge. He'd be a fool if he had by then.

And another typical extract:

> I had to fine T £3 yesterday for trying to bring a girl into hall. This hurt him a lot – and, honestly, it hurt me as much for I love him dearly. I offered him a fortnight's gating in lieu, but he preferred the fine. I warned him in a fatherly way not to get his fingers burnt – and half an hour later he appeared in chapel for the first time this term.

I was also elected to the College Council, which ran the college. All elections to fellowships and appointments were made by this body, which also made the administrative and financial decisions necessary to run the college. The Master, the President, the Bursar and the Senior Tutor were there *ex officio*; the remaining eight were elected. It took up an awful amount of time, some four hours every fortnight, sometimes longer; and then there were committees. (The only committee I really enjoyed was the wine committee.) But it was interesting, not least to see the clash of interests. I learnt to dread that remark: 'Master, I object on principle . . .' This usually meant that the person concerned was objecting on prejudice. All this left less time than I would have liked for pastoral work with undergraduates, but I had in turn two quite outstanding chaplains, Denys de la Hoyde and Alan Pyburn.

Just before I came there had been a putsch in the college which became known as the 'Peasants' Revolt', partly because Bauer means peasant and Peter Bauer (later Lord Bauer) had been the candidate put up by the peasants to break the monotonous way in which certain Fellows regarded themselves, once they were on the College Council, as entitled to continuing re-election. Two of the four tutors were also deprived of their tutorship. Stanley Dennison, then Senior Tutor, had taken a leading part in this. Although it benefitted the college to have new blood in the running of its affairs, the way in which the revolt was conducted left some deep wounds, and one of the tutors concerned was so hurt that he only came into college thereafter to teach or to come to Sunday chapel. It was part of my job to try to heal these wounds so far as I could (and that was not much). This meant listening to both sides.

The College Council was naturally the scene of continuing power struggles; and involvement in college politics was to a certain extent necessary. The Council met fortnightly after lunch until the evening.

The Master became increasingly conservative. He was frightened of electing new Fellows. Every Fellow had a right to bring in a guest for dinner, and he said that if we went on in this way, the whole of hall could be full of Fellows and their guests so that there would be no room for any undergraduates. In fact Fellows, who had one free meal a day in hall, usually chose lunch, and went home to their families in the evening, so there were scarcely more than a dozen or two on an ordinary evening. He and Eileen Chadwick found the Lodge very inconvenient; but the College Council naturally wanted them to continue to live there. And so it went on, and in the end the Master resigned.

There ensued a mastership election. One such is described by C. P. Snow in *The Masters*, but that election seemed tame compared with ours. For example, a favourite candidate was a professor in Oxford. His opponents said he was living with his secretary, and I was despatched to find out. I reported that there was no evident sign of cohabitation. Of course there was not. Then that faction which wanted a more radical candidate but who were frustrated by not amassing enough votes suddenly changed sides, and said they would vote for the most conservative person imaginable. But then it was realised that this person would only be Master for two or three years before he had to retire and then they hoped that they would get their own candidate in, second time round. And so it went on. I persuaded Professor Sir Nevill Mott to stand. In his autobiography he has written that his Mastership was not the happiest period of his life; and I think that most of the Fellows who were in Caius with him would agree with that. At least, I tried to comfort myself, it was better than it would have been under the other candidates.

The president of the senior common room presided over the mastership election. He was Sir Ronald Fisher, Professor of Genetics. As befitted a professor of genetics, he had a large family, all daughters, eight of them, I think; but they did not live in Cambridge. He lived a bachelor-like existence. He was not overgenerous in money affairs; and when he found that if a professor slept in his free rooms in college, money would be deducted from his university salary, he decided to sleep in his laboratory, although of course he continued to have his rooms in college. He was very shortsighted, and devoted to his pipe. When retained by the tobacco companies to testify against the carcinogenic properties of tobacco, he developed a theory that if smokers developed cancer, they were going to do this anyway, so why deny the poor blighters the pleasure of smoking? He was quite brilliantly clever, and he is best known as providing the statistical basis for the theory of neo-Darwinism.

Ronald was also a professing Christian, although he was essentially an individualist and had his own personal interpretation of the Christian faith. He wore a different hood (from his many honorary degrees) every Sunday night in full term when he attended college chapel. He even preached there occasionally, although it would be fair to say that few people could understand what he was driving it. I had a great affection for him, and he struck up a correspondence with my second daughter Janet, then I suppose aged about nine or ten. When he did *The Times* crossword every day, which he finished with all despatch, he left blank interstices of words 'down' and 'across', saying that it was a waste of time to write them in; indeed it is said that he died doing *The Times* crossword in hospital in Australia. At any rate he decided that the fairest way of conducting the election was by means of the 'single transferable vote', which unfortunately few of the other Fellows could really understand.

One of the stranger episodes that happened to me as Dean concerned someone whom the college took in from Hungary after the Hungarian rising against the Soviets. I saw him when he arrived, as I did everyone else, and said to him: 'You can always ask my help, and it needn't be about religion.' I was very surprised one day when he turned up and said: 'I want help. I want to spy for Britain. What should I do?' I felt it was more a question of what should *I* do! Was it moral to help someone to spy? I came to the conclusion that spying was inevitable, and I had no good moral grounds to thwart him. I went to see the Chief Constable, who informed MI5. Eventually someone was sent down to see him in my rooms, after an extraordinarily convoluted journey to avoid observation. Unfortunately MI5 made my rooms the usual place for a meeting after the man was enlisted. He really wanted money, as his country would not give him any. But they paid his college bills without question, including his buttery bills. He discovered he could buy whisky galore in the buttery, flog it to fellow students, and get pocket money that way. He got some money out of MI5 but I doubt if they got anything back from him. They were justifiably alarmed when he took a party to Russia in the vacation and heard nothing for weeks. However, they all came back, and in the end MI5 gave the man up in despair.

As a tutor I had to interview people at the college entrance examination just before term, and another of my jobs was to chair the college livings committee. Almost all of our benefices were in East Anglia: after all, at one time the college only admitted students from Norfolk. I find this entry for 6 January 1960:

T came to lunch about the college living of Mattishall (Norfolk). I found I had met him at Westcott House refresher course. I remember one year he cycled in from Norwich to Cambridge. Ex-scholar of Peterhouse, all his life in a poorly paid country living; slow, shrewd, wise, he's the best kind of country parson. Entrance examination this evening with difficult co-interviewers. P is too absurdly charitable, and M is too sharp and too talkative. I wonder what they both think of me?

and two days later:

Long session with S over the college accounts [we had both been appointed by the College Council examiners of accounts], and at last it looks as though we have got out an agreed report. Very wearing; but a welcome change from reading scripts [from the entrance examination] which I usually do at this time of the year.

Gonville and Caius was then, after King's and St John's, the wealthiest college; and naturally bursars like to amass capital, and naturally Fellows want it spent on the four objects of the college; religion, learning, education and research. So one of the tasks for the examiners of accounts was to see where (if anywhere) money had been hidden away.

But term was about to restart. Three days later I write:

The whole racket is about to begin again. I feel very remote from it all after a vacation; and then I see the undergraduates again and I find myself loving them and caring for them; and after a day or so the stimulus begins to work and my tempo of living and ratiocination increases. But just at the moment I'm a little flat, like a soldier on D-Day minus one; a little self-pitying as I contemplate the end of a delightful 'leave' with my adorable family.

Here is an interesting entry for the beginning of term:

One of those rather scrappy days giving out loads of work for other people to do – bags of essays which I will have to listen to within the week!
   Interesting discussion at dessert . . . We were talking about traitors and I asked the Master [Chadwick] if he had known Fuchs [who betrayed our nuclear secrets], and he told me

he had had Fuchs as his research student at Bristol. F was known to be left-wing, was very quiet and nervous. Stayed with a Quaker family who for Quakerish reasons had put him up free. F had never written a word or communicated with them in any way since. The Master remembered how in a group discussion some research students had read like a play the transcripts of the 'treason purse' trials in Russia. Suitably F had read the part of prosecutor.

Everyone seemed to agree that P. G. Wodehouse's 'Great Sermon Handicap' is one of our best English short stories.

It was around this time that the scheme for Churchill College broke upon the university. There was to be a committee of trustees to receive money and to establish the college before handing it over to Fellows. It was said that the college would be on traditional lines, but when the scheme was actually published there was no mention of either a chapel or a dean. Barry Till and I went to see Noel Annan, Provost of King's, who was Chairman of the Trustees. (He was later Lord Annan, and Vice Chancellor of London University.) Annan said: 'You won't believe it, but we forgot!' He promised to ask 'the old man' (Churchill) who when asked said 'A quiet room will do.'

Annan said that the only way he thought we could get a chapel was to find a benefactor. I immediately sent in a cheque made out to the Churchill College Chapel Fund; and when it was accepted, I thought that at least we were on the right road. I then set about finding a donor. Unfortunately the rich people whom I knew were all Jews, who could hardly be asked for a chapel. There was, however, a wealthy priest whose father had served in the same regiment as I had been during the war. Timothy, now Lord Beaumont, after reading Agriculture at Oxford, had come to Westcott to train for the priesthood when I was Vice Principal there. He had come into his inheritance and had been immensely generous in giving away large sums, so that today he is no longer wealthy. He had financed *New Christian*, which under the editorship of Trevor Beeson had been a very successful Christian periodical, but which could not be sustained because it could not attract advertising. When I approached Timothy he responded most positively, offering to give the entire cost of the chapel on the grounds that his father had been a liberal who deeply disapproved of Churchill.

This decision did not commend itself to the Fellows of Churchill College, although they were still in the hands of their Trustees. In their plans the architects had placed the chapel right at the centre of the new college: plans had to be revised to move it to the remotest

corner of the site. The Fellows said that they would not administer
the chapel, and so a Churchill College Chapel Trust was formed.
Francis Crick, who with Watson discovered the double helix of our
genetic code, and was a member of Caius whom I personally found
very engaging, had become a Fellow of Churchill, but he was so
disgusted at the chapel that he resigned his Fellowship. He also
offered a substantial prize for the best undergraduate essay on
the best use to which a college chapel could be put! Fortunately
Churchill College engaged as chaplain Noel Duckworth who became
a friend of everyone in college; but later I found that the chapel
had fallen on evil days, served by an outside priest, with a secular
counsellor rather than a pastoral priest available to undergraduates
in need of help. The full story of the Churchill College chapel is told
in my biography by John Peart-Binns. I was no longer *persona grata*
at Churchill; and although other colleges invited me from time to
time to their feasts, Churchill never did.

It was during my early years at Caius that the benefice of Great
St Mary's, the university church, became vacant. Since it had no
vicarage, it had always formerly been filled by a wealthy clergyman
from Trinity College, which held the patronage of the living. However, John Burnaby, on behalf of the Trinity Livings Committee,
decided that next time round a change should be made. Caius was
the nearest college to Great St Mary's, and I remember Burnaby
coming round to ask me if I thought that college chapels could
stand the competition of a popular preacher at Great St Mary's. I
replied that I thought that this would stimulate religion as a whole
in Cambridge, and I was in favour of it. Enough other deans must
have given a similar answer, for he persevered with his project,
and Mervyn Stockwood accepted the living. Mervyn had made a
great reputation in Bristol, not least for his ecumenical ventures
with the Methodist Church. He was known to be a member of
the Labour Party. He was forthright in his preaching, with a great
sense of humour, and he transformed Great St Mary's overnight. I
and my family had been looking for a parish church since we had
moved to 'Springfield' and we went to Great St Mary's as soon as
Stockwood had come and had instituted a parish Communion. He
arranged courses of sermons for morning service and for an 8.30 pm
special student service, which was really a preaching occasion with
an opportunity for students to question the preacher on 'Mars Hill'
afterwards.

The undergraduates warmed to Mervyn's style, which mixed
serious theology with popular preaching and homely analogies.
Soon it was not unusual for the student evening service to have

an attendance of over one thousand. I offered Mervyn the use of my rooms while I was dining in hall after our college service on Sunday evenings, so that he could have a brief rest between his evening service for the town and his student service. Soon came the Suez crisis of 1956. It became known that Mervyn proposed to preach about the situation the following Sunday. This crisis sharply divided both senior and junior common rooms – some dons were not on speaking terms with one another – and the Vice Chancellor begged Mervyn to desist. He did not. Accounts of the lengths of the queues to get in have certainly been distorted as the years have gone by – I have even heard it said that the queues reached all the way down King's Parade to the Botanical Gardens; although not as long as that, they certainly stretched a long way. Mervyn preached a splendid sermon, and the occasion was a truly spiritual one. Thereafter Great St Mary's became a popular focus of the university; where, incidentally, boy might meet girl. His ministry was outstanding, and he also was assiduous in building up the town congregation into the largest in the city – and Cambridge was a very churchgoing place. He was a wonderful visitor. I remember once coming back to our house in 'Springfield', and finding him engaged in a spitting match with my seven-year-old daughter Catherine.

After a whirlwind ministry of three years, Mervyn was offered the bishopric of Southwark. He did not really want to leave what was for him the promised land of the university pulpit. Should he go? He invited a number of people to an extraordinary meeting in my rooms one night after the evening service. It so happened that the Archbishop of York was in Cambridge that Sunday, but he sensibly refused to attend. Mervyn asked us whether we thought he should stay or go. We all said that, although we enormously appreciated his ministry among us, we felt he was needed in the wider church, and that he should go. The only person to dissent was Ken Carey, Principal of Westcott House. He said afterwards that he did not think that Mervyn should be a bishop because his health would not stand it, and he would either die under the strain or would have to retire early. Alas Ken himself died from a tumour on the brain; but Mervyn Stockwood, who has recently died, lived into his eighties.

Mervyn Stockwood was succeeded by Joe Fison, a prophetic figure whose voice it was said could be heard in Oxford from the Broad to the High. Joe was always looking over his shoulder to Mervyn's successes, but he was a very holy man and when on form a preacher of the very first rank. He was, however, totally unsuited to the task of making administrative arrangements. I remember that he once called at our house, and as he took his handkerchief out of his pocket, a paper fell on the floor. It was the 'last final notice' of an electricity bill. Such was the method of appointment to bishoprics in those days that the Prime Minister's patronage secretary happened to hear him preach one day at Great St Mary's and was so bowled over that, again after only a three-year ministry, Joe was consecrated as Bishop of Salisbury.

On one occasion when Joe came back to preach at Great St Mary's, he said to me that he was going into his bedroom on the Sunday afternoon to compose his sermon, and nothing, absolutely nothing must disturb him. Soon the telephone rang for him, and I told the caller his message. 'Tell him his palace is on fire' came back along the line. So I did disturb him and he was aghast. All he could say was 'O dear! O dear!'. In Salisbury it could be said that his early death was of a broken heart, as he poured out his pastoral care on individuals and was totally at sea without the administrative expertise needed for coping with a huge rural diocese.

Shortly after Mervyn Stockwood left, he persuaded John Robinson (who had been his curate in Bristol) to leave the deanery of Clare College and to be consecrated as his Suffragan Bishop of Woolwich. John naturally retained his links with Cambridge. He fell ill with a slipped disc and during this enforced idleness he wrote a book published under the title *Honest to God* which, as a result of an *Observer* headline 'Our Image of God Must Go' became a best-seller with a sale of over one million copies. John invited a number of us from Cambridge to an extraordinary meeting at 12 Manor Road, his London see house. We had all been sent proof copies of the book, and asked our opinions of it. We all agreed that he should go ahead and publish it, but some of us thought that passages which could be misunderstood should be changed. However, now that the book was in proof, there was little chance of that; and when I wrote afterwards to John with some suggestions, he replied on the theme 'What I have written, I have written.' The Cambridge movement which began with *Soundings* was carried much further by *Honest to God*. A somewhat muddled book, it scandalised many older people at the time (including the Archbishop of Canterbury); but it is probably fair to say that it gave new hope and deepened faith to many more who felt the divorce between orthodox belief and current ways of thinking.

I think that the divinity faculty began to realise, with all this popularising of 'Cambridge Theology', that it ought to do more to bring modern theology in a relevant way to the attention of ordinary undergraduates. Several series of 'open lectures' were initiated, which proved immensely popular, and took place in the examination schools, as being the largest lecture theatre in the university; but even this could only with difficulty accommodate the numbers attending. Some of these series were later published. I gave one on 'Sexual relations before marriage' which drew an immense crowd (later published in *God, Sex and War*). This was at the time when conventional sexual mores were beginning to be challenged, and was therefore very relevant to the needs of undergraduates.

Earlier Geoffrey Lampe had enlisted Cambridge theologians on the subject of Holy Communion. This was long before the rules had been changed, which now allow anyone who is in good standing in a Church which believes in the Holy Trinity to share in Communion at an altar in the Church of England. In those days this was forbidden; and Anglicans who communicated at Free Church altars were considered *outré*. I was one of the thirty-nine whom Geoffrey got to sign a statement which justified what had earlier been the well-established practice of 'occasional Communion' in the Church of England. The media seized on this as a sign that Cambridge theology was beginning to make its presence known not just in academic circles but also within the institutional Church.

This was a time of hyperactivity on my part. So many opportunities seemed to be opening. I was invited to preach at many public schools on Sundays out of term, which I usually accepted, partly because I wanted to foster good relations between the schools and the college. I was on the Ordination Candidates Committee of CACTM (the Council's Advisory Council for Training for the Ministry). There I met many like-minded friends. Candidates were booming and we decided to promote a new large theological college. A substantial extension was built with church money to Queen's College, Birmingham. Although a new college was planned for Nottingham, the London College of Divinity was moved there in 1970 and renamed St John's College. The ethics examination of the General Ordinands Examination had been dropped, because it was thought that the syllabus at theological colleges was too large. This meant that clergy were being set loose with no formal training in ethics of any kind. I proposed that the exam be re-introduced with a more sensible syllabus, and the proposal was passed.

I have said little about life at home. Fortunately Elisabeth kept a 'little green book' in which some of the girls' *bon mots* were noted down when they were young. Perhaps, as one might expect in a clerical household, many of these concerned misunderstandings in church. One, for example, thought that the Communion Service was about 'meat and rice' (a mishearing of the words: 'It is meet and right so to do'). Another one asked: 'Mummy, what does conscious mean?', and after the word had been explained, said: 'No, I mean church – Conscious Pilate.' One was once heard chanting in the Creed, in place of 'Very God of very God', the excellent emendation 'Merry God of merry God'. The word in the weekly collect 'adversities' was difficult for them, for one was heard to pray 'Keep us, Lord, from all advertisements which may happen to the body.' They knew the origin of Guy Fawkes Night, for in planning fireworks, one said 'We'll have Roman candles – and catholic wheels.'

They learnt the facts of life. I once met their complaints with the words: 'Without Mummy and me you wouldn't be here.' One of them said 'Oh, *I* know, we did it in Science', and another interposed 'You always know when the staff are going to start on it – they talk about the birds and the bees.' 'We did the diagrams too,' she continued. They noticed I was overworking at college. One wrote in an essay on 'My Mummy': 'My mummy is called Elisabeth. She has grey eyes and black hair and she's always making a fuss about Daddy coming home at midnight or at one o'clock in the morning.' When Elisabeth once said: 'Bother, the Army & Navy haven't got a botanist's vasculum', one exclaimed: 'Ooh, Mummy's said a naughty word.'

As they got older, there were occasional visits to London to the theatre. I can remember returning at great speed one night from such an occasion, and noticing that a car was following behind us for some miles. Eventually it overtook us, and pulled me up. I was accused of going over seventy miles an hour, which was true enough; but it was 1 am, and the new speed restriction had been imposed for the first time from midnight. I thought that on this occasion the police were being somewhat overconscientious.

The children were happy. They did not have much to do with the university, although they remember the axolotl in the natural history museum, and seeing liquid hydrogen poured out in the Cavendish Laboratory. They were a great help when we entertained undergraduates. Janet used to divide them up into two categories: those who liked to talk about ideas, and those who liked to talk about food. They were well settled in Cambridge schools, and I did not want to move. However, I was becoming rather good at writing long academic footnotes to learned papers, and I felt a strong vocation as a priest, which I felt was hardly compatible with a full-time academic professorial post. I note this in my diary for 11 May 1960:

K suggested that I might become the first professor of theology at Makerere, Uganda. This is a vital and fascinating job, but I don't see how I can entertain the idea. In the first place, I don't think that E's spine would be strong enough; and then, what of our children? African education would be hopeless, and we have *no* relatives in this country who would be suitable, and really the children do deserve proper consideration and a home life of some kind. This is the third chair for which I have been sounded out in a year – first King's College, London, then Bangor, now this. And each of them has had to be turned down for what I'm sure are the right reasons. It would be so much easier if I had a clear plan of what the remaining twenty-five years or so of work should entail. But I haven't. I'm sure that I ought not to remain in Cambridge until retiring age. And I feel that I'll be moving off in a year or two – the feeling is strengthened by the departure of so many of my friends. The best thing seems to be to stay put until I am offered a job which I know is right.

As this shows, Elisabeth's health had not been good. Her back gave her much trouble, and she suffered also from a feeling of exhaustion, so that she had to rest most afternoons. We had had a succession of au pairs, mostly from Scandinavia. On the whole they were a great success, and we still keep up with many of them thirty years later. We did, however, learn that it was imprudent to go away together and leave the girls with them: undesirable parties could take place. One particular girl was most unsatisfactory, and finally got herself pregnant by, of all people, a Caius research student from abroad. (This proved a little awkward for me when his case was brought to the College Council.) She went home.

I had to spend a great deal of time with the Bye-Fellow who had succeeded Raphael Loewe. He was the Revd Emmanuel Amand de Mendieta, a Benedictine of a very good family in Belgium. He had become a convinced Anglican, and was received into the Church of England; and had married a young Belgian girl. He won the Cook Bye-Fellowship and there was quite a media fuss about his first celebration of Holy Communion as an Anglican in our college. I was determined that this should be low key, without the press. It was at 8 a m, admission was by ticket, and I had all the college gates locked; and as a precaution I posted a choral exhibitioner (who was also a boxing Blue) outside the chapel. I was nearly outwitted. The *Daily Express* sent down an old Caian reporter who got in through the college kitchens; but the boxing Blue was more than a match for him.

What on earth would happen to de Mendieta when his three-year

Bye-Fellowship ran out? He could not fend for himself, and he couldn't master either English idioms or English intonation at all well: when I made him see a speech therapist, I was told, somewhat strangely, that his tongue was not long enough to cope with the English language. He took everything very literally. According to my diary, I was driving him home from Oxford one day, and stopped at Bedford for lunch. 'There are hundreds of cafes here,' I said. 'Surely not a hundred?' he replied.

If I didn't take up his case, no one would. Archbishop Fisher, who had received him into the Church of England, and who had said he would take responsibility for his future, had written to tell me that it was I who must find him a job. Various kinds of research fellowships and posts all fell through. The college kindly gave him an extra year; but still nothing came. Then Dr Joseph Needham decided that he could qualify for a special Fellowship under the college statutes as 'a person of exceptional distinction in science literature or art'. De Mendieta's only real interest was a critical edition of the Greek texts of an early Christian Father called St Basil the Great. Needham made him put all his voluminous publications into a tin trunk, and the college porters had to lug this around to the rooms of members of the College Council (who had surely never even heard of St Basil). He did not get the Fellowship. What could I do? I wrote to every bishop as soon as I saw in the papers that there was a vacancy in a residential canonry. Letters always came back with impeccable excuses: the canonry was reserved for a particular post, etc. Finally I struck lucky: two canonries became vacant at the same time in Winchester. Dr Allison could not think of two sets of excuses, and off he went to be a Canon of Winchester until sadly he died a few years later, and his wife went back to Belgium.

Joseph Needham was a great character, who later became Master of the college, and healed most of its wounds still festering from previous troubles. In his younger days he had been a fervent Christian Socialist, with many writings to his credit. Although he did not get a First as an undergraduate, he was a brilliant biochemist, and at one time he and his wife Dorothy were the only married couple both of whom were FRS. When he was elected Fellow, the college was very conservative, and he was ostracised for his extreme political views. He told me that when he came to dine in hall in the evening, he had to eat in silence because no one would speak to him. During the war he was in China for UNESCO, and this combined with his socialism made him very uncritical of that country, as well as very knowledgeable about it. When the Chinese accused the Americans of dropping infected flies on the country,

Joseph endorsed the accusation, which greatly distressed 'Chubby' Stratton, who as Deputy Lord Lieutenant complained that he did not like to bring Americans into hall to dinner. Joseph had begun to write a History of Chinese Science, which no one really could review knowledgeably in this country, as they did not know enough about the subject. In the SCR we became wary of saying when anything was first invented (such as a watch) because Joseph could always tell us that the Chinese had invented it many centuries earlier. The History is so long that Joseph became worried whether he would complete it before he died. He is now aged over ninety, but there is now a Needham Institute in Cambridge to see that the work goes on.

Chubby Stratton, mentioned above, was a former Professor of Astronomy, through whose hands many famous astronomers had passed. He was also a keen member of the Society for Psychic Research, although as a very down-to-earth person, he believed all the phenomena could have a physical explanation, such as subsidence. Chubby was very old and conventional: in his room a Victorian tablecloth covered his table. He was a keen Unitarian, so that I did not have to officiate at his funeral. He had very bad luck: he travelled the world in order to observe a total eclipse, but wherever he went, it was cloudy. He was a very upright person, very keen on military affairs, and he took his deputy Lord Lieutenancy very seriously.

Another senior Fellow whom I ought to mention was Francis Bennett, one of those who interviewed me before I came. Francis was one of those invaluable Fellows who attend all possible college functions. He had earlier been Senior Tutor, and had a great love of the college. He was, however, very superstitious. I remember driving him to the institution of a vicar to a college living. I saw he was bowing and raising his hat. 'What on earth are you doing?' I asked. 'We have just passed a sweep,' he replied. I particularly remember him at the Shakespeare Society, where we met once a fortnight to read alternatively a Shakespeare play and one by another author. As a matter of fact, I felt that there were not sufficient opportunities for senior and junior members to meet, so I started a society for both, where every member had to read a paper on a subject of his choice. I called it the Sherrington Society after the great man (who was a Caian), and I think it still flourishes.

Paddy Hadley was the Precentor. He was Professor of Music, but basically a composer, with a particular love of folk tunes. His greatest pleasure was conducting the College Chorus, which in its religious aspect was the Chapel Choir. In his day it numbered forty-five people! I cannot resist this entry from my diary: 'I'm told that the Precentor got muddled in his practice for Sunday's anthem (old Caian Jeremy Taylor's "Heaven") and instead of "uncircumscribed treasure" sang "uncircumcised treasure".' I was devoted to Paddy. He always insisted 'Now, chaps, we are the servants of the chapel.' During the First World War he had lost a leg, and he wore a wooden one. I remember once, when we were interviewing candidates for Choral Exhibitions, the eyes of a candidate glazed over as he looked down at Paddy's leg. His sock was secured with a drawing pin. He could not know that it was a wooden leg!

Paddy loathed sermons. I had to warn visiting preachers that after their invocation at the start there would be an audible click, when Paddy held up his stop watch to time them. After ten minutes there would be audible sighings. As a result of his war wounds, Paddy used to have drinking bouts. The organ scholar Martin Neary (now organist of Westminster Abbey) was marvellous at ministering to him. Paddy's father had died at the age of sixty, and he was convinced that he too would die then; and so he retired to the Evelyn nursing home to await the event. When it did not happen, he came back, but resigned the Precentorship.

The visiting preachers in chapel varied in their style and content. One Sunday evening I invited the Revd F. A. Simpson, who had begun to haunt the college chapel for weekday evensongs, lurching about and wandering in and out of the chapel. Simpson was a Fellow of Trinity College and one of the great eccentrics of Cambridge, wandering around cutting grass edges with nail scissors and famous for his jams. The full story of this extraordinary man has been written up by Eric James in *A Last Eccentric*. Having written the first two volumes of his history of Louis Napoleon, universally praised as brilliant, Simpson produced nothing more, but remained a Fellow of Trinity until he died aged ninety-one.

Many are the stories that could be told: here I mention only one. In 1948 Simpson had published *A Last Sermon*. However, in the mid-1950s he began to preach around Cambridge a sermon on the Good Samaritan. He once prefaced it in King's College chapel by saying: 'You may have heard this sermon before, but I always say it is better to hear a good sermon twice than a bad sermon once.' I invited him to preach in Caius. He started off in fine style, but three quarters of the way through he stopped abruptly, said 'Oh my God' and rushed out of the chapel. I immediately announced the last hymn, and wondered if he had gone outside to die. The evangelicals were delighted, saying how good it was to hear a clergyman publicly calling on God. I found him outside after the service in good heart, and took him into hall where he ate a hearty meal. When I ventured to ask him what had been his trouble, he tossed it aside, saying 'A momentary *aphasia*, a momentary *aphasia*!' What had happened I am sure was that the old man had suddenly run out of steam. He always memorised his sermons, which were masterpieces of brilliant and moving rhetoric, even down to the last comma. He had suddenly forgotten how to go on.

I cannot resist two more citations from my diary:

M told me a strange story of C when he was Dean of J long ago. Undergraduates got screwdrivers and secured his 'oak' (outer door). He was seen leaning out of his window and wailing to the Master who was passing in the court below: 'Master, Master, I've been screwed in my rooms.'

Rather unfortunate text by the preacher tonight at this evening's sermon – 'Call no man Master' – and there sat the Master, impassive in his stall.

I have spent a lot of time recalling the lighter side of life among senior members; but in fact most of my time was spent with the junior members, and I felt privileged to have their friendship, which in some cases still continues. Many of them in later life have achieved distinction in various fields. Three are now bishops. There were those who became politicians such as Sir Terence Higgins or Kenneth Clarke, or European statesman Lord Tugendhat. David Frost was also an undergraduate. As a state scholar his performance was dismal, as he spent his time with the Footlights or Anglia TV, and we would have sent him down but for the plea of his Methodist minister father that he could not face his congregation if we did. Sending people down was one of the least pleasant tasks of the Tutors' Meetings, as was deciding the large number among the applicants who could not be admitted to the college. Lesser punishments were in the hands of the tutors.

As for the chapel fellowship, I had started what was called 'The Church in the College' to which all baptised members of the college belonged, whatever their denomination, providing that they accepted a basic Christian rule of life. The Church in the College would meet together once a term to discuss chapel policy, and very responsible people they were. The Free Church members were very loyal to the chapel as well as attending their own church on a Sunday evening; but it seemed that they gave more than they received. I can remember agonising discussions when the idea of concelebration with a Free Church minister was introduced. Only seven people were against this, but the meeting of over one hundred unanimously decided that rather than disrupt the chapel fellowship it would be better not to have this. This was an early introduction to undergraduates of the pains and joys of the ecumenical movement. Chapel attendances at that time were very good. We would have up to one hundred to the college Communion on Sunday morning, and eighty-five at 7.45 am on Ascension Day; and usually a pretty full chapel for college evensong in the evening. It was a time when the Christian religion was flourishing in Cambridge; many other college chapels had similar attendances.

Many pastoral problems came my way about which it would be inappropriate to write here. Anything could happen. A typical note in my diary 'W came and told me he was offering himself for the Methodist ministry. S wants to make his First Confession. Church traditions work differently, but God is glorified in all.' And another: 'I told an ordinand to stop teaching in a Sunday school – that's not what he's here for. In the evening a freshman burst in, breathed in my face and said: "I've a temperature of 103°." With a kindly voice which I hope disguised my self-interest, I suggested lying down on a sofa in my other room. Phoned for a taxi and got him into hospital in ten minutes.' Or again: 'C rang up and said he had someone with the most difficult Confession he had ever known and that he would like me to take it. I thought he had said "Commission" and said "O dear, but it may be fun." When I heard some details I was appalled. I feel quite incompetent for this sort of thing.' Or again 'B came for advice about a career: he was thinking of being a solicitor because he wants dealings with people – I fear he may be disappointed.' 'Spoke to G – he'd spent £7 [over £100 at today's prices] in one week on drink and tobacco "on tick" in the buttery. Denied he had been jilted!' 'B.D. to tea, he's going to start confirmation classes.' 'Difficult day with girls. W brought his mother to coffee at 11. She spent most of the time telling me W was a fool to get married this January . . . I visited T in the sick bay, and found his fiancée asleep on the floor. O well, I suppose one should be glad it was on the floor.' 'Appalling morning with three supervisions and a tutorial hour . . .' 'Invited all ten Church of England ordinands to breakfast . . .'

The pace was too hot to last. I see in May 1960 the following:

I have written nothing for two months, which was a period of great strain. It included all the end-of-term work, examination of Choral Exhibitioners, writing a whole course of lectures for Part II Theology on the Doctrine of Man, preparation and delivery of Holy Week lectures at Wells Theological College, addresses at St Margaret's Westminister on Good Friday, the opening of a discussion at 'Dons and Beaks' on the implications of the ending of National Service, etc. As a result of all this I broke under the strain during the first week of term and simply cleared out for a month leaving everything in the air. Appalling feeling of angst over lecturing, inability to sleep, stress and strain.

I recovered reasonably quickly, despite my father's death during this period; but I had to give up something, so I gave up the tutorship. Life continued, but as I had been a lecturer for six years, I took a year's sabbatical leave. Henry Chadwick had been pestering me about a commentary on the Epistle to the Hebrews which I had contracted to do, but which I had no time to write. I had written lots of learned articles, and I felt it was about time that I produced a book. (I don't count a paperback of a course of sermons in chapel called *Beyond Reasonable Doubt*.) I also needed time with my family. I 'sported my oak' (shut the outer door of my rooms) and buried myself in my commentary. There is no end to the reading one can do for a biblical commentary, so I decided that I would reach a particular point in the Epistle by the end of each week: that was the only way I could guarantee to get it done. And it worked. It is still selling over thirty years later. For my last term I knew I must get away. I accepted a Visiting Fellowship at the newly built St George's College in Jerusalem.

En route, I went to Rome, and attended among other things a General Audience of John XXIII:

> . . . finally found myself with best front seat of the lot. The Secretariat for Unity must have a lot of pull. Spanish priests chanted Gregorian to while away the time. The old man was due at noon, finally arrived at 12.20 amid tumultuous clapping, seated on a sedan chair, attended by a large suite. Swiss guards pure Gilbert and Sullivan, with majordomos in court knickerbockers of purple velour. The Pope looked white, anaemic, and very old, as though he might die at any moment, but started throwing his arms about and livened up when he began to talk, which he did for about twenty-five minutes, all about St Joseph, patron of the universal Church. He paid little attention to his Chamberlain, insisting on presentations before he spoke, and bursting into French for five minutes just when it was announced that he would pronounce the benediction. He had all (except his suite) with smiles on their faces and laughter on their lips. He must be the terror of his bureaucrats.

A wonderful man and a saint.

It was the first time I had been to the Holy Land, and in many ways I felt I had come home. It was not so much the sacred sites, many (but not all) of which were the invention of the Crusaders, but rather that this was the scene of sacred history, and Galilee was where Jesus had walked and talked. I had a wonderful time in Jordan and Israel, and in Jerusalem I made friends with the Ecole Biblique, and went with them on their annual outing on the Dead Sea. As Visiting Fellow at St George's I had to give a lecture, and I decided to talk about the Coptic Gospel of Thomas, and the relationship of its parables to those of the Synoptic Gospels, on which I had done a lot of work. I was rather taken aback when Père Benoit said 'We've put our Coptic scholars in the front' because I didn't know Coptic apart from Greek loan words, and had worked from a translation; but I got by. I also crossed to the Jewish side of the border, where I had to be careful, because Montefiore is such an honoured name. I found myself to a modest extent being shadowed, and I had a meal with the Minister for Religion (I doubt if that was the correct title).

It was while I was going to Mount Carmel that some post reached me from England, including a telegram from the Patronage Secretary at Downing Street asking me if I would accept the vacant benefice of Great St Mary's, Cambridge. (Because the Crown had taken away Joe Fison to Salisbury, the Crown had to replace him at Great St Mary's.) Of course I could not decide there and then – I had to talk with Elisabeth about it all, for one thing.

But I knew that I had to move on, and perhaps this was it? An invitation received on Mount Carmel – Oh God, what next?

Chapter Seven

THE UNIVERSITY CHURCH

Sabbatical leave gave me a little space to assess myself, and to see where I was going. I had greatly enjoyed my Cambridge university life, and I thought that the job that I was doing both in college and in the Divinity Faculty was worth while. But it was clear to me that I could not keep up the pace of life as both Dean of Caius and university lecturer in the New Testament, together with all the other jobs that were coming my way. Once again the old trouble was looming – I was not seeing enough of my family. I had been at Caius for eight years, and I had amassed a lot of influence in the college since I knew and was friendly with all the undergraduates, and the other dons were not; I had been on the College Council for some time, and had been a Tutor as well as Dean.

I began to realise that this was somewhat resented among some of the younger Fellows. Peter Tranchell, who had succeeded Paddy Hadley as Precentor, wanted to make the singing in chapel more 'cathedral-like' and less congregational. I knew that this would not attract undergraduates; but he had promised me that so long as I was Dean, the pattern of college chapel music would not change. I think that that irked him: at any rate he wrote a college play which was publicly performed and which consisted of a vicious attack on me as Dean, and I was very hurt. I wish I had a thicker skin. Although I liked to be forthright in what I said, I was very sensitive. Perhaps I had better go. Unless I was going to be a perpetual don, I certainly should go.

Life was very comfortable for me in college. I relished the fleshpots of the college kitchens, and the excellencies of the college cellar. I put on weight. I had tried to do something about this earlier, and had failed. I ate whole packets of All Bran soused in PLJ (pure lemon juice, before the days of skimmed milk), but this made no difference: it simply angered my digestive tract. This was before the contents of processed food had to be listed on the packaging, and I had not realised that the stuff was coated with sugar to make it palatable. Then I got hold of a book called *Eat Fat and Grow Thin* which seemed to promise all that I could want; but of course the result was that I grew fatter. The crunch came when I stripped to the waist one day on a rare heatwave in Wales. Teresa, Janet and Elisabeth jokingly called me in turn 'sloshy', 'bulgy' and 'impregnated with fat'. This became a kind of family taunt, and I did do something about it, but I soon regressed. It was not until pressures eased after my retirement that I was able to keep slim.

I think that my problems over weight were symptoms of a deeper malaise. I worked very hard, but I suspect that that was because I was a workaholic. Conditions were easy and it was a cultured and sheltered life guaranteed until retiring age – had I really been ordained for that? When Christ called me to his service, surely he was not calling me permanently to the academic life? I was becoming quite an authority in New Testament scholarship, but a layman could have done that quite as well as a minister of religion. In any case I was out of sympathy with current trends in New Testament scholarship, in which the Christ of faith quite eclipsed the Jesus of history. I found I had become a kind of worker priest, earning my living by teaching in secular institutions (even if religion was one of their aims), and trying at the same time to be a full-time priest to undergraduates: the result was unsatisfactory. Certainly I was learning standards of intellectual rigour which, when added to a passion for truth, resulted in a refusal to be put off by easy answers to the very real difficulties in formulating the Christian faith. But surely I was not ordained to spend all my life among an intellectual élite? And I had learnt that the intelligentsia had just as many limitations and prejudices as anyone else, and could even be childish. For example Sir Edward Bullard, a famous scientist in college who directed the International Geophysical Year, said to me when the sputnik first went into space: 'Well, that scuppers your God, doesn't it?'

Even more important, I began to realise that the kind of life I was leading did not really make for any progress in spirituality. I often had to work late at night, and college prayers after breakfast at 8.30 am made it hard to find time for prayer and meditation. I find this note in my diary: 'Made up my mind in future to spend twenty minutes a day on my private prayers: horribly ashamed to have to put this in my diary.' I needed a more spiritually ordered life. The habits of prayer and meditation, so carefully built up in a parish and at Westcott House, were becoming eroded. I did not enter in any way into 'the dark night of the soul': perhaps it would have been better for me if I had. But I felt inside myself a spiritual unease at the kind of life I was leading; I needed to get back into the mainstream of the Church's life.

That was one side of the picture, but there was another one too. I had had no experience of a parish other than eighteen months when I had been an assistant curate in Newcastle upon Tyne. Would I be any good as the parish priest of the principal civic church in Cambridge which also happened to be at the same time the university church of Cambridge? Could I cope? It is one thing to change your lifestyle when you move to another place: it is quite another to do this when you are moving less than a hundred yards to the church on the other side of the road. Would I be able to give up my scholarly interests at the drop of a hat? Would I be looking over my shoulder all the time? Mervyn Stockwood had been a brilliant parish priest who had filled the church. Joe Fison was a saint whose integrity and sheer spiritual power had continued this tradition. How on earth could I adequately follow these two giants?

On the other hand it would be more like a joint ministry with Elisabeth than anything else I had undertaken. I should be able to spend a little more time at home. I knew and loved the church, because it was both the university church and our own parish church which the family attended every Sunday. We had been founder members of the parish Communion which Mervyn had started – there were only seven in the congregation when it began, and on one very wintry Sunday there were only two families present: ours and the Robinsons. (That was right at the beginning: it soon mushroomed.) Elisabeth would still have her Cambridge friends – those who had not left. I think what decided me in the end, after I had talked it all over with Eliza, was that I could think of no good reason to say 'No'. I wrote to Michael Ramsey, then having left Cambridge (where I had got to know him as Regius Professor of Divinity and Chairman of the Governors of Westcott House): he answered me in his own hand with a very wise letter, and advised me to accept. I did.

The next question to settle was where I was going to live. 'Springfield' where we were already living on the edge of the Backs was nearer the church than the vicarage up Madingley Road which Mervyn had made Trinity College provide. Why should we move there? The college was prepared for us to continue to rent our 'Springfield' flat. The trouble was that I had to let the vicarage to pay the rent for the flat. Who would want a fairly large unfurnished vicarage for only a year? I did not dare let it for longer because it would be needed if for any reason I ceased to be vicar. This

was a perpetual worry to me all the time that I was Vicar of
Great St Mary's, but somehow or other I always managed to find
a tenant.

I had to be instituted during the academic year, which meant that
everything was a bit rushed before my institution in September 1954.
I had immediately to start booking up preachers: it was customary to
have courses of sermons at morning prayer and at the undergraduate
service, and that meant, with a Long Vacation course, no fewer than
seven courses a year, of eight weeks each. The right preachers had
to be found, as the Vicar usually only preached at each once a term.
And then there was the problem of the institution service. How
could I with integrity make the Declaration of Assent agreeing
to the Church of England's Thirty-nine Articles of Religion as
agreeable to the word of God? No doubt they were excellent for
the seventeenth century when they were composed; but they were
out of date for the twentieth century. Not only did they speak of
Christ being reconciled to the world – it ought to be the other way
round – but also they affirmed that all works done before the grace
of Christ had the nature of sin. To agree to that was to say that
everything done by my beloved Jewish parents was sinful. I knew
that that was just not true. My integrity revolted at the thought.
And yet, according to the law of the land, I could not be instituted
unless I did.

I hit on the compromise of a supplementary declaration. I did
that which was prescribed by law, and then I went on to affirm
that in making this declaration, I was not subscribing to each and
every article, but affirming that they were agreeable to the word
of God *at the time in which they were written*. There is a certain
cultural relativity about all doctrine. We cannot be expected to
believe all the same things in exactly the same way as people did
in the seventeenth century. I don't think that the Diocesan Bishop,
Noel Hudson, who instituted me, was particularly happy about me
doing this; but he certainly made no effort to prevent me. I wanted
to set the tone of my ministry there as one of intellectual integrity.
The law then still demanded that I read all Thirty-nine Articles aloud
at my first Sunday service; and when I preached, I explained about
the supplementary declaration. What I did of course did not pass
unnoticed in the press.

I suppose that it was this action which prompted Michael Ramsey,
after he became Archbishop of Canterbury, to invite me to join the
new prestigious Doctrine Commission which the two Archbishops
decided to set up; and the first task we were given was to consider
any possible changes to the Declaration of Assent. The Commission

Hugh in tender years

Camping out in Bagley Woods, Oxford as
an undergraduate, 1939/40

Lieut. Sebag-Montefiore in India, 1942

Ordained at Westcott House, Cambridge,
1948/9

Westcott House play 'The Zeal of Thy House' in St Edward's Church, Cambridge. Four angels, left to right: John Hoskyns, Frank Wright, Hugh Montefiore, F. G. L. O Van Kretschmar

Hugh and Elisabeth with Teresa and Janet while he was teaching at Westcott House

Duke Ellington conducting his 'Concert of Sacred Music' in Great St Mary's

Consecrated Bishop of Kingston-upon-Thames by Archbishop Michael Ramsey at Michaelmas 1970

On holiday in Spain. Left to right: Elisabeth, Lady Elizabeth Cavendish, Sir John Betjeman, Hugh and Bishop Mervyn Stockwood

Visiting a junior and infants school during a parochial visitation when Bishop of Kingston

At a phone-in at Birmingham local radio station with Maurice Couve de Murville,
R.C. Archbishop of Birmingham

The 'Urban Bishops Group'. Back row: Bishops Lunn, Montefiore, Thompson, Bowlby, Sheppard, Young, Booth-Clibborn. Front row: Mrs Montefiore, Mrs. Bowlby, Mrs Booth-Clibborn, Mrs Sheppard

Visiting a Birmingham pantomime at dress rehearsal

'You're always so controversial, Bishop': Mrs Thatcher at the National Exhibition Centre, Birmingham

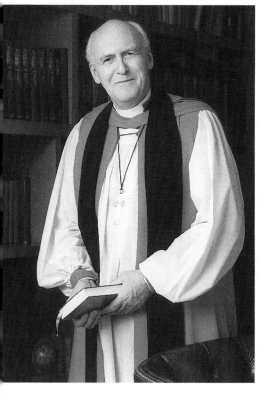

Hugh Montefiore, Bishop of Birmingham

Addressing the People's March for Jobs from the Cathedral Green in Birmingham in 1981

Billy Graham visits Bishop's Croft Birmingham

Nailing up a derelict house in
Handsworth to highlight the housing
shortage

At Dudley Road Hospital, holding a thriving premature baby who could legally have been aborted

On diocesan pilgrimage, near the Mount of Beatitudes on the Sea of Galilee (Bishop on left; right, Canon Ronald Brownrigg)

Elisabeth and Hugh shortly before retirement

On the way out: thousands of balloons are released as Hugh and Elisabeth leave the Farewell Eucharist

was chaired by Ian Ramsey, the lovable Bishop of Durham, who had earlier been Dean of Christ's in Cambridge and then an Oxford professor. He killed himself with overwork; even when recovered from a massive heart attack I found him once, during the afternoon break of a conference, holding a meeting of his staff. He had such a subtle mind that he could almost make black into white. He was a marvellous chairman of the Commission, greatly helped by Michael Perry (later Archdeacon of Durham) who made meticulous minutes. However, it was a very donnish affair, and I found myself the only parish priest on the Commission.

Our first task was to reconsider the Declaration of Assent to the Thirty-nine Articles. We tried and rejected various possibilities, such as writing fresh Articles for today (they would soon be out of date), or scrapping all mention of the Articles (as the American Church has done). Since the Commission comprised representatives of different shades of the Church of England, it seemed that we were in an impasse when we retired for the night after several meetings; but next morning John Austen Baker, then Chaplain of Corpus Christi College, Oxford, later Canon of Westminster and then Bishop of Salisbury, pulled out of his hat (as he did for us on other occasions) a formula on which we could all agree. This is embodied in the present Declaration of Assent, which consists of neither assent to each and every Article, nor of a general assent to them all. We affirm our loyalty to our inheritance of faith (which includes the Thirty-nine Articles of Religion, the *Book of Common Prayer* and the Ordinal) as our inspiration and guidance under God, and to the faith to which the historic formulae bear witness. This gives a positive way of looking at the Articles of Religion, without making them authoritative for us today.

Later on the Doctrinal Commission went on to consider various smaller matters. What does it mean to 'bless' someone? What ought to happen when the consecrated bread or wine at the Holy Communion runs out? What about prayers for the dead? I do not think that we produced anything of epoch-making importance on any of these matters. Our advice on the eucharistic elements was passed to the Liturgical Commission (which had earlier given no instructions about consecration of more bread and wine if these ran out during their administration). Our consultations did, however, lead us to publish a useful volume of essays about different aspects of the Eucharist. Mine concentrated on its symbolic aspect, which seems to me of greater import than the use of correct formulae. I thought that we would never get an agreed report on prayers for the dead. The evangelicals seemed to be adamant that a person's eternal destiny was fixed at the moment of death, so that there was no point in praying for people after they had died. We did, however, finally agree on a prayer, which was so clumsy and long-winded and all-embracing that I was surprised that it made its way into the *Alternative Service Book*: 'May God in his infinite love and mercy bring the whole Church, living and departed in the Lord Jesus, to a joyful resurrection and the fulfilment of his eternal kingdom.' Even the evangelicals couldn't object to that!

While I was on the Doctrinal Commission, Elisabeth was a member of the Liturgical Commission, on which she stayed for some fourteen years. Unbelievable as it may seem, that was about the only contact that these two commissions had with each other, on the occasions when we both happened to read each other's mail. I think that she enjoyed herself there a great deal, concocting all those new services. The Church of England was experimenting, what with Series 1, 2 and 3, and finally Rite A and B. Of course the minute revision of every service by the entire General Synod later on was hopeless. Looking back now on the work of the Commission, it seems rather pedestrian; but at the time it was something of a liberation to get away from Cranmerian English. We had fun together when it came to composing the new marriage service. We both loved the Seven Blessings of the Bride and Bridegroom in the Jewish service, and we tried to incorporate something of this in versicles and responses; and although the Commission of course altered it, traces of our work remain. I remember blowing off in the Synod about the new introduction to the marriage service, where the phrase 'knowing each other in love' was used as a euphemism for sexual intercourse. I said that I thought that the phrase would be unintelligible to the proverbial couple on the top of a Clapham omnibus. I fear that the phrase still remains.

Back at Great St Mary's we found when I began as Vicar that the attitude of the congregation to our three daughters had changed overnight. Formerly they were just taken for granted as members of the congregation: now they had become 'the vicarage girls', and their every remark and action was noted. This was very displeasing to them.

I had asked the Divinity Faculty if I could become a 'university lecturer part-time' as allowed by the university statutes; but (rightly, I think) this was refused. However, I continued for a year to give my lectures, to direct studies in theology at Caius and to continue New Testament supervisions to those I was already teaching. This was rather a strain; but I gave my lectures and took my supervisions at 9 am which left most of the day clear for parish work. But my back, which was my weak point ever since my laminectomy when I was at Westcott House as a student, gave way under the strain on several occasions, and sometimes I had to supervise lying on the floor.

I also continued for a time with my chaplaincy at the women's college, New Hall. When the college began, there were fifteen students, and two of them read Theology; surely the highest percentage of theologians in any Oxbridge college. New Hall was then on the present site of Darwin College, just opposite where we were living in 'Springfield', and Rosamund Murray the Principal (who later became Vice Chancellor) asked me to act as a kind of chaplain. The college grew and later moved to new premises next to the new site for Fitzwilliam House, whose chapel they shared; and I continued with the very much part-time chaplaincy. I had known Rosamund when she had been a don at Girton, where I had acted as 'under the counter chaplain' while I was Vice Principal of Westcott House. I used to go there one afternoon a week during a term, and sit, waiting for girls to come to me with their pastoral problems. When they did come, it was more likely to be troubles of the heart. This former link with Girton College was useful when I was Vicar of Great St Mary's, because we could not afford the stipends of two full-time curates, and Peter Southwell Sander became part-time chaplain of Girton College as well as continuing stalwart work at Great St Mary's. Girton was always sensible enough to choose a married man as chaplain: this was in the days before Girton (or indeed any college) had become 'unisex'.

I found I had entered into a great inheritance at Great St Mary's. At 7.30 am there was a daily Eucharist and matins, with undergraduates acting as servers and lesson readers; and similarly at evening prayer, which was followed by half an hour's silent prayer. This was a life saver! Before I had gone to Caius I had been used to a daily Eucharist, and I needed a rule of life which gave me proper time for meditation and prayer.

Sunday services seemed unending: Holy Communion at 8 am, parish Communion at 9.30 am, matins and sermon at 11, Holy Communion at 12, often a university sermon at 2.30 pm, evensong and sermon at 6.30 pm, followed by the university service at 8.30 pm. There was a visiting preacher to entertain to Sunday lunch, and another in the evening before the university service; and we used to keep open house for tea to undergraduates. It was a long day!

Apart from the early service and the noon Eucharist, congregations at each service when I arrived were seldom less than one hundred, and at the university sermon in the evening, if there was a full house (which included both galleries) there could be over a thousand. One of the curates, Ian Ogilvie, was keen on youth services, and we instituted these once a quarter for young people in the town during the vacations. Again we would get over a thousand for these services, which were a great pother to put on, arranging rock groups, etc, but well worth it. Cliff Richard came on one occasion, but was careful not to allow me to ask him questions about his faith from the pulpit. All sorts of young people turned up to these youth services, and we had to ask them to throw away their cigarettes or take off their cloth caps before they came in. Young people also came in from local churches which did not have this kind of service.

I always thought that the churches were rather lacking in initiative in not putting on more of these services for young people. The kind of worship which older people like was often very boring for their children. It still is, but now, I fear, the opportunity may have passed. We had so many young people that we started a 'youth service' for the town, young people visiting the elderly and housebound. The old and the young get on very well together. It was run by Richard Garrard, one of the curates, now Bishop of Penrith. It was a great success, with well over a hundred on his lists. We also ran for a time a youth club for the town. This could get rather rowdy, and we invited some of the more strongly built male members of the congregation to 'look on' during meetings. After a time, we dropped this, as it had no direct connection with the Christian religion, and it is a task which secular authorities should take on.

We were careful not to make the young people from other churches become members of our congregation. Had we done this, we would have lost the goodwill of all neighbouring clergy! It would hardly have helped the diocesan parish system. In the same way, quite a lot of people would come to us occasionally for a 'refresher' from lonely parishes out in the Fens. We were glad to see them but we did not want to make them regular members of our church.

Unlike my predecessors I decided that if I were to get on with my fellow clergy, I ought to play some part in diocesan affairs, and not act as though I was entirely extra-diocesan. As a matter of fact, the bishop did say that I ought to ask his permission before inviting people from outside his diocese to preach in Great St Mary's, but I am afraid that in this connection I did behave in an extra-diocesan way. I pointblank refused, saying that if I did, there could be a diocesan censorship of my ministry to university students, which would be wrong. (Those colleges which were ancient foundations were extra-diocesan. The 'visitor' of the college chapel was the Master and Fellows, and the bishop had no jurisdiction there.

When I was at Caius I always used to invite the bishop to leave his pastoral staff, a symbol of his authority, in the vestry.) But I had to show willing in other ways. I sat on the Ely Diocesan Board of Finance. I attended meetings of the Rural Deanery. In my final years at Great St Mary's I was even made an Honorary Canon of the Diocese. The duties were minimal: a service for all the canons once a year in Ely Cathedral, when a somewhat odd extract was read from the Venerable Bede about Queen Etheldreda (foundress of the cathedral) which recounted not only how she refused sexual relations with her husband, but also declined to wash and take a bath. In her view uncleanliness must have been next to godliness.

I found that in Great St Mary's we had mixed congregations. We would discourage all students from coming to the parish Communion; their place was their college chapel. We welcomed them only at the university service. Matins tended to be older folk, predominantly middle class, from the town. The parish Communion was a mixture of town and gown; some dons, mostly with families, and people of all sorts from the town. By contrast evensong consisted mostly of working-class folk from the town, until it was practically killed off, as were so many evensongs up and down the country, when BBC TV put on *The Forsyte Saga* in the evening.

There were of course the regular members of the congregation, and visiting them was a great effort. The actual inhabitants of the parish consisted of twenty seven people who lived in the centre of Cambridge! But the visiting area I reckoned to be sixty square miles, with people attending from some villages outside the city. I used to visit in a little red Mini, which I could just lodge inside the church precincts, and we bought Mopeds for the two curates, who bore the brunt of this as of everything else.

Before I had any letters of congratulation on becoming Vicar I had letters of complaint – about the bells of Great St Mary's. We were one of the very few churches in the land with a peal of twelve bells. To bellringers they made sweet music; but to anyone outside the church they made a quite terrible cacophony. I am not surprised that people disliked them. I can remember students in Caius front court having to evacuate their rooms on Monday nights, when practice took place. The bellringers were allowed to ring a peal only on Bank Holidays, when the marketplace (adjoining the church) would be deserted. But still these bells were there, and it was right that they should be used for the purpose for which they were intended. We invited Prince Charles to the belltower on his birthday (he was an undergraduate at the time). We rang a short peal and toasted him with champagne. I found that bellringers are often fanatics.

In Selwyn College there was an annual dinner of campanologists from all over the country. They had their own subculture and their own newspaper, *The Ringing Times*. In Great St Mary's there was a Master of the Belltower, and the ringers were the 'Ancient Society of Cambridge Youths' (despite the fact that some of them were over seventy). They were often a difficult lot. One Sunday just as evensong was about to begin, I was told that fighting had broken out in the belltower. Should I start evensong, or go up to the belltower and sort it out? I decided on the latter, and made the long ascent, only to find that when I arrived tempers had cooled. So down I came again, and had to start the service somewhat short of breath.

Again, we had some difficulty with the choir over the parish Communion. This was the central service of the day, and I was determined that women as well as men should fully participate. But the choirmen would not allow the ladies to join them. Very well, there was only one thing to do: form a parish Communion choir, which we did, with some of the less traditional of the main choir among them. We were now running three choirs – the main choir for matins and evensong, a parish Communion choir, and an undergraduate choir for the university service.

Again, there was some trouble about women servers. Why should men have the monopoly? But in those days female servers were unusual. This difficulty was surmounted by the Vicar's and the churchwarden's daughters being among the first. Then there was the distant altar, up in the sanctuary, beyond the choirstalls. The congregation were resistant to a nave altar. I hit upon a successful idea. English congregations do not customarily refuse presents. When a curate who was leaving asked me about a present he could give to the congregation, I suggested a nave altar. The strategem worked, although I recall a normally quiet and peaceable single lady, leaving the church on the first day of its use, shaking her fist at me and saying: 'Vicar, you've taken away my long walk to God.' Surely the one certain good of the parish Communion is that it symbolises that God has already drawn near to us.

One of my first actions on becoming Vicar of Great St Mary's was to break off negotiations between the church and Gonville and Caius College. These concerned the future of St Michael's Church, a hundred yards away, and which was joined to the benefice of Great St Mary's. It was in disuse. Mervyn Stockwood had nearly given it to the Roman Catholics, who found that Fisher House was getting too small for their needs. Joe Fison had heeded the siren words of our Bursar and was proposing to make it over to Caius for their library, which was becoming too big to be accommodated in college. I had heard as a Fellow of Caius that the Bursar was making a good bargain, as of course one hopes bursars always will. But now I had changed sides. The property was Great St Mary's only physical asset. No matter that Caius had already bought the churchyard, and had built St Michael's Court on it earlier in the century. St Michael's Church was a most valuable site in the centre of the city.

The church had no hall – and St Michael's could be transformed into one. It was a very ancient building full of historical associations. St Michael's Hall had been centred on it before it had been incorporated into Trinity College at its formation. All college chapels were based on St Michael's chancel, which was their prototype. George Pace of York was our church architect, and he got out plans for a skilful transformation, which kept the chancel intact, formed the Hervey de Stanton Chapel at the side, made a hall out of the nave, and introduced rooms upstairs. I opened an appeal, and we managed to carry out the transformation most successfully. Most people in Caius no longer know about this episode; but at the time it hardly endeared me to my former colleagues. Recently the college has paid some £6 million to the university for the purchase of the Squire Law Library to accommodate its library.

We had a weekly 'staff meeting' at which sermons for the past Sunday were criticised, duties allocated for the following week, visits we had all done were briefly described, and note taken of any sick who had been left unvisited, while topics for discussion were raised or policy issues decided. I suppose that is what happens in all clergy staff meetings. The junior curate had to take notes and produce typed minutes by the time of evensong. I am not sure that I was always very good as a pastor – I would forget faces, and pass people in the street without recognising them. I think the curates did a lot of covering up for me! At least two families left the congregation, I know. Still, I did my level best.

My first job was to get to know the regular congregation, and so I went visiting as much as I could. It is a great pity that visiting is no longer so fashionable among some clergy as it used to be. People enormously appreciate a clergy visit in their own home, and it also helps greatly to 'fix' someone in the mind of the visiting clergyman. Unfortunately our congregation was so spread out that sometimes one could only visit two people in an afternoon. I had two most loyal and hardworking curates to assist me; I was always fortunate in my assistants, without whom I could have done nothing. Dr Loewenfeld, the church treasurer, had once looked after the Kaiser's estates in Germany. He came to Britain as a refugee, and Lord Macnair, a

Fellow of Caius (formerly Chairman of the International Court of Justice at the Hague) had helped him to set up as an international lawyer. He kept our money straight. We always did have difficulty keeping our outgoings and income in balance, especially as we had the largest 'quota' in the diocese to pay to central funds. We used to charge for going up to the top of the tower, which gave an unrivalled view of Cambridge. (It was carefully wired in, to prevent suicides.) Volunteers sat at the bottom clocking up sixpences (and later, shillings). We paid for a curate this way! But the staircase was narrow, and once two fat ladies met halfway and got stuck – only temporarily, I am glad to report.

We were fortunate in the perks we received as university church. Originally Cambridge University simply consisted of Great St Mary's, where all events took place – that was before the foundation of colleges and halls of residence back in the Middle Ages. All formal meetings of the university used to take place within Great St Mary's, and university sermons still are given there. In recognition of this, the university generously paid the salary of a full-time verger. Trinity College, our patron, also took their duties seriously, and paid for the upkeep of the chancel. We had two organs – the university organ and the parish organ.

Cards giving details of our morning and evening courses of sermons were delivered to all ten thousand undergraduates. This custom was started by Mervyn Stockwood. It was a great expense and a great undertaking. We tried to make it the most distinguished card that any undergraduate would receive. Jim Bezzant, the Dean of St John's, took objection to the practice, and ordered the porters to throw his college's allocation into the river Cam. 'I have not become Dean of this college to preside over my own destruction,' he said. Bezzant was a very intelligent New Testament scholar, but a rather tragic figure, whose marriage had gone awry. We used to invite him to meals from time to time, for he was very lonely, as was evident from his inability to stop talking. It was necessary to employ considerable tact to gain the goodwill of the deans and chaplains who would naturally look on Great St Mary's as a potential threat, unless we made it crystal clear by our actions that our ministry was complementary to theirs, and not a substitute. My having been in the past chairman of 'Deans and Chaplains' meetings helped greatly in this approach.

It must not be imagined that we were the only church in the city which undergraduates frequented. Little St Mary's, the most prayerful and beautiful church in the city, attracted the high churchmen. King's College chapel attracted those whose idea of worship was beautiful music. Then there were the evangelicals. CICCU (Cambridge Inter-Collegiate Christian Union) have for many years been very strong. As Dean of a college I found that I could only cope with them by friendship (if permitted), by pulling their legs, and by telling them how their views were unbiblical. The more extreme among them tended to be biblical fundamentalists. I remember an undergraduate, who is now a diocesan bishop, saying to me one day in the court: 'Dean, it *would* help if you were a Christian.' CICCU members tended to frequent the Round Church, one of the only three churches in Britain built on the crusader model. For the more central evangelicals there was Holy Trinity, where the famous Simeon had been vicar in the last century, and on which the Cambridge Pastorate was centred. Whether it be town or gown, there seemed no end to Cambridge churchgoing in those days.

Despite the fact that our church seemed to flourish, I realised that all was not well with the Church as a whole. Great St Mary's, because of its unique position, could not be typical of the Church of England. I thought that leadership was badly needed if things were to improve in the country as a whole. What should be done? I organised a private conference in Cambridge to see if any agreement could be found. We were twelve in all: a very mixed bag, some vicars, a lawyer, a laywoman, a professor, and so on; only one or two firebrands. I will quote at length from the working paper that I wrote for this occasion, because it would be in almost exactly the same words if I were to write it today:

The malaise affecting the Church of England is mainly spiritual. She has not yet come to grips with the new age of science, technology, sociological and psychological insights, secondary and university education. She has not yet spoken with real conviction a clear, comprehensible and credible Gospel Message to the distracted and uncertain world of the mid-twentieth century. Always conservative in nature (for her main task after all is to conserve the Gospel) she has been overtaken by the speed of change. Man is changing his ecology with unprecedented speed: the Church of England is advancing at her usual sedate and ceremonial pace.

If the Church of England is to shake herself and rise to her present pastoral opportunity, she must find a tremendous release of energy and enthusiasm. She will be required to live dangerously, experiment widely and to co-operate fully.

It is perhaps hardly surprising that nothing came of this conference, because we did not agree among ourselves about what was needed and what could be done. I suspect that the same would happen if a similar conference were called today.

Our policy so far as the undergraduates were concerned was to bring to Great St Mary's pulpit the best preachers in the country, and beyond, and to expose them to the full Christian Gospel, expressed in terms which they could understand. How could they be expected to live out the Christian faith in their lives unless it was relevant to their situation? I remember some great occasions with a very full house. Martin Niemoller came from Germany to preach on a Remembrance Sunday. He arrived with a very bad cold, and when my wife asked what she could do for him, he said: 'I would like an old German remedy – hot tea with a lot of rum in it.' When she offered to help him, he took the bottle from her hand, and poured out a whole teacupful. Malcolm Muggeridge was in his heyday, and could speak most movingly, especially in the days when he had not yet fully embraced the Christian faith. He and Kitty were great fun to have to stay. James Stewart, Professor of Theology in Edinburgh, gave what for me was the most moving sermon of all, on the theme of the Holy Spirit, to the refrain 'Listen to the wind, Nicodemus, listen to the wind.' Trevor Huddleston also had the power deeply to move students. Albert van der Heuvel, later leader of the Dutch Reformed Church, gave what I remember as a most memorable sermon on Easter. And so one could go on. Colin Morris (from Zambia, and later to become Chairman of the Methodist Conference), John Robinson, Lord Denning and many others were among the preachers.

I was determined to have some Roman Catholic preachers, which at that time was forbidden according to the rules of that Church. I thought if anyone could get round this, it would be a Jesuit; and I was right! I invited Fr Thomas Corbishley to come and give an address which would not be part of a service. The Bishop of Northampton, in whose Roman Catholic diocese Cambridge lay, was at the time in Rome for the Vatican Council. Corbishley saw him briefly, and said: 'By the way, I've been asked to give an address in Great St Mary's: it's not part of a service' and permission was given. We had the ordinary university service, and after the last hymn I said 'This service is now ended: we shall sit for a short violin solo as a voluntary.' At the end of this Corbishley preached. I was most moved by his beginning 'At the start I want to say that we Roman Catholics want to offer you an apology . . .' I wonder whether we, in those circumstances, would have had the grace to do the same.

By far the most prestigious Roman Catholic preacher I had was Cardinal Jan Willebrands, the head of the Secretariat for Christian

Unity in the Vatican. On the Saturday I gave a 'cardinal's lunch party' for him in Caius, and he preached at the Sunday evening service. Unfortunately his sermon did not make much impact on the students or on people at large, partly because it was delivered in rather halting English as Dutch was his mother tongue, and partly because it was couched in low-key language more like a lecture, and hinged on the Greek word *tupos* from which the English word 'type' originates, and which is hardly a popular 'turn on'. Nonetheless I regard that sermon as the most important theological utterance from Great St Mary's pulpit since Archbishop Geoffrey Fisher preached about the Free Churches 'taking episcopacy in their system'.

Willebrands' approach to unity looked at the matter from the other end. He recognised different 'types' within the Christian Church, and so he was really validating its diversity. Each church has its different traditions, which express themselves in their distinctive liturgy and spirituality, canon law and theological method. 'We find the reality of a *typos* in the existence of a long and coherent tradition, inspiring love and loyalty among men and women, forming and maintaining an organic and harmonious totality of complementary elements, each of which supports and reinforces the other.' He was obviously taking his model from the uniate churches of the Eastern tradition which acknowledge the supremacy of the pope; but he applied the concept more widely to other churches. No doubt such ideas are out of fashion nowadays, with growing Protestant fundamentalism and Roman Catholic centralism. But the tide will turn, and one day Jan Willebrands' sermon will be seen as prophetic of the future, with different churches expressing the one faith in different ways, united in communion through a reformed primacy in Rome with its bishop seen as *primus inter pares*, the first among equals.

I invited Billy Graham to come and preach; and he accepted. He and Ruth were charming guests, and he would speak confidingly about most intimate matters. He seemed to sit reasonably lightly to his 'advisers'. I fell for him. I discovered to my horror that I had invited him to preach the weekend before the Tripos Examinations were to start. I saw that there were queues around the church waiting to get in. I said to him 'Billy, please cool it. I want all your congregation to become Christians, but I do not want them to fail their examinations.' He preached a splendid sermon on the Holy Spirit (it was Whit Sunday).

Of course one never knew what preachers would say. I stopped only one. John Pearce–Higgins, Provost of Southwark, an expert on the spirits of the dead, was discoursing on 'Easter and paranormal phenomena'. After forty minutes he had only reached a discussion of discarnate bodies over the Alps when he said: 'I've been going on for rather a long time.' I replied: 'You have' and announced the next hymn. I hope he forgave me. I also thought it would be good to have professing Christians among the prominent politicians of the day to speak. Among them were Ted Heath (who had been on the staff of the *Church Times* at one stage), Alec Douglas–Hume, George Thomas and George Brown. The last named had been characteristically rude to undergraduates at a tea party earlier, and decided after the sermon that he would act as policeman in holding up the traffic afterwards to allow my Mini to back out of the church; another characteristic action duly noted by the press.

The most remarkable occasion was when I invited Kenneth Kaunda, President of Zambia, to come and preach. A keen layman, he was then quite young. He arrived with his staff, and they took over my study in the church. I had asked the police to provide proper cover; and they only sent two men into the organ loft. When I protested, they replied: 'Had it been a European statesman we would have provided a full bodyguard, but since it is an African head of state, he is bound to be popular among the students.' How right they were! He is the only preacher I have ever had for whom, when he ended, the undergraduates stood up in their pews, clapped and gave a standing ovation.

Among the politicians I asked was Enoch Powell, then Minister for Health. I invited him to preach in a course focusing on social justice, but he was adamant that he would only preach on 'The Athanasian Creed' (which is printed in the *Book of Common Prayer*, but is neither a creed nor by Athanasius). I said I would ask him some other time. I approached him again the following year, and again he insisted on speaking on the Athanasian Creed. Realising I could not deflect him, I gave him his head. The undergraduates, who were present in large numbers, listened open-mouthed as he discoursed in a thoroughly Calvinistic vein on the large number of casualties which God had foreseen in his plan of salvation – and that from the Minister of Health!

The most impressive politician was Michael Stewart, Wilson's Foreign Minister, who had flown back that afternoon from a Scandinavian conference. A man small of stature, he was also a Methodist lay preacher, and he likened himself to Zacchaeus who had climbed up a sycamore tree to catch a glimpse of Jesus. He gave an impression of integrity and real humility.

I also arranged some courses to give students an overview of the Christian faith as a whole. Tony Bridge, later Provost of Guildford, was among the most foul-mouthed and brilliantly successful of our preachers. Harry Williams, Dean of Trinity College, was at that time at the height of his powers, after the publication of his Trinity College sermons, *The True Wilderness*. He gave a very memorable course of three in-depth sermons 'On being human', 'On Christian experience' and 'On belonging'. But the most effective preacher of all, without doubt, was Michael Ramsey, the Archbishop of Canterbury. He had a wonderful combination of oratory, sincerity, theological acumen and wit; and the students loved him. I remember him saying once from the pulpit: 'Some people think that Bibles float down from heaven – some with apocryphas and some without.' He gave a course of three sermons too which were greatly appreciated.

A good number of these sermons were published in *Sermons from Great St Mary's* and *More Sermons from Great St Mary's*. We also ran a sermon service. Many more people read them than heard them. The spoken words were taped, edited, duplicated and then posted literally to hundreds of people who had subscribed to them.

We also had some other activities for undergraduates. C. Day-Lewis spoke once – I remember him and Jill Balcombe, his wife. sitting over breakfast talking until lunchtime. On another occasion W. H. Auden came and read his poetry. He had helped himself very liberally to wine before the occasion, as a result of which we were rather late arriving at the church. But he was well oiled, and recited his poetry from memory for a whole hour; pretty accurately too, as we discovered afterwards, when we compared the tape with the printed text. This was the only time I was really alarmed about the galleries, which were grossly overfilled; I feared a terrible accident. No one had stopped people coming into the church, which was overfull.

The other occasions where I feared disaster were the annual advent carol services. Every undergraduate was given a candle, and the service began in pitch darkness. And then from one candle all the rest – well over a thousand – were lit in the building. It was a very moving occasion. Prince Charles, then an undergraduate, used to read one of the lessons. (I was taken aback later, at the Trinity College Review, to hear him mimicking me in a skit.) In those days all undergraduates had to wear gowns at night, and as they were crammed together, each year I thought a candle was bound to set someone's gown on fire; and we had only two small fire extinguishers in the building. But it never happened. (As a place of worship we did not have to observe fire regulations.)

I invited Duke Ellington to give a concert in Great St Mary's. To my great surprise, he accepted. He himself paid all the expenses of the visit for his entire band, including the fares from the USA. Of course the occasion was a sell-out and we had a large screen relay in the Senate House across the road. The Duke performed his 'Concert of Sacred Music', which was quite wonderful and made into a record. The song I remember most vividly was about creation: 'In the Beginning'. Such concerts meant a very great deal of hard work for our indefatigable overworked verger, George Clarke.

For one thing, a stage had to be constructed. To my surprise we were asked by Garfunkel, after the Duke's successful concert, whether he too could give one. The Parochial Church Council, probably wisely, turned it down. We did not want to overwork our staff, nor should we forget that we were primarily a place of worship.

St Michael's provided a good venue for smaller audiences. I staged there some courses of lectures on the Christian faith when we were not having courses of sermons on this in the church. I was determined that the undergaduates should be able to listen to a reasoned exposition of Christian beliefs during their time in Cambridge. We also had a lecture in the church by Frank Lake on psychology and religion. I did not subscribe to all Frank's theories, but he had a great gift of making psychology relevant to religion. Sparrow, the Warden of All Souls, Oxford, commented adversely about such goings on from the university pulpit; but then he had not heard the lecture.

I also arranged some 'teach ins': these were popular at the time. There were some set speeches, but everyone could join in and the events went on for two or three hours. It gave people an opportunity to hear all points of view, and to make clear their own views on some relevant and contested subject. We had one for example on Anglican-Methodist reunion, then much in the wind. Quite a number of people involved in the negotiations came down from London to join in. In some ways these occasions are preferable than just being 'talked to' in a sermon. After the Sunday evening student service, however, we always held a session called 'Mars Hill' when people could question the preacher. I will always remember one irate student asking the Archbishop of Canterbury how he could reconcile his Christian ministry with driving around in a huge Rolls Royce. 'Well,' replied Dr Ramsey, 'in the first place it's a Ford . . .'

During my time at Great St Mary's, because I was known to be Jewish I was consulted quite a lot by couples wanting to get married, of which one partner was Jewish. I used to advise them to take every possible step to avoid hurting their parents on either side. They usually did not know that, in Jewish thought, Jewishness passes through the mother rather than the father. I also used to advise them to think out the question of the religious upbringing of any children they might have before they got married; and unless they could settle this, not to get married. Also they must count the cost beforehand. It might mean that one of them might be cut right off from their family. But the decision of course was theirs, and no one else's.

Only on one occasion did I inform a parent in London that his son and daughter had decided to be baptised; and I greatly regret having been persuaded to do this by the chaplain of a college who had not the nerve do it himself, and especially as I did not even know the two people concerned. The parent concerned swept down to Cambridge next day, and so far as his daughter was concerned, tried to remove her from the college; but she was of age, and the Mistress said that her bills would be paid if she decided to stay. The incident got me a bad reputation in the Jewish community. The president of the Inter-University Jewish Federation, after he had given an invitation to me to speak at a seminar, had to ask me to withdraw because of pressure from the Chief Rabbi and the withdrawal of funding from a Jewish trust for the seminar.

The last half of my time at Great St Mary's was the period of student unrest in Britain. Students took over university buildings and wanted to run the universities. One of my daughters at the time was at Oxford, and remembers some excitable scene in which she was involved, when the Proctor swept up. He was Henry Chadwick, now moved from Cambridge to Oxford (he seemed to do this not infrequently). Of course she had known him well at Cambridge as, like me, he had three daughters. With a courteous flourish he took off his 'square' (mortar board) and bowed to her courteously; and she said she had never felt such a fool in her life.

In Cambridge there was an attempt at a student university, tumultuous debates at the union, one or two mild occupations, and a demand by students to share in the running of the university. (They had no idea of the tedium of university committees.) I had sent the Vice Chancellor my impressions, and advised that the way forward lay in consent rather than conflict. Owen Chadwick was the next Vice Chancellor, someone for whom (with his wife) I have a great affection and respect. In his time he had been a rugger Blue, and was well known to have been exuberant himself. He charmed the student leaders, and all settled back to normal.

I learnt that Monsignor Gilbey, the Roman Catholic Chaplain, was retiring. He was immensely distinguished, a marvellous pastor, but very old fashioned. (For example, he kept his telephone hidden in a commode.) He refused women entry to the Newman Society, and as a result was leaving the university unsung. I was glad to organise a farewell dinner for him in Caius.

I was beginning at this stage to join in church deliberations at the centre. I had ceased to be a member of the Ordination Committee of CACTM. But it was felt by some clergy that the Ely diocesan representation on Church Assembly was too trad. Francis Palmer, the Vicar of Holy Trinity, proposed me for election as Proctor in Convocation, and to my surprise I was elected. I now had to attend meetings of the Clergy Convocations and the General Assembly in London. Thank goodness these have been (almost entirely) merged into General Synod, which is bad enough, but not nearly as bad as its two earlier predecessors. In particular the Convocations were a kind of fancy dress parade. Clergy had to wear cassock, surplice, scarf and hood, while bishops paraded in their rochets and red chimeres. I remember one occasion when John Robinson (also a clergy member) once broke off in the middle of a sentence, only to resume his sentence two hours later! This was because a debate had to stop when the Upper House (the bishops) retired for their private deliberations, and start again when they returned.

Among other matters that were discussed, the negotiations with the Methodist Church went on and on. I can clearly remember a vital occasion when (without many people present) the question of the size of majority needed to secure the passing of the measure came up. Dr Ramsey, the Archbishop, was in the chair, and he said 'Oh, I think 75%. That is what the Methodists required when the Primitive Methodists and the Wesleyans joined up; and I think we should do the same.' At that moment I realised that the vote was going to be lost, because the Church of England is so constituted that it is practically impossible to secure a 75% vote on anything at all! Nonetheless we had to go through all the motions until the final vote. By that time the Methodists had agreed to go ahead, and the Church of England jilted them at the altar at the very last moment. To cap and crown it, when the final vote was given out and it was realised that the day had been lost, clapping broke out in the gallery. Ramsey made an eloquent speech in favour but he had left it too late to declare his hand. As he remarked, there will never be another scheme so good as this one. And that, in fact, has been the case.

During my time at Great St Mary's, I had been asked to give some lectures in the diocese of Leicester, and I chose as my subject marriage and remarriage in church. Perhaps for this reason I was invited by the Archbishop to join a commission chaired by Professor Howard Root (then of Southampton University) to look into the matter of remarriage after divorce, with particular reference to remarriage in church. It was interesting that two members of our commission, who had begun by being against such remarriage, changed sides during our meetings, and we were able to produce a unanimous report. But it took several years for us to achieve that, and the report lay in the future.

Fairly early in my time at Great St Mary's I was surprised to get an invitation from the chaplains of all the New Zealand universities asking me to visit the country, and to give open lectures in each university. I did not think that it was an invitation that I could refuse, since I could go during the Long Vacation, which was of course their winter term. My mother kindly offered Elisabeth and the children a holiday in Ireland while I was away, which eased my mind somewhat. I find among my diaries one entitled 'Diary of a Strange Journey'. I went via America, and stopped off at San Francisco to give a seminar for Bishop Pike of California at the Church Divinity School of the Pacific (the Anglican seminary) in Berkeley and discovered that there was a hard sell for me to become Professor of Theology there, which I did not take as seriously as perhaps I should. I felt that I did not want to move our daughters to American schools. However, when I spent a sabbatical leave there many years later, I much enjoyed the ethos of the place and its idyllic setting.

I embarked again, to stop off at tropical Honolulu, only to find that my baggage was missing and I had lost the cheque I had been given at CSDP. Fortunately the airline gave me $28 to clothe myself and get shaving gear etc. I realised with horror that I would arrive in New Zealand in mid-winter with only a tropical suit to wear! After a search throughout the southern hemisphere no one could find my baggage anywhere, and I had to make arrangements to get more ecclesiastical gear sent out from England. Then at last it was said to be lying unclaimed at Sydney addressed to a Mr Herbert, and would meet up with me at Christchurch. I landed at Auckland amid hoar frost and sat shrouded in Qantas blankets. The luggage didn't actually arrive until two days later in Christchurch. Air journeys are splendid when they go right, but hell when they go wrong.

As I look back over my diary of that visit, I see that I was given a very heavy programme, sometimes four public addresses in a day, although I also had some rest days during the six weeks I was in New Zealand, and one short break in the middle when we stayed in a 'shack' belonging to a chaplain and his family amid wonderful scenery in Queenstown. My main task was to give open lectures in all the many universities and university colleges of the land. I also visited halls of residence and seminaries, and addressed meetings of clergy and laity as well as preaching in the cathedrals. All the preparation of course had to be done before I left, except for those occasions when I found I had to speak impromptu. I recall, when preaching in Wellington, that the front rows were filled with men clutching Bibles. I gathered that they all came from Nelson, which was an evangelical and rather fundamentalist diocese, some of whose members had disliked my approach to the Bible and were intent on showing their disapproval. The university chaplains had not arranged for me to visit that particular diocese! The attendances wherever I went seemed fantastic: there were never less than a hundred, and sometimes four or five hundred. I am sure that this was not because of my presence. It was rather because the kind of explosions which ensued from *Soundings* and *Honest to God* had not yet taken place in New Zealand (apart from Lloyd Geering of Dunedin who had denied the physical resurrection of Jesus). Many Christians there were yearning to hear a preaching of the Gospel in terms more relevant and credible than the traditional approaches.

I was overcome by the beauty of the country, whether it be the Southern Alps, or the water around 'windy' Wellington, or the coastal area near Dunedin, or the gold workings of Otago or the boiling mud around Rotarua. I shall never forget the Maori farewell to the retiring Bishop of Christchurch, which I was able to witness. I made a resolution to come back with Elisabeth, which I was able to achieve in 1978, due to the kindness of Bishop Alan Pyatt of Christchurch, with whom I made friends on this first trip. I travelled usually by plane from city to city in order to fulfil my schedule. I remember one occasion when during the flight it was not possible due to the weather to land at *any* airport, but luckily that crisis had passed by the time we were actually due to land. The students and indeed everyone were very friendly, and I fell in love with the country. I was struck by the way that (in those days) everyone referred to the UK simply as 'home'.

During my time in Christchurch I stayed with David Thorpe, who was Vicar of St John's. His wife, Rowie, was the daughter of my mother's cousin Peter de Pass, who was regarded as 'unsatisfactory' and sent to sail before the mast to New Zealand, where evidently he made good. Christchurch was originally an Anglican settlement (just as Dunedin was a Presbyterian one). It was a prime example of what happens when one leaves things to the planners. Back in England they thought it would be a good idea if all the houses faced south; but of course in the southern hemisphere this is the equivalent of houses here facing north!

When I was in Auckland in the North Island I was also moved to see the old Benjamin home belonging to the family to which my maternal grandmother belonged. The family had been among the original settlers who landed in the Bay of Plenty. The house is now part of the university. On the way back I stopped off at Sydney, and duly admired the opera house under construction; and again in Cairo, where I visited the Pyramids and explored the inner parts of this vast city, something I would not dare to do now.

I came back to find everything in order; and of course the curates had greatly enjoyed my absence, which gave them a chance of doing things by themselves. I was very fond of the team who worked with me, but I think they had a lot to put up with, and I was not very good at delegating, so that it was good for them to have this period while I was away.

I soon returned to my normal schedules. One of my preoccupations concerned the environment. Although today one can hardly open a newspaper without reading about some environmental issue, in those days one was regarded as a freak if one was concerned with such matters. I had been interested ever since my ordination in Newcastle, when I came across a book written by Michael Roberts, himself a Newcastle man, who later became Principal of a training college and a writer of wide interests. This book was called *The Estate of Man*. Almost all the facts subsequently proved wrong (there were far more petrol reserves than he had anticipated) and almost all the arguments were proved right. I realised for the first time that our resources were limited and that we were using them without thought for the future. I realised again for the first time that we were causing pollution which would affect our health. I began to take note of what was happening, and to make cuttings from newspapers on the subject. The English translation of a German book by Gunter Schwab called *Dance with the Devil* fed my passion. This concern with the environment still continues unabated into my retirement.

I wrote my first contribution on the subject in a symposium published in 1966 and called *The Responsible Church*, put together by the chairman of the Church of England's Board for Social Responsibility. In 1969, I was invited to give some lectures at Queen's College, Belfast. I recall the occasion vividly because the chaplain said to me 'We're having a little local trouble here between Catholics and Protestants but it will soon blow over.' How wrong can you be! By this time I had gathered together a great deal of information about the current state of resource depletion and pollution, not least from DDT. I incorporated these into the lectures which were subsequently published in book form under the title *The Question Mark* and later in a paperback *Can Man Survive?* I was flattered when the editor of *The New Scientist* called them 'quite unique in being so well informed'. The matter came before the Church Assembly in 1970 when the report *Man in His Living Environment* was debated, at which I and Lancelot Fleming (Bishop of Norwich and former member of the Scott Polar Institute at Cambridge) both spoke. I recall that I had become something of a fanatic. Once laid low on my bed with flu when I was due to preach at Great St Mary's on the subject, I insisted on rising, putting a cassock over my pyjamas, and managing to enter the pulpit to give tongue. But then people never do know what is worn under the cassock, do they?

Bishop James Pike, whom I had met when I stopped off en route to California, decided to spend a sabbatical term in Cambridge. This colourful character, after a successful ministry in New York, became more and more outspoken and eccentric when consecrated Bishop of California. He seemed to believe more and more about less and less. He believed he could solve in a few days problems which had perplexed scholars for years. 'Hugh, I'm gonna crack the secret of the Dead Sea Scrolls,' he said to me once as he went into a Cambridge bookshop to order every book written in English on the subject. He made Great St Mary's his headquarters; but he was so addicted to tobacco that it proved impossible to get him to take his cigaratte out of his mouth as he walked through the entrance of the church into the vestry.

The real reason for his visit, he confided, was that his son was hooked on some form of boot polish, and he hoped to get him off this by bringing him to England where drugs were then mercifully still rare. Tragically, he failed; and the boy committed suicide. Pike was greatly affected by what he considered to be messages sent to him by his son from the dead. He actually said to me once: 'Hugh, it's kinda strange: I didn't used to believe in resurrection, but my boy's messages are making that belief come back.' Pike finally met his end by the Dead Sea. He was searching for the historical Jesus; but his car ran out of petrol in the wilderness, and he descended down a steep nullah in a vain search for water to drink; quite a parable of his life.

Back in Cambridge my ministry continued. One of the delights of Great St Mary's was that I was brought into touch with ordinary people. Everyone has about them something special and individual. I found that some apparently ordinary people were in fact among the saints of God. The sacristan was one of these. She faithfully laid out vestments every day (she still does) and kept the linen spotlessly clean. She is a dear woman. People of all sorts used to man the tower and the bookstall: gasfitters, housewives, travelling salesmen, builders and so on. One of the wonderful things about a church congregation which I don't think you find elsewhere is the splendid mix of people. Of course one has to be careful. This person does the flowers, that person does the catering, so and so looks after the lettings of the hall. One must not step on anyone's toes. We had a full-time verger, George Clarke, who loved the place. He was a small man, but he could walk with more dignity, holding a verger's wand, than anyone else I have ever seen. No job was too much for him. What I loved about the place was that you could find a bursar of a college rubbing shoulders with an estate agent or a stone carver on the same committee. It was a privilege to be told intimate secrets by members of the congregation, to baptise their babies, to prepare their growing children for confirmation, to marry couples and to say the commendatory prayers at a deathbed. The more 'ordinary' people were, the greater privilege it was to be admitted into their hearts and homes.

There was also the less 'ordinary' side of the job. I believed that the pulpit should be used to speak the word of God in a relevant way to a contemporary situation, whether it was 'town' or 'gown'. This led me into some difficulties. Soon after my institution as Vicar I was asked to preach a university sermon, and I decided that instead of talking about matters far from home, it would be appropriate to consider the present functioning of the university in the light of Gospel principles. Since the university sermon was then printed in the weekly *Cambridge Review* it had a larger audience than the small assembly of determined dons who put on their gowns and made their way to the university church at 2.30 pm on a Sunday afternoon. I am afraid that my effort was not appreciated. As a result one particular opponent, a Fellow of Trinity College, whose daughter was in the same class as Catherine at their school, gave a present of a kitten to her in order to annoy me. The trick rebounded: 'Tig' became a friend of all the family.

Then there was a terrible row over the Garden House Hotel riot. Some undergraduates got out of hand, and there was a bad fracas at the Garden House. Judge Stephenson decided that he must inflict exemplary punishments of up to eighteen months imprisonment which meant the end of the career of some students. This seemed to me very unjust, and on the following Sunday in the pulpit I questioned the morality of exemplary punishment for the people concerned, and said that what they had done was not so very terrible. 'Just think what it would be like if Cambridge were a garrison town, and ten thousand soldiers lived here instead of ten thousand students.' This remark let loose fury from the army. Field Marshal Templer, who I think was in charge of the Tower of London at the time, aimed salvos of rage against me in *The Times*.

Trouble blew up in the autumn of 1967 over an interfaith service in Great St Mary's. The World Congress of Faiths was holding a conference in one of the colleges and asked for a service in Great St Mary's, as the civic and university church. There were Buddhists, Hindus, Jews and Muslims. After thinking through the matter, I said 'Yes', providing I could vet the order of service. In those days interfaith services were frowned on. A Commonwealth Day Service in St Martin's-in-the-Fields that year had to be cancelled because of official disapproval. They now take place annually in Westminster Abbey with the Queen present.

I decided to go ahead. Attempts to get the Archbishop of Canterbury and the Bishop of Ely to veto the service fortunately failed. It seemed to me extraordinary that Christians should not worship with those of other faiths. Jesus died for the sake of all mankind, not just for an élite. He did not teach us to pray the Lord's Prayer in an exclusively Christian sense. Are we not all children of God? Yes, Christians do pray 'through Jesus Christ our Lord' and members of other faiths do not. But it is a strange faith that concludes that God does not hear their prayers on this account. The idea that I could not pray alongside my Jewish brethren struck me as almost obscene. I was, however, careful to ensure that nothing in the service should offend members of the Christian or other faiths, and I insisted on preaching myself, which was the only way in which I could censor the preacher. I do not suggest that there should be regular interfaith services, but I couldn't see what was wrong with it on a special occasion such as this. Canon Wansey did. The Rector of Woodford, Essex was a great protester, whether about infant baptism or the appointment of bishops or whatever. He organised an anti-service on the pavement outside. Fortunately, the Lord took my side, and opened the doors of heaven. The protesters were rained out.

And there was the reordering of King's College chapel. Michael Jaffé (later in charge of the Fitzwilliam Museum) persuaded his fellow dons to spend thousands of pounds lowering the floor of the chapel so that it could accommodate at its East End the famous Rubens picture of the *Adoration of the Magi*. I noticed that this involved the cross being removed, and there was now nothing to mark out this famous chapel (which was regarded by some people anyhow as a humanist temple) as a place of Christian worship. Its

Master at the time was a charming anthropologist who could not keep off the subject of religion; and I think that David Edwards, who was at that time Dean of the college, was somewhat embarrassed by his presence at so many services 'for purely anthropological reasons', as he put it.

At any rate I made some remarks to the effect that King's College had decided to spend thousands of pounds in order to remove the emblem of the Cross, which was based on fact, and to replace it with a famous picture, which was based on myth. This again did not meet with a universally favourable reception, although I noticed that in future a small cross was placed on the Holy Table (although not of course tall enough to interrupt the line of sight to the aesthetic masterpiece of Rubens).

During the transformation of their chapel, David Willcocks, the famous organist of King's College, asked if the choir could sing evensong in the afternoon in Great St Mary's, for which of course permission was readily granted. However, without the tall vaulted roof of King's College chapel, the voices of its choir sounded depressingly ordinary, and so the experiment did not last long; and I think that the choir was given accommodation by its rivals in St John's College.

There was also the matter of college feasts. I fear that I myself am naturally rather greedy, and I enjoy my food and drink more than most. Colleges in those days kept very good tables. I had been on the wine committee at Caius, and I knew how much was spent on wines at feasts; and for our Perse Feast, for which Stephen Perse had left a modest sum 'for an exceeding in diet among the fellows' there was then no budget and the sky was the limit. Poorer colleges did not have so many feasts: richer ones had many. Trinity College for example had a feast on every red-letter feast day in the calendar, even on the evening of Christmas Day. Some Fellows, sated by their Christmas lunch with their family, used to come in for a repeat performance.

When I was Dean of the college, undergraduates used to remonstrate with me about all this, but I used to shrug it off. I came to the conclusion I had been wrong. We were now constantly being brought up against starvation in the Third World. 'War on want' lunches of bread and cheese were held by students. I decided one Harvest Festival, while thanking God for our lovely food, to raise the question of this excess. Of course it was seized on avidly by the press. I admitted, in what I said, that I myself enjoyed feasts, but I did not think they were justified on the present scale. Dr Joseph Needham, Master of Caius, agreed with me, and that college removed a course from its evening meal. One professor's wife wrote to me to the effect that I had probably saved her husband's life by what I had said! But, as one can imagine, my sermon did not go down well among senior members of the university as a whole. I noticed that I was never again invited to a feast at any college other than my own.

My greatest trouble during my time at Great St Mary's arose from a lecture I was invited to give to mark the centenary of the Modern Churchmen's Union at Oxford. I was not a member of the Union myself, but many non-members were also invited to this series of lectures, including the Archbishop of Canterbury. These talks were all published later under the title *Christ for Us Today*, edited by Norman Pittenger. The subject of my lecture was to be 'Jesus the Revelation of God'. The journey from Cambridge to Oxford was a disaster. I was giving a lift in my Mini to William Frend, Bye-Fellow of the college and editor of the *Modern Churchman*, who was also due to give a lecture. Unfortunately I had neglected to see that my radiator had sufficient water. After a dozen or so miles, it started to spout steam, and was evidently badly holed. I had slowly to make my way home, stopping every so often to beg some water from a wayside dwelling. Then we had to get another car, and make our way to Oxford. Naturally we arrived very late, in fact just before I was due to give my lecture.

I still think that the lecture was rather a good one. My argument was that, if Jesus was to reveal God, then there would have to be certain aspects of his character which did this. I analysed those characteristics which he had in common with mankind, those which he shared with the Jews of his day, and those which were peculiar to himself. Among the last named, I especially noted his self-identification with those who were despised in the world's eyes. I pointed out that he was believed not to have been procreated by his legal father, that he was born away from home like a displaced person, that during his ministry there were times when he did not have anywhere to lay his head, that he suffered the most ignominious kind of death known to the Roman world, and that he died between two revolutionaries. It was as though God, in becoming man, was determined to identify himself with the most despised and unfortunate of his human creation.

I then speculated that it could be that he was also homosexual in orientation. If so, this would fit in with these other points I had made about his identification with the outcast, for the Jews hated homosexuality. I went on to suggest that there could be pointers in this direction. He had not married, and Jewish males were supposed to have produced a male heir by the time that they were twenty, unless they were Rabbis, which Jesus was certainly not; and at the Last Supper St John uses a somewhat strange phrase about him leaning on the breast of the beloved disciple. All this took up barely a page in a twenty-page lecture; but the press were there, it was during the silly season, and it was blown up into a colossal scandal.

I realised that something had gone badly wrong when I was woken up in the middle of the night with a message that the *Daily Express* badly wanted to speak to me. I drove back to Cambridge, and as I got in the front door of our flat, I heard the telephone ringing. I took the receiver off the hook, and a voice said: 'Have you any comment on the Archbishop's statement about you?' Well, of course, I did not know anything about a statement, but the Archbishop, urged on by his lay assistant, had been persuaded to issue a statement, saying of course that I was utterly wrong. That was only the beginning of troubles. All the papers took it up. I was subjected to a barrage of reproof. Over two thousand letters arrived, some of them 'more in sorrow than in anger', but most of them written in a state of fury. Of course these people had no idea of the context in which I was speaking, but had only read a few sentences taken out of a long lecture, and published in the press. Pride of place must go to a Belfast telegram: 'Bible Protestants of Ulster abhor your smear on Christ and charge you with diabolical blasphemy – Ian Paisley.'

I sent a copy of my lecture to the Archbishop and to my Bishop, Ted Roberts. The Archbishop wrote in a very kindly way, ending: 'I am sorry you have been involved in a turmoil which I hope will die down.' The Bishop, when he heard the context in which I had spoken, was simply splendid. He said: 'Hugh, I want you to preach on this next Sunday evening, and I will come and sit under you just in front of the pulpit.' So I did. There was a large congregation, and I explained just what I had said and why I had said it. Of course it was inevitable that there were some members of the congregation who were somewhat distressed. The churchwardens, however, stood by me very strongly, and there seemed to be nothing to do but to ride out the storm. I was, however, grieved that I had caused such pain to so many people, and also that it had given people an occasion to speak ill of the Christian faith. But, as I reflected in my sermon, to say that Jesus could have been a homosexual in orientation was roughly the same in our contemporary culture as it had been in the first century for him to die a criminal's death on the cross.

I had until then been receiving a good many invitations to preach or lecture at clergy gatherings. I felt that I was in rather a privileged position in Cambridge compared with the parochial clergy, without any specific duties during the three months of the Long Vacation, so that I ought to help as much as I could. In retrospect, I think I did too much of this, and I could have better spent the time with my family. Before the storm over the Oxford lecture broke, I had accepted an invitation by a bishop in a West Country diocese to lecture at a diocesan conference of all his clergy. Naturally what had happened affected my standing in the Church. After the storm had broken, one of his clergy (the bishop evidently funked it) rang to tell me that it had been decided that, after the rumpus, it would be better if I did not come; but would I care for a free holiday in a caravan in the diocese instead? No, I would not!

Strangely enough only a couple of years ago I received a similar invitation from the same diocese to lecture to the clergy. I replied that I was indeed free on the day when I was invited, and I would be glad to accept, providing there would be no repetition of what happened twenty-five years earlier when exactly the same invitation had been summarily withdrawn. 'Of course not, Bishop,' said the clergyman in rather shocked tones. Nonetheless I was not entirely surprised when a fortnight later he rang again and in an abject voice he did precisely that! This time, I was told, the reason was shortage of money. Nothing will induce me ever to accept another invitation from that diocese.

This episode of my Oxford lecture lay in the files about me which all the media kept, and it was continually trotted out. Even when the announcement was made some nine years later that I was to be a diocesan Bishop, it was alleged that I had said that Jesus was a practising homosexual. I had said no such thing; indeed I had been at pains to point out his celibacy. I was at Lambeth Palace at the time for a bishops' meeting, and I immediately rang up the Director of the BBC and demanded that an apology should be broadcast on all future news bulletins that day which contained a mention of my appointment. To my surprise this request was carried out.

By this time I was feeling the strain of keeping up the ministry at Great St Mary's. I had no one left in Cambridge really in whom to confide; most of my friends had left: Barry Till from Jesus to be Dean of Hong Kong, Simon Phipps from Trinity to be one of the Coventry team, Bob Runcie from Trinity Hall to be Principal of Cuddesdon, George Woods from Downing to Birmingham. I had been at Great St Mary's for seven years, while both my predecessors had been vicar for only three. It was more and more of an effort to think up the next courses of sermons. It was more and more difficult to find the right preachers for the courses. I was on medication, and my doctor told me I needed a break from this whirlwind non-stop ministry. But what could I do? I felt I had to go on. After the débâcle a year or two earlier about the Modern Churchmen's Union lecture, I was a kind of leper. We now know, through Owen Chadwick's biography of Michael Ramsey, that he suggested me to the Crown for a bishopric, and met with the reply that the Patronage Secretary did not think that Mr Heath's colleagues would approve. Apparently this was the first time that the cabinet had been brought into the appointment of bishops.

Oh God, what next? Nothing came my way. I suggested to my old college Caius that I be appointed to a vacant bye-fellowship in theology, but this (quite rightly I think) did not meet with approval. Again, when a vacant living appeared in the Fens, I cast a fly in that direction; but quite rightly that too was rejected. There had been talk earlier of me becoming Principal of Ripon Hall, but that was not really my style of churchmanship. The Bishop of London had suggested that I become Chaplain of London University, but when the authorities of the Catholic Apostolic Church (sometimes known as Irvingites) got wind of it, they said they would forbid me the use of the Church of Christ the King which belonged to them and was loaned to the Bishop and used as the university church. Although I pointed out to the Bishop that an outlawed chaplain would appeal to students, he dropped the idea like a hot potato. The only concrete proposal that was put to me was, by the kindness of a friend, that I should take charge of a diocesan retreat house. I really could not see that I was in any way fitted for that. It appeared to me that my ministry was finished, apart from the freehold of the Great St Mary's living which I held, and which no one could take from me. I could not leave; and at the same time I could not go on. I still believed that if God wanted me to serve in any other way, he would put something before me. Indeed, my lack of success over the bye-fellowship and the country living confirmed this conviction. But he didn't. I was particularly distressed because, although personally I had recovered from the 'homosexual orientation' lecture, it had left a deep scar in Elisabeth, who had found that Cambridge university society somewhat closed ranks against the Montefiores. This kind of situation often bears more hardly on a wife than on her spouse. She developed a real fear of any publicity of any kind; and I am not surprised.

One day my back played me up again, and when my curates arrived in my study for a staff meeting, they found me lying on the floor, proposing to conduct the meeting on my back. When they told me I should take a break, it became clear to them that I had passed the stage where I was able to make arrangements to do this. Accordingly, Barney Hopkinson, one of my curates, bless him, stepped over my body, picked up the phone, and rang up the diocesan bishop. He replied: 'Tell Hugh he is off duty now, and I will come over to see him and make arrangements'; and he was as good as his word. I think I believed in episcopacy then more than ever before! Elisabeth and I managed to get away up to Wales, and to stay at Abergwesyn, where, if I remember aright, I spent a lot of time repointing a stone wall, and trying to repair another which had tottered to its ruin. I regained my sanity somewhat, and managed to regain my poise as well. Of course Cambridge wanted to know what was wrong, and a rumour circulated that I had had a stroke; but Eliza was simply splendid in choking off even the most importunate enquirer.

Fortunately all this took place during the Long Vacation, and I returned to Cambridge able to face another academic term, as well as to take on the role of Vicar of the parish. The homosexuality row had seemed to elate me, because I knew I had been unjustly lambasted. But this was different. I was frightened now of spiritual aridity. I was able to carry on for the present; but I knew that this situation could not last. I had done my time there; I *must* go elsewhere. But still I did not know where, if anywhere, that would be. I only knew I could do nothing about it myself.

As so often in the mysterious workings of providence, when I did find out what next, it was from a quarter in which I least expected it. My old friend John Robinson had ceased to be Bishop of Woolwich, and had returned to his old stamping grounds in Cambridge. He was now Dean of Trinity College. He asked me one day to lunch with him, which seemed perfectly natural, and we discussed matters of scholarly interest to us both, and also Cambridge gossip. Naturally I thought that that was all there was to it. And then casually after lunch, shortly before I was preparing to leave, he said: 'Oh, Hugh, have you ever thought of being Bishop of Kingston?' To this I naturally replied that such a thought had never entered into my head, and it was out of the question anyway. But he replied 'Oh, no it's not. Mervyn asked me to ask you. Think it over and tell him what you think.'

Further questioning about this utterly improbable and unexpected suggestion evoked the answer that the Archbishop would approve the appointment (he had to be consulted because he might have refused to consecrate). As the Archbishop apparently told Stockwood later, he was the only person in the Church of England who would have had the courage to invite me to be his suffragan. It seemed that the question 'Oh God, what next?' might have been answered, if only because I had to move and no other move had been suggested. Of course it was not settled yet; and in any case I had to talk it over with Elisabeth. Providence does work in the strangest of ways.

Chapter Eight

SOUTH LONDON

Yes, we went to South London, and I became Bishop of Kingston upon Thames, but I've only recently discovered how I came to be offered the job. Just after the death of Mervyn Stockwood in January 1995, I received a letter from Canon Eric James, which I have his permission to quote:

I've decided to tell you a story which I'm sure you've never heard.

One Friday evening – I think 1969 – I was dining in Trinity. [Eric at the time was Chaplain of Trinity College, Cambridge where Lord Butler was the Master.] 'Rab' told me to come and sit next to him. He was presiding. To my embarrassment he opened the conversation – as tho' he was addressing the whole Hall – with the question: 'What can you do for poor Hugh?' He then explained that by some mischance what you had to say about Jesus and homosexuality had been reported in 'some Balkan newspaper' and had been reported back to Britain by the ambassador and 'got into H.M.'s red boxes' so that 'she'll never consent to him getting a bishopric'.

'The man's given all he's got to give at Great St Mary's and is going downhill' he said. 'What can *you* do?' I immediately said I could do nothing. I wasn't in that league. 'Oh yes you can!' said Rab, 'Do what you can!'

It so happened that I was due to have lunch with Mervyn the next day – Saturday – as I often did. Lunching on the lawn, I said what Rab had said. 'Poor Hugh' said Mervyn pensively, and we talked about possibilities; but none of them were realistic. As I left Mervyn said: 'I'll have a word with John [Robinson] about Hugh. We can't just leave him.' A few days later Mervyn rang and said 'Eric, I thought you'd like to know, as a result of our conversation,

I've decided to ask Hugh to be my suffragan. Whether I shall succeed in getting him is another matter.'

He did succeed in getting me. I was thrilled to go. I don't really approve of the old boy network, but it certainly helped me then in my parlous situation.

It so happened that this move to London coincided with the departure of our three daughters from home. Teresa, the eldest, had got married after taking her degree at Nottingham University before we left Cambridge, and she was then living in the Forest of Dean, and grandchildren were beginning to appear. Janet had gone to Lady Margaret Hall at Oxford to read English, and went straight on from there to an Assistant Lectureship in English at Liverpool University before becoming a lecturer in Canterbury at Kent University. Catherine our youngest was not yet launched on the world, but she was at that time engaged to a student from Jesus College whom she had met in Cambridge, and she had taken a short-term job before studying to be a social worker at the London School of Economics, so although she had a room in the house for a few weeks when we first moved, we did not see much of her.

I realise that I have said little about my daughters so far, and one would hardly guess from what I have written that they share a very large part of my heart. I have done this for two reasons. When writing memoirs it is difficult to make continual short references to the family. Also I did not want to embarrass them; but enquiries have shown that I was wrong to think this. So I will now include something about our family as they grew up.

Teresa was born when we were in Oxford. Janet was born two years later when we were in Cambridge and I was at Westcott House. Catherine was born at our home in Cambridge. We were delighted to have three daughters. Having been brought up as one of three brothers, it was a pleasant change to be (apart from me) a purely female household. I prefer the female sex. Women can be beastly to one another, I know; but by and large they are nicer than men. They understand the graces of life. Girls tend to be cleaner, more hardworking and more sociable than boys. In any case Elisabeth always said, probably rightly, that it was a good thing that we did not have sons: I would have given them impossible targets to live up to, and would not have had a good relationship with them. I am appalled at the present possibility of choosing the gender of one's children. A child is not a commodity to be bought or ordered; children are a gift from God to be loved and cherished for their own sake.

For Teresa life really started in Newcastle, where for a time she went to a very indifferent nursery school run by St George's, the church where I was curate. Back in Cambridge, as they grew up, they went to Chesterton Preparatory School at the end of the road where we living, down by the river Cam. Reports differ about the headteacher at that time there. Certainly on one occasion she made my youngest daughter very unhappy, but by and large they prospered there. We went on family holidays, and we had au pairs from abroad to help. Cambridge University at that time seemed to run on au pairs: they enabled dons' wives to cope, and they provided girlfriends for undergraduates. I remember that when Teresa was young and I was a student at Westcott House, we had Ruth from Basel who used to practise her opera singing in the morning by an open window. What the neighbours thought I didn't like to think; but they never complained.

Later on, Elisabeth was ill a lot. Her back played her up, and she suffered later from a feeling of exhaustion and also of nausea. She had often to rest in the afternoon. What the real cause of all this was remains unknown. However, a retired chaplain from the Leys School in Cambridge had a gift of healing in his hands, and after he had laid them upon her her feelings of nausea completely disappeared. He came to me once when I was laid low with gastric flu just before a great festival; I felt shafts of cold air from his hand, my stomach rose and fell, and later in the day I got up well. When Eliza was ill, the children obviously saw more of me, and I had to attempt the cooking. Fortunately on one of these occasions a haunch of venison arrived during the time I was at Westcott House from one of the students there. I remember one Christmas when I had to get the Christmas dinner in the oven, and then go out and preach a sermon before dishing it up. Because of Elisabeth's ill health, it was necessary to have awaybreaks without the children. We used to get in an elderly lady to take charge, who spoke in proverbs, and it was only later that we discovered how much of a disaster she was. Again, we used to send them to Farleys, the children's home then run for St Julian's, which was a rest home started for returning missionaries which later extended its welcome to clergy and their wives. Again, we only discovered later how much they disliked it there too.

The children each in turn left the Preparatory School to go to the Perse School for Girls. Stephen Perse had been a Fellow of Caius, and he had founded the Perse School. In his will he left his own college in charge, but unfortunately the Fellows disgraced themselves, taking the money and running down the school, and an Act of Parliament had to be passed transferring control to Trinity College. A girls' school was later formed. This was what was known as a 'direct grant school'. It was on a private foundation but received government grants which enabled clever children from poor homes to get a good education. And of course there were lots of dons' children there too. It rightly had a high reputation. Two of our girls did Classics, and there was a brilliant Classics teacher. I was horrified, however, at their Biology (or 'bilge' as they called it). They had to learn their notes by heart for examinations. I was particularly interested in the school because Caius was still allowed two Fellows on its governing body, and when I became a Fellow there, I joined the school governors, among whom were Dr Polkinghorne of Trinity College (now Master of Queen's College), and Mrs Barker the wife of the headmaster of the Leys School (now Lady Trumpington, a government minister).

I think we were a reasonably happy family, even if one did once stab another (not very seriously); and again one of them had a tendency to lie for a long time under the dining-room table when feeling put out. At any rate they are all great friends now. They were at times quite entrepreneurial. At 'Springfield' we had a walnut tree which bore copiously, and one of them would get up early, put the nuts in a sack, and flog them to a trader in the marketplace. There was a large room at one end of the house, out of which two small bedrooms had been carved. This was their territory, and I used to complain that they kept it in a 'quagmire'. In fact, when they were young, I used from time to time copy barrack-room inspections, and make them 'stand to their beds', usually finding some unmentionable dirty underwear underneath. One of them remembers me teaching her to read, another remembers Bob Runcie reading to her *Mrs Tiggywinkle*, and two of them were taught the piano by Lindy his wife.

We did not, for obvious reasons, see much of my side of the family, so that their Montefiore cousins were not well known to them, although they knew and were very fond of their grandparents (my parents) who always showed them kindness. My mother occasionally came to Cambridge, but sensibly stayed at an hotel. Once she got ill there. Fortunately I was able to take into my confidence Tony Sills our very friendly GP who got her into a nursing home, and eventually she got home. I was quite incapable of dealing with her, but Elisabeth was splendid. I usually ruffled her up, but she would eat out of Eliza's hand.

Elisabeth had three brothers and a sister, and ten nephews and nieces. She was closest to her sister Catherine, and her brother Michael, formerly in the Diplomatic, but later a priest and Archdeacon of Sheffield. They were not of course in Cambridge, so most of the girls' friends came from school. Elisabeth's mother, Granny Paton, or Granny P. as she was known, used to come and stay with us, and they would stay with her. She was a great favourite. From time to time, at a crisis, Phoebe Paton, Elisabeth's sister-in-law, would help out: I remember one ghastly occasion when she got her hand stuck in our mangle. Phoebe was married to Elisabeth's brother Bill, later Professor Sir William Paton FRS, Professor of Pharmacology at Oxford. He was a brilliant and innovative scientist, whose research made possible drugs which relaxed muscles during operations. He was responsible for the introduction of drugs for high blood pressure, and the exploitation of North Sea oil would have been impossible without his contribution to the physiology of deep sea diving. Bill and I were directors of 'Paton Books', the bookshop we set up for Eliza's sister Catherine. A professor and a bishop: we were an unlikely pair.

When we went on holiday, we tended to rent a small house, going for several years to Penrhos, near Llanbedrog on the Welsh coast. It made more work for Elisabeth, but there were au pair girls with us, and it left us freer. Later, when we got the Old Vicarage at Abergwesyn, we used to holiday there. The girls naturally loved the wild scenery and the walks, and we had people to stay from time to time; but I get the impression now that they could have done with a little more social life. There was pony trekking in the neighbouring Llanwrtyd Wells, and one year they went on that. It was a terribly tedious journey in those days from Cambridge to Abergwesyn. Extreme measures to eradicate boredom in the back seats were usually ineffective; and of course from time to time the children were sick. I find this in a 'family log' by one of the girls: 'When we had gone ten miles from home we discovered that Mummy had forgotten the lunch, so we had fish and chips instead. When we arrived here it was about four o'clock, so we were all very hungry. J. and I were sick on the way, but I was more sick than J.'

We realised that we had never taken the children abroad, as we had our Welsh holiday home. So one year we all went to Venice and the Italian lakes. Another year we took a package trip to Malta. We all went one year to Korcula, a small island off the coast of what was then Yugoslavia, together with Richard and Ann Kindersley, friends who had been in the Diplomatic Service in that country and could speak the language. This was a great success, including climbing the local mountain on the mainland. It was called 'Sveti Ilija'. Sveti means saint, not sweaty, but it was so hot that we had to do the climb at night. We all drank Grk, the local wine. Although the island was under communist rule, it was run by a former mayor, an arch fixer called Anerić. He organised for us an orgy of a lunch one day, after which we were all so grossly extended that we had to lie down on the floor outside. We kept on thinking that each course was the last one, and then another came. Once when we remonstrated, he replied: 'The salad is helping to eat the porks.' Later, as the girls grew up and went off on their own, there were fewer of them to take on these holidays; fortunately Elisabeth wrote up a diary of all our holidays abroad, so that we have detailed reminiscences.

I used to produce 'soap serial stories' for the children. There was Roddy, who was I think an idealised version of what I would have liked to have been as a child. The most popular story concerned a family I called Burbidge. My ears still perk up when I hear of someone real with that name. 'Give us a Burbidge' they would say at supper; and I usually acceded. Unfortunately these Burbidges (or rather, their daughter Clytemnestra) won a pig at a country fair, and kept it in their back garden (strictly illegal, I later found). I had located them in Park Parade, a Cambridge residential street. It was particularly awkward when Dennis Nineham was made Regius Professor of Divinity, and his family bought the very house in Park Parade where I had located the Burbidges and their pig. They had to move.

We did a lot of entertaining of undergraduates at home, and the girls used to help a lot. I gather they got quite a reputation for this. One of them tells me that she was told: 'Oh, you must be of those Montefiore girls who are so good at making conversation at undergraduate parties', which, far from flattering her, flattened her. We had sometimes lame ducks from college to stay with us during term from among the undergraduates. Institutional life is ghastly if you are suffering from depression; but the influence of the girls and a home atmosphere was very therapeutic. One of those who stayed with us is now a distinguished professor.

And then, all too quickly, they grew up and went away. Looking back, I greatly regret that I did not spend more time at home with them. I used to think that it was more important to stay in college seeing undergraduates, or as a Vicar visiting members of the congregation. Now as I look back I am not so sure. I wish I could have known them better then and shared their lives more than I was able to do. It is a difficult choice, and I fear that many clergymen have the same regrets as I have. And now that we were in London, the birds had flown the nest.

I suppose everyone has a favourite saint. There was no doubt who would be the pin-up for my episcopate. It was my namesake, St Hugh of Lincoln. If I could model my time as Bishop on him, that would be best. I loved the collect for his feast day:

> O merciful Father, who didst endow thy servant Hugh
> with a wise and cheerful boldness,
> And didst teach him to commend the discipline of holy life
> to kings and princes;
> Give us grace like him not only to be bold
> but also to have cause for boldness,
> even the fear and love of thyself alone;
> Through Jesus Christ our Lord.

St Hugh, unlike some other medieval saints who were against the Jews, actually stood up for them. He loved the world of nature: his emblem is that of a swan, because the natural world loved him too. He was a humble Bishop and greatly loved in his diocese. He always took the option for the poor and underprivileged, and even withstood kings in order to do this; for example, by insisting on fair compensation for those whose houses were demolished by CPO to make room, by order of the king, for his priory. Although he had a sweet and loving temperament, he was easily roused to anger by injustice. I felt a great love for and even identify with St Hugh, because I was called by his name. I did not know what lay ahead for me as a Bishop, but I did know I wanted to follow in the footsteps of St Hugh.

There were quite a few matters to be settled before I could be appointed Bishop of Kingston upon Thames. Great secrecy surrounded the appointment. Mervyn Stockwood, the Bishop of Southwark, who got easily bored unless some drama was afoot (and who was rumoured to stir things up when there was none), made me call myself 'Mr Johnson' when I rang him up. That was all right until he forgot what he had asked me to call myself. He wanted David Sheppard, the Bishop of Woolwich, to vet me to see if we could get on together. David and Grace came down to Cambridge to a meal, and then I was to go and stay with David at his mother's house in the country. This was all attended by extraordinary secrecy. We had to meet in mufti at a London railway station like two spies at a rendezvous, and then go off in a cloak-and-dagger manner to stay in the country with David's mother. Luckily we got on well together, and it was settled that I should come.

I felt that we needed a break before a new start, and we went on an Hellenic cruise, to Greece, Crete and the coast of Turkey. Henry Chadwick was one of the guest lecturers. I will never forget him lecturing about the various monasteries as we passed along the coast of Mount Athos. I have an enormous respect for him as a polymath, but as we cruised down the coast he spoke with such great conviction and in such detail as he pointed out the various monastic establishments, their differences and specialities, that I recall asking him afterwards if he had ever been on Mount Athos. 'Of course not,' he replied.

Where should we live? That was a matter which had been preoccupying me in Cambridge. The previous Bishop of Kingston had shared a house with his sister, a schoolteacher, which was quite unsuitable for us. Archdeacon Reg Bazire was told to find another one for me, but he could only go by what the estate agents sent him, and they were all hopeless. Reg was a wonderful old man, who had been on the China mission field and together with Eileen his wife they had lost all of their possessions no fewer than three times. They then started life again in England. Eileen was still a strict evangelical who could only be persuaded to drink gin if she were told it was funny-tasting water, as the diocesan bishop did once; but Reg had broadened out into more central churchmanship.

I decided that I would have to find my own house. As I had been living on the edge of the Backs in Cambridge, I was determined to live near an open space in London. We came up from Cambridge, hired a car and drove round all the commons of south London. We then found just the right house; something inside me said: 'This is where you are going to live.' It was on the south side of Wandsworth Common in a row of shops, with over a mile of open space over the road. The last owner was a dentist who had extracted teeth in the room marked out for my study. It was a small house of character, with a charming small garden, and many rooms. An alleyway would easily be converted into a garage with an 'up and over' door. I found myself bidding for it against someone who wanted it for a cat home!

Then a Church Commissioner came to see it. It was then in rather a seedy area (it's very upmarket now), and next door there was a house in multi-occupation with most of the furniture dumped outside when the Church Commissioner came to inspect it. Naturally he was not impressed and muttered something about there being only nine inch brick. They refused to buy it for me. In those days houses in a run-down part of London were cheap, and with my mother's help I bought it for myself. As we now know, the Church Commissioners are not very good at investing their money in real estate. At any rate, it is the best investment I have ever made.

Before I was consecrated, Mervyn Stockwood didn't want me to talk about the homosexual row, but the Evangelical Council issued a statement, saying that I was being unorthodox in my speculations, because according to orthodoxy Jesus was 'perfect in every way'. I could not help pointing out that they simply did not understand the meaning of the Greek word *teleios* in this connection: it meant that Jesus was 'complete' in every way. He was fully man and fully God; as the Latin phrase went, *totus in suis et totus in nostris*. My riposte did not go unnoticed, but thankfully it did not make another storm. Mervyn obviously wanted me to make a good impression on the diocese, and to put this episode behind me. He decided I should speak to his diocesan Synod before my consecration and without prior notice. On this occasion the Synod was taking place in Church House. I was told to secrete myself in the lavatory until I was summoned, which I did. It went well.

I needed all the impedimenta of a Bishop. Fortunately at Great St Mary's a member of the congregation, Loughnan Pendred, was a woodcarver, and he made me a lovely pastoral staff of walnut wood, with a carving of a sheep and the Good Shepherd on it. I needed a pectoral cross, which was made with his own special treatment of silver by Gerald Benney, now a well-known silversmith. I had picked him earlier to make a huge cross for Caius College chapel when the college wanted to give itself a present for its sexcentenary. I suggested that it also gave a present to God. Then there was my ring. It was a present to me from the lady to whom I had given a ring twenty-five years previously. It was designed by a Cambridge man and made by Michael Murray. I had to sit for the designer just as one sits for a portrait. A bishop's ring must reflect the light and be large enough to be noticed, but not so large that it obtrudes itself. Mine has the Chi Rho (the first two letters of Christ in Greek) in silver superimposed on a gold ring both on the two sides and on the front. At the back there is a small star of Bethlehem. Later in Malawi, which is linked to the diocese of Birmingham, I was given an ivory pectoral cross in the form of a Canterbury Cross. This is a very precious possession which I still wear as a pendant on my shirt front.

The day of the consecration arrived, Michaelmas Day 1970. The Ramseys had kindly invited the whole family to stay the night before at Lambeth Palace. After dinner the Archbishop said to me: 'Now, Hugh, I want you to come with me to my study for a few minutes.' I thought to myself 'This is it. But surely he can't go back on it all now that all the arrangements have been made?' When I got there, it was not as I feared. 'I always want to give a new bishop a few tips,' said the Archbishop; 'I advise you to take off one Sunday in four to do

some reading. It is what I do myself. Nobody knows where you are.'
Of course I didn't, and what is more I don't think he did either.

The consecration was held in Southwark Cathedral, and was a
glorious occasion. There was the threat of an interruption by an
ill-wisher, but it didn't materialise. (It was the old service: it is
not until the new service came in that the congregation was asked:
'Is it your will that he be consecrated?') David Willcocks of his
great kindness brought down King's College chapel choir to sing
an anthem and lead the singing. I was most uplifted and thrilled to
be given this new responsibility. When I had said in despair: 'Oh
God, what next?' I never dreamed that it would be this.

The person to be consecrated is allowed to recommend the
preacher for such an occasion, and I suggested Geoffrey Lampe,
who preached a most memorable sermon. He reminded us of the
ancient custom of exorcism before baptism, lest evil spirits be sealed
up within a person. He suggested that various manifestations of the
spirit of fear still seemed to be sealed up within some members of the
episcopate. One is the spirit of prelacy (not personal self-importance
so much as giving too much weight to episcopacy). Others are the
spirit of devotion to the status quo, the spirit of not rocking the
institutional boat, and the spirit of not washing the dirty institutional
linen in public: 'spirits which hate to be reformed and which make
the Church an ineffective agent of the Kingdom of God'. I must
quote at greater length his words on my teaching ministry, as they
have been with me throughout my episcopate:

> The chair of a bishop has always been a teacher's chair. If he is
> an honest teacher, it cannot be a chair from which prefabricated
> answers, dogmatic assumptions or prescribed orthodoxies are
> handed down on authority for his people to take or leave. The
> bishop's teaching must be concerned more with questions than
> with answers. He has to try to ask the important questions, to
> help the rest of us to ask them too, and to get us to go along
> with him in his search for possible answers. For then he can
> trust that the Holy Spirit will, in the end, lead us into all the
> truth which we do not now possess. He will find too that the
> unity of the Church in this present age is a unity in asking and
> searching together and not, as has often been wrongly supposed,
> a unity in possessing agreed answers. If a bishop is not an honest
> and open-minded enquirer, he cannot be a teacher. This was well
> understood by the great bishops of antiquity: by Cyprian, when
> he said that the bishop should not only teach knowledgeably but
> also learn patiently, by Augustine when he distinguished the two

senses of 'teachable' as applied to the bishop: 'able to teach' and 'able to be taught'.

After the consecration we went back to our house, where we had been living for a month beforehand. Strangely enough, my first experience of being a bishop was of extreme loneliness. At first nothing much seemed to happen unless you made it happen. In a parish there is a wonderful support team; curates, a parish secretary, a verger, churchwardens, organist, the parochial church council and so on. You live in a vicarage, and there is perhaps a parish office in the church. People pop in and see you all the time. But as a suffragan bishop you just live in a house, you say your morning prayers on your own, you are left to your own devices a very great deal. It took me some time to get used to it.

I had an area for which I had special pastoral care, although I was not formally in charge of it. The other half of the diocese was the Woolwich area, where David Sheppard was suffragan. My area stretched from Church Ditton beyond Kingston and on the way to Guildford, down to beyond Reigate, and eastwards to Waterloo: quite a chunk of south London. It comprised the London boroughs of Lambeth, Streatham, Wandsworth, Richmond, Kingston, Merton and the borough of Reigate. There were some ten deaneries, each with a rural dean – a somewhat ridiculous title for someone who may live in the inner city. I had two archdeaconries, each of which usually comprises three or four deaneries. There were over a million people who lived in the area. So it was as large as a small diocese, but of course it was a constricted area: less than eighteen miles from one end to the other. I had to get to know the clergy, the churches, the institutions (two prisons, remand homes, many hospitals, masses of schools) and above all the people. The first thing to do was to go on visits with Elisabeth to all the parishes to meet the clergy. These visits were organised by each deanery. I had to go in the daytime, which meant that I did not meet children who were at school or wives who were at work; but still, we learnt about them, their ages, their names, their special characteristics. It gave me some idea of the area. I enjoyed these visits tremendously, and so I think did Eliza.

I also enjoyed the extreme contrasts of the diocese. What for example could be more different than a picturesque (and slightly bogus) rural parish outside Reigate, an inner-city parish in Battersea, and an upmarket parish like Kew or parts of Richmond? I enjoyed most of all being in the real world. Just as I had experienced a great sense of relief when I moved from the somewhat hothouse atmosphere of a theological college to a Cambridge college, so also

I felt a sense of liberation in being in the real world after the rather sophisticated atmosphere of Cambridge. I have to admit that I was somewhat 'thrown' when I first arrived by the number of West Indians in the inner city, and to a lesser extent the number of Asians. I had not lived among them before; in Cambridge they were confined to the occasional research student. In particular parts of my area, such as Brixton, they were in the majority. At first I was slightly frightened of them, but as I got to know them, I began to appreciate them enormously, and in some ways prefer them to Whites; particularly their sense of humour, their vitality, their friendliness. I found, however, that in the Brixton area the police did not seem to share my good opinion, and appeared to be prejudiced against them. The 'sus' law was still operative, so that West Indians could be arrested simply on suspicion. I was surprised that there was not trouble. The Brixton riots happened after I had left; but in my opinion they were long delayed, and could have happened much earlier.

South London in the last century had been a very churchgoing area. Churches had been built, so it seemed, every few hundred yards. Some of these had been closed before I arrived; but more had to go. The body charged with investigating this was the Diocesan Pastoral Committee. Great care was taken to see that everyone had their say before a decision was taken, and when it had to be taken to ensure that it should be made fairly and on high principles. But the trouble in London is that parish boundaries do not mean much, and so a church could lose or gain a congregation, whatever the area might be like, depending on whether it had a bad or a good vicar. We had a full-time clergyman, Colin Scott, as Secretary of the Pastoral Committee, who later became a Bishop. When David Sheppard left to go to Liverpool, I took over the chairmanship from him. We closed a few more churches, and joined some together as 'team ministries'. I didn't care much for these: they usually seemed to be formed out of weakness rather than out of strength. I suspect, now that the Church Commissioners have lost a lot of the Church's money, more churches still will have to be closed. However, this must not be regarded as failure; south London was far too overchurched. This is a general fault of the Church of England. The Roman Catholics, who have a slightly larger active membership than ours, have built far fewer churches which therefore tend to be fuller; and they seem very content with the situation.

Next, I had to learn to do my new job. I went to see how David took a confirmation. I went with Mervyn on a visitation of a parish. And then I started out on my own. You learn from your own mistakes. There is no one to put you right. You just have to get on with it. I was used to central Anglican worship, but I had to get used to other kinds as well. I had no fewer than five changes of raiment; chasuble (for high church), cope and mitre (central), red chimere (low church) and black chimere (very low church). These designations are of course only approximate. I really didn't mind what garments I wore, and was happy to wear what the vicar wanted. I didn't mind whether I stood for Holy Communion behind the Holy Table, or in front, or (very low church) knelt at the 'north' side of the table. I was greatly heartened by the confirmations. They were lovely occasions. Once upon a time people came forward to confirmation because it was the done thing to do; but no more. I discovered that those who were confirmed sometimes were laughed at in school because of this decision. There was a real integrity about them. It was the same with the adults too. After a heavy day I would drive out to a confirmation feeling exhausted, but the service actually refreshed and uplifted me. It was chatting up the families which was the most tiring part, and as a result I would on occasion drive home from a distant parish at the far end of the diocese too tired even to speak.

As for catholic worship, I gradually became (as I liked to think) a bit of a dab hand with a censer, and I simply loved sloshing people (or rather 'asperging' them) with holy water. But I did not know all the drill. However, Catholics are very good at telling you what to do. I learnt that when a strange man in an amice bears down on you, and you don't quite know why, just make the sign of the cross, and the odds are that he will go away again. As for Evangelicals, I grew to love their simplicity, but I disliked their habit of discarding surplus bread and wine after Communion; and I preferred to consume it all myself, even at the risk of becoming a bit swimmy. I found the kind of doggerel they sing (called 'choruses') very trite compared with the grandeur of the church's marvellous hymnody; but that perhaps is simply my personal preference.

I learnt to appreciate the strong points of each type of churchmanship. I liked the objectivity of catholic worship, its colourfulness, its dignity, its corporateness, its sense of transcendence, its link with churches down the ages, and its use of all the senses (touch, smell, taste, sight and hearing) in traditional worship. I loved the simplicity of evangelical worship, its concern for scriptural truth, its emotional quality, its personal element, its feeling of assurance and its total commitment to Christ. I also appreciated aspects of middle-of-the-road worship; its emphasis on truth and our search for truth, its appeal to reason, its intellectual integrity, its serenity, its admission of doubt as well as its affirmation of belief. I refused to identify myself with any church party. I hate labels. The glory of the Church of England is that one can take what is good from all the strands of church life and make it one's own.

I went, early on during my time as a suffragan bishop, to St George's House, Windsor, a centre started up by the Duke of Edinburgh and Robin Woods, then Dean of Windsor, where church people and others could meet in conference. This residential course was on man management and administration. Secular experts spoke to us. I had never before considered the theory underlying good management: it came with all the freshness of novelty when I was taught about consultation, peer assessment, and all the other things one ought to know before taking on an administrative post. Nowadays I think notes are produced to help new bishops. These were badly needed.

Mervyn had begun to undertake a visitation of the whole diocese, but it was beyond his capacity to visit and spend the night in all the 350 parishes of the diocese. So he called in David and myself to help. I enjoyed these visitations enormously. There is no better way of finding out what a parish is really like. I can't think why all bishops don't carry them out. The visitation would start with evensong on Sunday evening, when one would preach; and this would be followed by a question and answer session afterwards. Then one would go to the vicarage, take one's shoes off and relax; and in this way it was possible to be in a really warm relationship with the whole vicarage family. The next day one would worship with the staff, take Communion to the sick, visit the housebound, go round the various institutions or offices or factories in the parish, and simply walk the streets and get to know the parish. After evensong, there would be a meeting of the parochial church council, when one would go through a questionnaire that had been answered beforehand, and discuss policy. Eliza only came with me on one visitation. The bed was too small, and neither of us got much sleep! We did not risk it again. On another occasion, I was going to visit an evangelical parish in mid-winter. I know just how cold vicarage bedrooms can be, so I took the precaution of taking a flask of brandy. There was a knock on my door, and I hastily put it on the top of the wardrobe. Unfortunately I forgot to retrieve it. It was three months before I plucked up enough courage to tell this very evangelical vicar what had happened. It was still there. What he thought, I don't know, but at least I got it back.

There was one practical result of a visitation in Wandsworth Borough that I remember well. In the course of walking the streets of the parish concerned, I was shown an old-fashioned printing works. When I went in I found that it was the only place in Britain where a particular form of printing from plates could be carried out (by hand) and that all sorts of treasures were to be found there, such as the original plate of 'The Stag At Bay'. The local borough had put a compulsory purchase order on the building, offering it an alternative location; but this small firm could not afford to move, and was doubtful if its gear could be set up elsewhere. I appeared at the public enquiry, together with Brooke Crutchley, the Printer of Cambridge University Press; and we won! I have hanging on my wall a print from a plate of Constable, which was given me by the owner, and of which I am very proud.

Only one parish refused to receive me on a visitation. It was an extreme evangelical church. My churchmanship was under suspicion. I decided that I would go and give a lecture to the parochial church council on the true doctrine of the atonement. I pointed out that the theory of penal substitution (that Christ paid the penalty for my and their sins) was immoral, and was not even truly a scriptural doctrine. He did for us what we could not do for ourselves; but how could he suffer the actual penalties of everyone in the world? They wouldn't add up. The parochial church council didn't like it, because this unscriptural doctrine was one of their fundamentalist beliefs. Mervyn said that, if I wanted it, he would put a 'visitation order' on the parish, which in effect would mean inhibiting the vicar and my taking charge of the parish on his behalf during the period of the visitation. I did not think it was worth the hassle. Because Mervyn was the diocesan Bishop the parish was prepared to receive him, and so he carried out the visitation instead of me. The parish was very pernickety. When there was a vacancy in the benefice later it was for some years without a vicar because the churchwardens continually turned down suggested candidates.

As I got to know the clergy and their wives, so they would begin to bring before me their problems. The excellent borough deans would be able to deal with most of these. Borough deans were not the same as rural deans, who were parish clergymen: they were archdeacons or priests set apart to exercise pastoral care over a whole London borough. Morale was high in the diocese, owing to Mervyn Stockwood's strong leadership. It was interesting to me how great a difference good leadership could make. I seldom found that among non-churchpeople there was any antagonism towards the Church. At the same time I found that, among the million or more people in my area, Christian commitment was confined to a comparatively small number. There is no focus or centre to south

London; it consists of a lot of overgrown villages. While the vicar could be to some extent a *persona* within his own small patch, insofar as it still had a village atmosphere, a bishop was not a natural focus for ordinary people (as in most dioceses of the country), but only for church people. I think that this was as true for the diocesan bishop as it was for me as suffragan. The diocesan of course had his cathedral, and we had seats there too, one on either side of him. But I had no see church as such, although the parish church of All Saints, Kingston upon Thames served as such. This is a very ancient church indeed, and there is still a stone preserved where Saxon kings were crowned. It is also a very beautiful building with a fine musical tradition, and I was glad to have a special connection with it.

Within the diocese I was given special tasks. One of these was to be chairman of the Readers' Association. Readers are volunteers trained and commissioned to preach and to take services (other than the Holy Communion). Although some of them were a bore, I learnt to have a tremendous respect for them as a whole. All the work that they did (and in some cases it was a great deal) they did for nothing. All they would take was their travelling expenses. These men and women (women had only been admitted fairly lately) were very committed. In many case they had a higher IQ than the clergy. I do not think that the Church of England could cope without them; they filled in during sickness, holidays, or a vacancy in a living, as well as helping in their own parishes. I was thrilled at the quality of new Readers (and the numbers of them) whom I admitted to the office. Later on I was to become the Chairman of the Central Board of the Church of England, and I was able to see and appreciate their work on a still larger canvas. I wish that more attention could be given to their training, and that their office could be more respected.

Another task which I was asked to take on was the chairmanship of the Diocesan Board of Education. Since I had worked in higher education for nineteen years in Cambridge, it might seem that I was naturally fitted for such a job; but I found that I had an enormous amount to learn. We had in the diocese a church college of education, and full-time chaplaincies in the two modern polytechnics in south London (now universities). There was all the Sunday school work in the parishes. We had a very large number of church schools, primary and secondary, well over one hundred. I had known little about church schools before I came to London; I think, God forgive me, that I had almost despised them. I found that they were among the great treasures that the Church of England possesses, that they were oversubscribed, showing just how much parents appreciated them, and that they were in no way 'churchy'.

Under the 'Butler' Act, passed during the last war, a new system of schooling was set up, under which there were two kinds of church schools. Some were 'controlled schools' which had all their finances paid for them. These had some foundation governors but they were in the minority. We only had one such school. The rest had a majority of governors elected by the church, and they did not fully, like other state schools, come under the control of the local borough's director of education (or, at that time the Inner London Education Authority, which has since been disbanded by a Tory government). The responsibility of the governors for the school was very great, and so far as the fabric of the building was concerned, the government grant was then only 80 per cent and the rest had to be found by the governors. Of course they could not do this on their own: the diocese helped them. We could achieve this through the sale of sites of schools which were no longer required; and in London the value of the site could be very high indeed, especially in some parts of inner London.

When I first came, I found the financial affairs were rather muddled, and I set up a commission under Robert Beloe, who had once been a director of education. (He had also been the Archbishop of Canterbury's lay secretary, and he had persuaded the Archbishop to issue that statement about me after my infamous lecture; but we got on very well together.) This commission discovered an extra million pounds! After this we decided to employ a full-time financial director. Fortunately I had an experienced Schools Committee, with some very experienced ex-head teachers on it; and I had much need of their advice, especially in the large grants we were giving for the rebuilding of schools when we could get government permission to do this. Our schools were usually very old, some of them built a hundred years ago, and were greatly in need of this rebuilding.

I used to go round these schools a lot; and I was filled with admiration for their head teachers and staff. I was also very moved by some of the worship in the morning assemblies, which seemed to me far more real and heartfelt than some in which I had participated in parish churches. I think that the parents appreciated these schools for several reasons. They knew that the children would be taught something about God. They knew that the schools ran on rather old-fashioned lines of teaching and discipline, in an age when it seemed in many state schools as though the children set the agenda. And they knew that there was a Christian atmosphere of caring about the schools, and often quite a close connection with the parish church. It amazed me that there was not more enthusiasm for our schools among the senior clergy. I could only imagine that they did not know much about them. Church of England schools are not sectarian. They were set up as part of the Church's contribution to the education of the nation. There was nothing Church of England about them, except in one particular neighbourhood where there was great pressure to get children into a church secondary school, and where the governors (who were responsible for admissions) did require a certain proportion of Church of England membership. In all these schools the teaching of Religious Education was important, but far more important was the Christian atmosphere of the school.

As a result of my work on our Schools Committee, I had to participate in ILEA committees. I found that there was considerable prejudice against our schools in ILEA, which was presided over by (Sir) Ashley Bramall, due I think to jealousy. We were accused of discrimination against Blacks; quite unfairly, I believe. When I could investigate any particular accusations, I found that the schools were very popular, and West Indians, notoriously bad timekeepers, had applied after all the places had been allocated. I had to chair ILEA's Standing Advisory Committee on Religious Education. There was a humanist member as well as representatives of other faiths. The Church seemed under continuous attack. I found David Konstant, at that time one of the Roman Catholic area Bishops of Westminster diocese, was also a member and a great support. I was delighted when we were able to set up the first joint Anglican–Roman Catholic secondary school on terms mutually agreeable to all parties.

While I enjoyed my work in connection with education enormously, it was also the cause of the greatest sadness during my time in Southwark. I do not want to rake up old scores now when I would hope they had been laid to rest, but it would be dishonest of me not to make any mention of the matter, although I will not mention any names. Before I came to Southwark, the Senior Adviser on RE who had recently arrived had told me that he planned to stage a Commission of Enquiry into our secondary and primary schools, and asked for my goodwill, which I gave so far as I was able to do before I had started the job. The Commission then started on the few secondary schools in the diocese. It seemed to me that the Commission worked, perhaps necessarily, in rather an inquisitorial manner. During Lent the following year Bishop Mervyn Stockwood, who suffered badly from his chest, was lent a cottage in Spain, and invited the two suffragan bishops and their wives to join him (along with Sir John Betjeman and some others). Unfortunately David and Grace for very good reasons could not come.

During our absence the Bishop's Council (which had only recently been set up under the Synodical Government Measure) met and authorised the Commission to start work on the primary schools, of which there was a great number. I was distressed that this had happened in my absence without asking me or the Schools Committee of the Board of Education, especially as I found that the primary school head teachers, whose morale badly needed boosting in the inner city, were very nervous about the whole undertaking; and on the advice of the Schools Committee I would not have sanctioned it. When I came back from Spain and discovered what had happened, I refused to join in, and the project had to be dropped. This caused grave distress to the Senior Adviser on RE and to one of the Residentiary Canons, both of whom left the diocese feeling that they had been badly treated. It took me a long time to get over the distress generated by this episode; but I am still convinced that I did the right thing.

Work on the Pastoral Committee, Readers' Board and the Board of Education took up a lot of my time which was not spent directly on pastoral work. There were many evening occasions, institutions of new vicars, weekday confirmation services, lectures to give and groups to address. I also gave quite a lot of energy to the financial affairs of the diocese. As a result of considerable pressure, Southwark diocese, despite having many inner-city areas, was able to pay the highest stipends of any diocese. But in a time of inflation it was a constant worry. Indeed some of us felt that the giving from the diocese could not keep up with requirements, and a group of us, laymen and clergy, met for breakfast at our house before work to consult on this subject. How wrong we were! Giving has triumphantly kept up with inflation; and with the loss of endowed income due to the Church Commissioners' speculations it will have to continue to do this.

There were weekly staff meetings under Mervyn Stockwood the bishop, and these were always fun. At the very first one of all that I had to attend on becoming suffragan bishop, I misjudged that amount of traffic early in the morning, and so I arrived a couple of minutes late. As I came in, Mervyn said in a rather authoritarian voice, meaning I think only to show disapproval, 'Bishop, we don't usually allow anyone to join us who comes in late.' I thought that two could play at that game, and I replied 'I am very sorry, Bishop, but I misjudged the traffic', and walked out. But I was never late again! Every so often we used to have 'three bishops' meetings', which were hilarious. Mervyn and David and I used to go off for the day. A very wealthy and charming Roman Catholic lady regarded it as her ecumenical work to provide us with a meeting place, and to entertain us. So we started with a bathe in her swimming pool. It was essential after that to get in as much work as possible before lunch, because the food and drink were so remarkable (with caviare on one occasion flown in from Iran) that it was hard to concentrate in the afternoon before we took our sauna and departed after tea.

It was fortunate that we three bishops got on so well together. Indeed it was essential. Southwark in those days (before Croydon was added on to it) was not divided up into official areas. I disapprove of this system, because it means that a large part of his diocese is a 'no-go' area to the diocesan bishop; and in such a case it is very difficult for him to know his diocese and to give effective leadership. We had in Southwark informal areas; that is to say, each suffragan was informally in pastoral charge of half the diocese, but the diocesan bishop was overall in charge of the lot, and used to minister freely wherever he wanted. This seems to me to be sensible, but it did mean that a suffragan might give a ruling one week, and be contradicted by the diocesan the next week. But such troubles could easily be smoothed over with a little goodwill – and there was a lot of goodwill. The legal area system was introduced partly because many suffragans felt that they had no more authority than an assistant curate in a parish. I never felt like that in Southwark; but that was, I suppose, partly due to the personality of the bishop and his determination to make the system work.

On one occasion when I was in Southwark we had a residential meeting of all the clergy. It was difficult to find somewhere large enough to contain us; but we ended up at Butlins at Clacton-on-Sea. At the time there were not many holidaymakers there, and I don't think we were awakened in the morning by Redcoats to the sound of 'Wakey Wakey'. However, I found myself drawn into the ordinary life of the camp. I hope that was the only time in my life that I will ever have to judge a 'knobbly knees' competition. How does one discriminate between knobs of that kind? The bishop had decided that on this occasion the home team had to give the lectures, so it was a busy time. Jilly Cooper was sent by the *Sunday Times* to report on proceedings. I'm glad she regarded me as 'suave and elegant in lavender flares and striped shirt' (this was the first and last time that those particular epithets ever have been or ever will be applied to me), but I was sorry that she reported that I have one of those 'frightfully frightfully' voices. I hope it isn't true.

Elisabeth and I did a lot of entertaining of clergy and their wives: there were a very large number to entertain. The Southwark clergy, perhaps taking their cue in this (as in so many other things) from the strong leadership of their diocesan bishop, seemed to have an insatiable thirst for wine. Elisabeth was, as always, splendid at arranging these parties, which entailed quite a lot of furniture shifting to make room in our smallish house. But this did not give her enough to do now that the girls had all left home, so she took up her old profession of almoner (by now they were called Medical Social Workers) at St James's Hospital just round the corner. It was an old hospital, and has now been demolished, but with a nice feel about it, and she greatly enjoyed having this other source of interest for her talents. She was also busy on the Liturgical Commission.

Meanwhile the report of the Marriage Commission of which I was a member had been published. We were glad to be able to produce a unanimous report. We were concerned not only with the theology of marriage, but particularly with broken marriages and whether, if there was a remarriage, this could take place in church. The law of the land permitted this (and enabled a vicar who was unwilling to officiate to make his church available to one who was willing). But an Act of Canterbury Convocation required the clergy not to make use of their liberty under the law. We proposed that this Act should be rescinded, and that the full marriage service could be used, at the discretion of the officiating clergyman, with a preface explaining that there had been a previous marriage which had been dissolved by due process of law. There would be no question of hiding the past, but this would enable people to make a fresh start with the blessing of the Church.

This report was published soon after General Synod came into being, amalgamating the old Church Assembly and the Convocations of Canterbury and York. Our report was too radical for many people; the new Synod refused even to discuss it. The members of the Commission were not even thanked for the long hours of work which they had put in, until the chairman wrote to the Archbishop to protest. When I became a suffragan bishop I had lost my seats in Convocation and the General Assembly which I had held as a representative of the clergy. I was thoroughly frustrated by the attitude, towards marriage, of Synod members whom I used to watch from the gallery, especially as the Synod was almost equally divided among itself. It refused a motion to discover the views of the dioceses. I even tried myself to find out what these were, but this proved impossible on my own.

However, the rebuff to our report was by no means the end of the matter. Continuing pressure led the Synod to set up another Commission on the same subject. People no doubt hoped it would produce different conclusions; but the differences were marginal. It agreed in principle that remarriage should be able to take place in church. I had written the appendix on the New Testament doctrine of marriage in our earlier report, and also together with Lady (Helen) Oppenheimer the appendix on vows (how could a person in good faith take life vows to two different people?). These two appendices were very unpopular with the more conservative members. They hoped that the new report would rubbish them; but I am glad to say that our position was vindicated.

This second report gave rise to years of continuing debate in the Synod. It was finally agreed in principle, by a large majority, that remarriage could in certain circumstances take place in church; but there was no agreement about what those circumstances should be. The options became very complex; and when the question was referred down to dioceses, the conditions of the Synod's preferred option were so complicated and intrusive as to be thought unworkable, and the dioceses rejected them; and so the whole question was dropped. It would have been far better if the recommendation of our original report had been adopted, and the matter left to the incumbent's discretion. The present situation is untenable. The blanket prohibition of the old Act of Convocation has never been rescinded, yet Synod has agreed (by a large majority) that there are in principle situations where a remarriage could rightly take place in church, but was unable to identify what these situations might be. The authority of the old Act of Convocation is questionable in these circumstances; and many clergy feel justified in going ahead and remarrying couples where they think this appropriate. When I later became Bishop of Birmingham, I invited the clergy to tell me (anonymously) how many such remarriages they had carried out in a year, and I was surprised to find that the number reached treble figures.

Meanwhile the Doctrine Commission, of which I had been a member since its inception, continued to meet. After the sad death of Ian Ramsey, Maurice Wiles, the Regius Professor of Theology at Oxford, was appointed chairman. While he was an excellent chairman, it may be doubted whether it was wise to appoint to this post someone who by his books had shown himself such a radical churchman. Members of the Commission felt that they had been fobbed off with odd jobs which had come up as a result of the needs of the Liturgical Commission. We wanted to get our teeth into something more fundamental. And so we were asked by the Archbishop to say something about 'the nature of the Christian faith and its expression in Holy Scripture and Creeds'. The seventeen members of the Commission contained evangelicals, catholics and radicals, and this made agreement very difficult indeed. All the other members of the Commission were working in the academic field (including one layman). Whereas I had before been the only parish priest, I was now the only Bishop on the Commission. In the end we had to content ourselves with a short report of under sixty pages, with two appendices and eight individual short essays. One appendix was on the unity and pluriformity of the New Testament, and the other on the origins of the creeds.

Our report was called *Christian Believing*, and perhaps the chapter headings will give some idea of what it contained. We started with the 'Adventure of Faith' and went on to consider 'The Pastness of the Past', 'The Nature of Religious Language', 'The Christian and the Bible' and 'The Christian and Tradition'. Once again, the Synod refused to discuss the report, which was generally rubbished by many of its members. This was a sad decision. If only these matters had been properly aired, in particular the due weight that should be given to tradition and to the pursuit of truth, a great deal of the steam would have been taken out of the uproar caused by remarks made later by David Jenkins, the former Bishop of Durham, which, I think has done the Church of England more harm than good. He caused such offence and such violent reactions precisely because the Church had been kept in the dark for so long about these very valid questions raised by critical thinking on the part of many faithful Christians.

I wrote the last of the personal contributions in *Christian Believing*. I was concerned about the way in which theological truth differed from other kinds of truth, about the appropriate criteria for adequacy in establishing theological truth, and how this may be properly communicated to others. I was adamant that ultimate commitment is not to a body of dogmatic statements, but to the living God. 'I commit myself wholly to the living God, the divine Reality who confronts me in my own being and in the world around me and who is transcendent beyond it as well as energetic within it. This living Reality demands my total allegiance, and so too does Jesus.' Acceptance of the dogmas of traditional Christology can only be provisional, for all the respect that is due to them. 'The mystery of Jesus is greater than any formulation about him. As a Person he is compelling and when he calls me to follow, I cannot but obey.' 'All our dogmas are partial, and our doctrines provisional. It is not by these, but by my prayers and my life that, as a disciple of Christ, I make my ultimate affirmation about God, creator, redeemer and sanctifier.'

I was glad to have set myself the task of writing my own contribution, even though it only takes up ten pages of print. I really had to declare where I stood and what were my fundamental beliefs. It had taken me a long time to be in a position to do this. In a sense, my whole love affair with theology, ever since I had come to Westcott House as a student, had been concerned with working out intellectually the meaning of the faith to which I had been converted and by which I lived. As a don, this had been particularly difficult, because dons ought to see all sides of a question. There were many radical voices raised against the historical basis of the Gospels, and the authority of the rest of the New Testament; and I had to work my way through to a position which satisfied me. Although the Gospels were written for faith, and not as historical evidence, I believed that they could be shown to contain a great deal of reliable historical material about Jesus and what he said, although no certainty could be attained. I felt that that desire for certainty was misplaced. If life proceeded by faith, intellectual enquiry could only proceed by probability – but some things were much more probable than others. I also felt that liberals no less than conservatives were motivated by (often unconscious) presuppositions which determined their conclusions.

This is not to say that I had not 'gone public' about what I really believed much earlier than this. In Gonville and Caius College I had published a course of sermons under the title *Beyond Reasonable Doubt*. Listening to eminent preachers at Great St Mary's had helped me, as did the books which I managed to review. While I was there, I published another course of sermons under the title *Truth to Tell*. I also had to think out my ideas about a loving God and the problem of evil for a series of Passion Week lectures at Lincoln Theological College. These were subsequently published under the title *Awkward Questions on Christian Love*.

There is a sense in which everyone who takes confirmation classes has to be clear where he or she stands. As unofficial chaplain to New Hall, and as Vicar of Great St Mary's, I had quite a few people passing through my hands. One year at the church we had as many as fifty young people as candidates. Young candidates were still coming forward, but the numbers were beginning to drop, and I remember feeling bad in Cambridge that my bishop had to return from his holiday because I sounded the alarm about this, perhaps too loudly. There were also quite a few adults, although not as large a percentage of the total as today. Lots of people wanted to get married in the church because it made such a beautiful setting. I could not see anything wrong in this, provided that one of them had qualified to be on the electoral roll of the church: to do that meant six months' regular attendance. One year the adult confirmation class was entirely made up of fiancés and fiancées who had found during that six months that they wanted to be real members of the church. I wrote out some notes to give them at the beginning of each session. Someone persuaded me to get them published, and so they were, under the title *My Confirmation Notebook* (or *Confirmation Notebook* as it is now called). This was published first in 1968, and it is still going strong. It must have filled a niche. In fact it is my only real bestseller! When I was in Birmingham I was asked to revise it, and when I said I didn't think this was necessary, I was asked if I would mind if a critique was made of its contents. I had to agree to this. I was so shaken by its criticisms that I revised it forthwith. I mention the book here because it gives in short compass my view of theology as a whole.

Taking confirmation classes concentrates the mind wonderfully on what one really believes. So all this had helped me to focus my intellectual understanding of the Christian faith, and led the way to the contribution I made to the Doctrine Commission's *Christian Believing*. My thinking did not end there: I hope it never will. As I will explain in a later chapter, circumstances conspired to make me think hard about the relationship between Christianity and culture, and this led to an extension of my theological thinking, not in contradiction to what had gone before, but as a further development.

After General Synod had been functioning for a year or two, it was decided that suffragan bishops could elect a few of their number to sit in the House of Bishops and to be members of the Synod, I was fortunate enough (or unfortunate, depending on how one loos at it) to be among the first so elected; but I felt we were there somewhat on sufferance. The earlier General Assembly had been largely taken up with the abortive Anglican-Methodist conversations, but at least a new canon had been passed allowing members of churches which believed in the Trinity to be welcomed at Anglican altars. In General Synod much time was being taken up with remarriage in church and ecclesiastical matters. I fear much of its work was not very profitable. It had been based on a parliamentary model, which is essentially adversarial, whereas the whole concept of a Synod should be the coming together (*sunodos*) of representatives of the whole Church for consensus. Archbishop Ramsey often used to preside over the old General Assembly with his eyes shut, and one could not tell whether he had drifted off to sleep or not; at any rate he was never 'caught out', so one presumes he was awake. By contrast, his successor Archbishop Coggan, when he presided over General Synod, was always brisk and alert. Other people, including clergy and lay people, were also appointed to chair the Synod, so this duty did not always fall on the Archbishops.

Mervyn Stockwood decided, rightly I think, that there was insufficient dialogue between bishops and academics. He turned to me for
help to get something going. Some five or six bishops and an equal
number of academics began to meet of an evening during the period
of Synod, usually at the vicarage of St Matthew's, Westminster,
nearby. I personally did not contribute much more than the name
of this gathering: 'Caps and Mitres' ('Caps' refers to mortar boards
worn by academics on formal occasions). I don't think that there
was much real exchange, because the academics were usually very
radical, comprising Don Cupitt, Dennis Nineham and John Drury
among others, and the bishops tended to be more conservative. But
it did mean that we understood each other's position better, and I
think that something of the kind ought to take place now. Perhaps
it does.

There is one event which sticks in my mind during this period.
I have already mentioned Robert Beloe who used to be the
archbishop's lay assistant. His wife had been a member of the
governors of Finnart House in Hayes, the Jewish approved school
where my father had been chairman for many years. She arranged
for me to speak, I think it was in the local synagogue, about my
position as a Jewish Christian, and how I viewed the Christian faith
from the Jewish point of view. I was very graciously received, and I
remember the occasion as the only real dialogue between Jews and
Christians in which I have ever been fortunate enough to engage.
Although naturally the Jews did not agree with me, I was given a
very fair and respectful hearing; and I have always been grateful to
them for that.

It was during my time in south London that I became more
fully involved with the media. I was not unacquainted with this
in Cambridge. In particular I used to make the journey from
Cambridge to Manchester and back once a week for fairly long
periods to be a kind of resident cleric in a TV programme called
Seven Days, quite different from the later programme of that name.
(I remember once when I had been talking in the programme about
our need to forgive I was horrified to find myself confronted with a
lady whose brother had been murdered, and his body dissolved in
acid: if ever there was an acid test, this was it.) There was another
series which was later published under the bizarre title *We must
love one another or die*. At that time Anglia TV was very active,
and I used sometimes to make programmes for them; I recall one
on Albert Schweitzer which was filmed in Great St Mary's. When
we came to London the work intensified, partly I think because I
lived in close proximity to TV studios. And I did some writing for

the press. Mervyn used to write articles for the *News of the World*, and occasionally he would turn the task over to me. For a time I was a kind of resident cleric once a week on the *Today* programme of BBC Radio 4, which I think had not long started. Mervyn was very relaxed about all this. He always allowed me to do what I thought right, although obviously if I was unable to participate in some decision-making process, I had to face the consequences if a decision was taken of which I disapproved.

We took short breaks at times. Sometimes I could take a weekend off and Elisabeth and I could go on 'Citybreaks', as they were called. I recall a wonderful trip to Paris for the weekend. We got into a couchette at Victoria, and got out next morning at the Gare du Nord in Paris. The whole coach was shunted on and off a Channel steamer without waking us up. I recall a gorgeous picnic on the banks of the Seine, and wandering together along the West Bank. On another occasion we went to Prague, but we had much difficulty getting a visa, I suspect because I had been speaking at an Amnesty public meeting about illegal imprisonments behind the Iron Curtain. In fact we could only get the visa through the good offices of Mervyn, who had made a habit of cultivating Eastern European embassies. Elisabeth was rather shaken to hear Czech military at Prague airport mutter the word 'Montefiore'; but all passed off well in that beautiful city, except that there was a break-in to our bedroom during the night with a master key without waking us up; all I lost was money.

On another occasion we went to Budapest, another lovely city, especially Pest. We also made off to Madrid and Vienna on similar weekend trips, and we had an interesting break in Brussels where some friends we had made in one of the parishes had joined the bureaucrats in the European Community there. For a post-Easter break we once hired a car in Greece and went touring. We were in Delphi for the Orthodox Easter, with an extremely long liturgy, fireworks at midnight on Easter Eve, and lambs roasted in the open on spits for lunch on Easter Day.

In 1974 Elisabeth had to have an operation on her hip because of arthritis. She needed a holiday afterwards which did not involve walking. We went by sea to Bergen in Norway, and then up by coastal steamer (which delivered the mail, etc) all the way to Kirkines by the Russian border. It was a lovely trip, even though for part of it there was perpetual daylight. We enjoyed the short twenty-minute stops at out-of-the-way coastal villages, although we had to be careful not to be late, or we would have been stranded for a week on isolated Norwegian islands. The sight of the Lofoten

Islands was of surpassing beauty. On another occasion we went on the Southwark diocesan pilgrimage to the Holy Land. I had been there before on my sabbatical leave; but Elisabeth had not. It was the Easter period, and I remember walking to the Church of the Holy Sepulchre in driving hail. What I recall most about the trip was having to engage in public dialogue with Professor Verblovsky on the subject of the Holy Land as part of the covenant of God with Abraham.

Perhaps the most memorable of all these trips was a short jaunt to Rome. I had met Monsignor Purdy when he had worked in England; he was then at the Secretariat for Christian Unity in Rome. We invited him for a meal, and as I had been at a general audience of Pope John XXIII, we asked if we could gain admittance to one of Pope Paul VI. Imagine our amazement when a grand invitation arrived next day for a private audience. I doubt whether the Secretariat would have such clout these days. Perhaps an excerpt from Eliza's holiday diary would not be out of place:

H dresses up in cassock, etc, E in silk shirtwaister, gloves and mantilla. H advises being buttoned up to the neck – 'accoltato'. Off we go in taxi in time to go to St Peter's. We go off as instructed to rather grand staircase at end of left colonnade, which is ravishingly beautiful. H presents letter of invitation to Swiss guards. A gentleman in frock coat opens it, guards salute. Some more steps and more guards and salutes, a lot more steps, a guard, a courtyard, more officials. A lift, another guard, and finally a rather grand room with more officials outside, only one is a photographer and not an official and asks permission for a photo. The room, where vestments used to be kept, has a highly decorated gold ceiling with paintings round the top of a secular kind. It seems odd that I should be so *very* modestly dressed with a female up aloft naked to the waist, not to mention all those putti. However we sit in solitary state until an American cleric appears who tells us about protocol, practically nil. After about a quarter of an hour clapping tells us His Holiness is near. He comes, old and smallish, with his retinue. One of them removes his scarlet cloak and he comes to his seat and has chairs brought for us. The young American translates and we are very warmly welcomed. [We speak about student religion.] We attempt to kneel for a blessing but he won't have that – 'H is my brother' and he helps me up, thank goodness. He gives us each a medallion, which I call handsome. Off we duly go – there are seven more people for him to see and he has already had a general audience.

I was very much struck by him, but I hope, if I ever get to heaven, that it won't be quite so intricate to gain admittance.

It was during my time as Bishop of Kingston upon Thames that my interest in matters environmental quickened. There was a church leaders' conference in Birmingham in 1972, and I arranged the ecological section, managing to get such people as Barbara Ward to come and speak. I was invited by Teddy Goldsmith to sign his 'Blueprint for Survival', but I refused, because I did not think that all his facts could be substantiated. The previous year, in 1971 I had been invited to give the fifth Rutherford Lecture at the Polytechnic of Central London, which I called 'Doom or Deliverance'. This was a resumé of the environmental situation in which mankind, I believe, now found itself. It attracted considerable attention, including a leader in *The Times*. I was invited by the Commonwealth Ecological Society to their Hong Kong meeting, and flew out for the inside of a week, although I was decidedly swimmy in the head when I took a confirmation the morning after my return!

Towards the end of 1972 I found myself invited by Jimmy Goldsmith (Teddy's brother) to undertake a study of transport from the environmental point of view with £34,000 generously provided by his Ecological Foundation. This would be an enormous undertaking. The funds were such that a report would have to be completed in a year. I had at that time a pretty hazy knowledge of transport matters, and I soon learnt that these are very complex, and the subject of whole courses in some universities. After consulting with Mervyn, I took on the job. It meant a whole day's work every fortnight, and much reading of position papers. I was very fortunate to secure the services of an independent expert on transport, Stephen Plowden, who was seconded to us from the firm which then employed him. It was really his energy, enthusiasm and enterprise which enabled us to carry the work to fruition in the required time. We managed to get premises near Leicester Square at a peppercorn rent, and to hire an excellent secretary and research worker. I remember spending my Christmas break writing to suitable people to ask them to be members of the 'Independent Commission on Transport' as I decided to call it. We could not have anyone with a vested interest in any particular mode of transport, but we had to have people who were experts in various aspects of the subject.

I was pleasantly surprised at the number of people who accepted my invitation. We had twenty-three members and four consultants. These were very varied in their interests and expertise, and even included Sir John Betjeman who contributed as tailpiece to our report his poem with its conclusion:

'You're balmy or plastered, I'll pay you, you bastard –
I *will* overtake you, *I will*!'
As he clenches his pipe, his moment is ripe,
And the corner's accepting its kill.

The report itself was a serious contribution to the subject, and we managed to get a cheap paperback edition of 364 pages published in 1974. Perhaps we were too detailed, but we wanted to give statistical data, and to argue our case in detail. We ended up with no fewer than ninety-two specific recommendations. It became in some places a standard textbook. It was, I think, the first systematic treatment of our transport problems and we made a plea for an integrated national transport policy – something which, for the last twenty years, every government has so far ignored.

I remember the great difficulty that we had in getting an agreed report on time. We finally hired a room in a railway hotel, and since there was no time to write down our many decisions about the wording of our final report, I dictated them as we made them in the small hours into a dictaphone. In order to get the publication out on time, I had to go down to the works where it was being printed to get the proofs. I wrote a personal statement at the beginning explaining how, as a bishop, I had agreed to set up the Commission and to chair it. Alas, our recommendations met with little success from successive governments intent on motoring expansion. It is only lately that the truths which we adumbrated in 1974, that more roads make for more cars, and greater attention needs to be paid to public transport, are becoming generally accepted. These are being thrust home by the physical incapacity of our country to accommodate an ever increasing number of cars, reinforced by the weighty and authoritative report of the Royal Commission on Environmental Pollution in 1994. We urged change, not only for environmental reasons but also for the sake of the poorer members of our society who do not have access to a car. (I knew something about their difficulties, for I had accepted the chairmanship of the Pedestrian Society a few years earlier.) We did not condemn the motor car, but we believed that considerable restrictions should be placed on its use. Once again, I was glad to be involved in secular matters on which the Christian faith had a real contribution to make over the values which should govern their regulation.

In 1976 I was invited, together with David Gosling, by the British Council of Churches to hold a public enquiry about commercial fast breeder reactors. (David was then a lecturer at Hull University. He later went to the Environmental Desk at the World Council of Churches, and is now in a parish near Cambridge.) It was thought that supplies of uranium would shortly become scarce, and at that stage a breeder reactor would become necessary to produce energy from the nuclear residues. In fact, supplies of uranium have not become scarce, accidents or near accidents have stopped the construction of new nuclear plants in most countries, and fears have very rightly been expressed about a totally nuclear economy. In 1976 it was thought that the construction of a protoype breeder reactor was imminent.

We planned public hearings on 13th and 14th December 1976 at the London International Press Centre. I chaired a nine-member panel, consisting of top experts in various fields, nuclear, economics, moral theology, etc. We invited submission from no fewer than thirty-three expert witnesses, and questioned them on their submissions. Once again I was surprised how well people responded to a secular problem with religious undertones when invited to co-operate by a member of the Church. Tony Benn was Energy Minister at the time, and he fully co-operated with us. I will always remember calling to see him at his Ministry. He said to me: 'Let's get out of here to somewhere where the civil servants can't hear us', which we did.

He gave the opening address. He was against the breeder reactor but had to be circumspect about what he said. It was not our task to reach conclusions on the matter, but to expose the arguments for and against, and to investigate the various aspects of energy need and production, including alternative energy resources. We looked at the question in four aspects; future needs and resources of society, risks, economic and technological feasibilities, and alternative sources of energy. I gave an epilogue, which consisted mostly of theological reflections on the subject, in which I expressed the fear that a fully nuclear economy could well deteriorate into a totalitarian state because of the security measures that would be needed. A transcript of the whole proceedings was published in 1977 under the title *Nuclear Crisis: a question of breeding*.

A couple of years earlier I had urged the Doctrine Commission to consider the theological aspects of environmental matters; but they were busy with other matters, and lacked the expertise. They did, however, invite Archbishop Ramsey to set up a working group, to work in conjunction with the Doctrine Commission, 'to investigate the relevance of Christian doctrine to man in his environment'. There were six of us in this small group, which I chaired; Donald Allchin, Don Cupitt, Mary Hesse, John Macquarrie and Arthur Peacocke. I thought we ought to have our final meeting in a setting of natural beauty, and we conferred at our house in Abergwesyn. We managed to put everyone up except for Don Cupitt, who slept at the neighbouring farmhouse. (This was still in the days of his orthodoxy, before he lost belief in the reality of God.) We presented our findings to the Archbishop in 1974, just before his retirement; a shortish report with appendices, which was published under the title *Man and Nature*, to which the Archbishop wrote a preface in his retirement. It was, I think, the first theological work of its kind to deal especially with environmental theology, and the distinction of the members of this small working group ensured the quality of the report.

Another matter blew up, concerned this time with air travel. For many years there had been work done on the Concorde project, shared equally between Britain and France. There had been vast cost overruns, and I suspect that most members of the government knew that it should have been cancelled. But it had got to the stage that so much money had already been spent that there would have been a greater uproar if it had been cancelled than if it was brought to completion. It was due to take off and land at Heathrow, and would come in to land over that area of Southwark diocese that was under my pastoral care. There was, and still is, an organisation known as HACAN, the Heathrow Association for the Control of Aircraft Noise. I was invited to be its president. I was impressed by the quality of those who worked on its behalf, all voluntarily. The moment approached when the Concorde project was coming to fruition, but in order to make the profitable Atlantic crossing, permission was needed for it to land in the USA. In HACAN we calculated that if it was refused permission to land in America, it would be difficult for it to take off at Heathrow. Accordingly we decided to give evidence at the public hearings to be held in Washington by the American Transportation Minister. Unfortunately the hearing would take place after Christmas; the chairman and other members of the committee were unable to attend. But it was during my post-Christmas break in 1975, and I volunteered to go. This offer was eagerly accepted.

I do not need to enter here into all the disadvantages of Concorde. A distinguished economist has said that the Concorde, together with the Advanced Gas Reactor were two of the worst civil investments in the history of mankind. (The third was the Russian Concordski. He had omitted the Pyramids and the American manned space flight programme because these were not really investment projects.) The Concorde needs so much fuel that it can only carry ninety-nine passengers. It is so expensive that only the rich can afford it.

The sonic boom does not disperse as ordinary bangs do owing to the sonic shape of the vibrations. There was fear that it could interfere with the ozone layer. None of these matters, however, were my concern. I spoke against the Concorde in Washington on one ground only, that of noise: Concorde far exceeded in noise the permissible limits. Naturally before I spoke, I had done considerable research on the subject. Environmental health officers in Hounslow had warned mothers not to take babies in their prams under the flight path of Concorde. I said that its noise could not be compared to hell, because hell goes on for ever: it was more like purgatory, and it could be compared to the pain of a gall bladder, intermittent but intolerable while it lasts.

My speech was televised in America from coast to coast, and received adverse publicity back here in Britain, something which I had neither expected nor desired. Lord Boyd Carpenter hit out with a savage attack, and so did Gerald Kaufmann, the government minister concerned. Wing Commander Norman Tebbitt (as he then called himself) joined in with others. I was regarded as highly unpatriotic, and newspaper enquiries were even made about who had paid for my fare (it was paid by HACAN). Unfortunately I lost the battle, and Concorde was allowed to land in the USA. The newspapers, desperate for something to be proud of, praised Britain as gaining with France a 'first' with supersonic aircraft. It was indeed a beautiful machine, and a marvel of modern technology; but I still hold by my phrase by which I described it: 'technology gone mad'. Should not the Church speak out about such things?

These environmental matters, however, were only a sideline. There was plenty of work to be done. Towards the end of my time in Southwark there was a period of galloping inflation in the country, where no one seemed to want to work, and there was a general air of impending disaster. I was invited to give some lectures at Advent 1975 in the cathedral which were later published under the title *Apocalypse*. My theme was that the end of the world was at hand; not the end of a final 'big crunch' or cosmic explosion, but the end of the world as we know it with unrestricted use of resources, Western supremacy, and ever-increasing consumption. My argument was biblical, and was well received. I believe that what I said is now coming to pass.

My main preoccupation was the care of the clergy and parishes in my half of the Southwark diocese. I had lost the companionship of David Sheppard, who had gone north to be Bishop of Liverpool. We had persuaded the Bishop of Southwark to go off on sabbatical leave, which he had not taken during all the years he had been its Bishop.

Mervyn asked me to see the Vicar of All Saints, Margaret Street, Michael Marshall, in great secrecy, as David's possible successor: he was keen that all three bishops should work well together. This made me begin to feel rather old, because when Michael was an undergraduate at Cambridge I had directed studies at Sidney Sussex College, and I had supervised him in the New Testament when he read theology there. Of course I was delighted to serve with him, and he was duly appointed and consecrated.

By 1978 I had been in Southwark for over eight years, and it would not be long before I reached the age of sixty, by which time it would be unlikely that I would move on to any other job. The Deanery of St Paul's fell vacant, and I did not give it a thought; but Dr Coggan, who by now was Archbishop of Canterbury, told me later (perhaps not altogether wisely) that he had written a three-page letter to Callaghan the Prime Minister urging my candidature for the vacancy. I have heard it said that there was pressure from Jews in the city (including cousins of mine) against such a move. Whether or not it is true I have no idea, but it would not greatly surprise me if it were. I am so very glad that no offer did come to me to go there; I would have hated it. I learnt later what a very unhappy place it was then. And so I soldiered on, still enjoying my job and the opportunities that arose. I only hoped that, when the time for Mervyn Stockwood's retirement drew nearer, I should find his successor as congenial and warm-hearted as I had found him. 'Oh, God, what next?' seemed likely to be ultimately answered by retirement.

And then one day my faithful part-time secretary, Joan Bate, came rushing downstairs and shouted at me: 'You're going to be the next Bishop of Birmingham.' 'Oh, no, I'm not,' I replied, for I had seen no indication whatsoever that I would ever become a diocesan bishop, and Birmingham seemed an unlikely choice. She insisted that she had just seen it in the papers, and had been rung up about it on the phone. I must read the wrong papers.

I found that an unholy row was indeed brewing up on the subject in Birmingham, where I was regarded as a front runner. This would be the first vacant see to be decided by the Church. It would inaugurate a new system by which the Church put forward two names, and the Crown (acting through the Prime Minister) chose one of them. I discovered that there was a campaign being orchestrated against me in Birmingham, consisting of the local paper (the *Birmingham Evening Mail*), some Anglo-Catholic churchmen in the city, and a city alderman, Anthony Beaumont-Dark, later to become an MP. He said he would be happy for me to be Bishop of Outer Mongolia, but not of Birmingham. He objected to my using the name of the city by which to sign my name. The secular objection against me was my environmental stance. It was feared that I would run down Birmingham's staple product, the motor car. The row spread to the national press. Bernard Levin wrote an article in *The Times* called 'There was an old Bishop of Birmingham . . .' I remained discreetly silent, and refused to comment. Then there was a leak from the Crown Appointments Commission (despite terrible oaths of secrecy) which made things worse. Archbishop Coggan who was due to pay a visit to Russia, actually gave me his Moscow telephone number in case things got too hot.

I knew nothing about Birmingham, either as a civic or an ecclesiastical centre, other than that it was the second city of Britain and that most people who did not know the place avoided it. But when the offer did come from Callaghan (carefully wrapped in two envelopes and marked 'Very Secret') I knew I had to accept. If pressure from the press and a certain sector of the Church could circumvent the choice of the new Crown Apppointments Commission on the very first occasion that it functioned, it would fall into disrepute, and the Church's small step towards self-government would be frustrated. Once again providence had brought me a totally unexpected move. 'Oh God, what next?' was now answered by one word – Birmingham.

Chapter Nine

THE SECOND CITY

Before we went to Birmingham, I thought that Elisabeth and I ought to have a real break. Not that we had been without holidays when I was working in the Southwark diocese. But the old vicarage at Abergwesyn seemed very far away; and when we did go there in the summer, I seemed to spend most of the time getting the garden back into order, and trying to tame the giant hedge. The house was too big for the two of us: the girls went there with their friends, and there was always quite a lot of tidying up to do when we arrived. We determined that we would sell, and we were fortunate to find a buyer who did not seem too perturbed by the latest dry rot. We were very sad to see it go, because we had spent such happy times there, and it had been a kind of family home.

Our holiday, before we went to Birmingham, took us to much more distant parts. I had promised to show Eliza the beauties of New Zealand, and off we went in our winter but New Zealand's summer. Bishop Pyatt of Christchurch and Bishop Mann of Dunedin had kindly helped to arrange the trip. I preached for my living, of course, while I was there, staying so far as possible in parsonage houses. It was fun watching the albatrosses at a spot on the coast just south of Dunedin, but the really exciting part of the trip was when we hired a car and went down the west side of the South Island, stopping over at Hokatiki en route and seeing the glow worm dell there, and then on down the narrow coastal plain under the shadow of the Southern Alps to the Franz Joseph and Fox glaciers. At the southernmost end of the South Island, before the road runs out there is a 300-mile parish, and we went down as far as we could. Earlier we had been to the North Island where we were looked after by an old Caian called Douglas Myers who had been a server of mine at Caius, and taken to see the sights. He was newly married and seemed to have become a tycoon, owning most of New

Zealand's wine – he took us in his helicopter to his country cottage by the coast. I also managed to see some Benjamin relations, connected with me through my maternal grandmother. We were greatly struck by the friendliness of people in remote areas of great natural beauty. The whole trip was a great success and we returned in good shape for the Great Birmingham Adventure.

When I got back, before I could become a diocesan bishop, I first had to go through several hoops. First I had to be elected by the cathedral chapter of Birmingham. Since some of the people who so strongly opposed me were members of the chapter, this could not be regarded as a foregone conclusion. In the old days if a cathedral chapter refused to elect the Crown nominee, it was subject to the penalty of *praemunire* (forfeiture of all goods and chattels); but the penalty had been abolished a few years before my election. This duly went through.

Then I had to pay homage to Her Majesty the Queen in Buckingham Palace. I drove there in my little red Mini, but it seemed rather incongruous compared with the grandeur of the Palace setting. The ceremony was organised by the Clerk of the Closet (John Bickersteth, who at that time was Bishop of Bath and Wells and whom I knew from school). It had to be witnessed by the Home Secretary who was dressed in a morning suit (Merlyn Rees at that time). A new diocesan bishop has to swear an enormous oath unchanged from the time of Henry VIII, to the effect that 'no foreign potentate or prelate hath any jurisdiction in this realm of England'. I had no difficulty in swearing allegiance to the Queen for whom I have an enormous admiration. She has in my judgement done more than anyone else to keep together the greatest voluntary association of nations ever seen on earth, the British Commonwealth of Nations, and here at home she is so much more experienced than any of her chief British Ministers. After paying homage, there is another odd ceremony which is a kind of 'benefit day' for the ecclesiastical lawyers (and believe me, they thrive on this kind of benefit). This ceremony, known as the Confirmation of an Election, consists of proving that I am who I am, Hugh Montefiore, and not someone else! In the old days it also had to be proved that one was not a bastard. I was allowed to bring a lawyer as a 'friend' to accompany me, and my old friend Hubert Munroe came along. It contains all kinds of legal gobbledegook, such as 'I veritably porrect'. Strangely enough a bishop's pay begins from the time of the confirmation, even though he may not have yet been consecrated.

My ministry in Birmingham began with my Installation, or Enthronement as it is usually (and rather unfortunately) called; an occasion when representatives of the Church and the city gather in the cathedral. I was installed by mandate of the Archdeacon Bernard Pauley. It was an oppportunity for me to tell people what my style would be like, what gospel I would be preaching, and how I intended to set about my job. I see from Elisabeth's New Zealand diary that I worked on the sermon during the trip. I began, 'Our first priority is God'. It went well, and when I came outside the cathedral to 'bless the city', I was serenaded out by a West Indian metal band.

My first job was to meet people. Once again visits were organised to all the vicarages in the diocese to meet the clergy and where possible wives and children. I was given a good welcome. Bishops are in a position of power and influence, and so it is sensible to be polite to them; but I found a genuine friendliness and openness, despite the press campaign. As a matter of fact I think most people were a bit ashamed at the attempts to stop me coming to Birmingham, and as a result I had a bit of a honeymoon. I had a Polaroid camera, and I wanted to take pictures of the clergy families, so that I could fix names and faces in my head. This was greeted with some such remarks as 'Would you like our fingerprints too?', but I only had one blank refusal. There were other groups to meet when I first came. I decided that I would try to make my ministry as personal as I could, and so I would not spend time on committees. I would only chair my informal weekly staff meeting, quarterly meetings of rural deans, the Bishop's Council and Diocesan Synod, and meetings of those concerned with the ordained ministry in the diocese. Others could chair the various boards and committees.

We had moved into 'Bishop's Croft' in Harborne, only about two miles from the city centre, not far from the university in Edgbaston. It was a gracious house, and of course far too big for us. In fact for some of the time we let the attic rooms as a flat, although this was a bit of a problem because there was only one front door. This still left us with six bedrooms and three bathrooms. There was a huge free-standing chapel. I simply could not see myself using this. To heat it in the winter would be a ridiculous waste of money; to use it unheated would, I thought, be suicidal. I had decided to make my own chapel in a very large bedroom at the end of the long first-floor corridor. I had a beautiful wooden altar made, and soft furnishings for the windows. I asked my old friend Derek Haywood, who at this time was Secretary of the London Diocese, if he had some spare furniture from the London redundant churches, and he kindly sent up a lorryload on 'permanent loan'. It was essential to get arrangements for worship satisfactorily settled. I had been allowed to have a domestic chaplain, Jonathan Tinker, who was already working in the diocese and who knew the ropes. We had a daily Eucharist as well as the daily offices, and a period of silence every morning. Without this worship and silence at the start of the day, I could not possibly have done my job.

Then there was the question of where I was to work. I started off in the Bishop's suite in the Diocesan Offices, which were only about a couple of hundred of yards away, part of the Church Commissioners' estate which was not licensed to me. I hated it there. I did not want to be associated with bureaucrats, good job though they do. If I were to be father-in-God to the whole diocese, I must work not from an office, but from my house. Bosses work from offices, but fathers work from home. I had a wonderful study in the house – the old billiard room before it had become a bishop's house; and the Church Commissioners agreed to install bookcases there. Also there was Elisabeth to be considered. I could not leave her alone in that huge house all day long to lead a purely solitary existence. If I worked from home, she could see and even entertain my visitors and feel part of the whole show. We wanted people to come into the house. I held all my official meetings there, whether it be rural deans, staff meetings or the Bishop's Council. Evening meetings began with a buffet supper which Eliza provided. I found that this changed the whole tone of the meetings, making them more friendly and less formal.

The only problem with these new arrangements was that there was not room for an office both for my domestic chaplain and my secretary on the ground floor. We eventually solved this by accommodating my chaplain upstairs, leaving him a little isolated perhaps, and reducing our sleeping accommodation to a more manageable four bedrooms.

The house itself was Georgian, built on the site of an old manor house. Just over the road was Harborne Manor, which used to belong to Joseph Chamberlain, but which had been turned into a Roman Catholic retreat house; and the parish church was opposite 'Bishop's Croft'. In front of the house there was a paddock, which the Commissioners let out to someone to keep her horse! There were three acres of garden, and far more ground which belonged to the Church Commissioners, but was not licensed to me. This estate was massive: it even included Harborne cricket ground. The garden was in a mess; but Eliza, who had green fingers, got the Royal Horticultural Society's help. They drew up (on graph paper) a new design, which she triumphantly turned into reality. The garden was far too large for her to manage on her own; but the Commissioners gave me a chauffeur. It was not my style to be driven around in state:

I preferred to drive myself, or if I was too tired after an evening confirmation, to be driven by my chaplain. (I drove rather too fast, and seemed continually to be stopped for speeding, although I never quite lost my licence. This was always reported in the press and seemed greatly to endear me to the Brummies.) Albert, my chauffeur, kindly agreed to look after the car but to spend most of his time tending the garden. A whole wing of the house had already been divided off, and was a self-contained two-storey maisonette in the gift of the Church Commissioners at the far end. For part of my time the director of the Birmingham Stock Exchange lived there.

Downstairs was ideal for entertaining. In addition to my study, there was a lovely split-level drawing-room which could be divided into two rooms, also a panelled dining-room, a large kitchen and a breakfast room. There were vast cellars, ideal for grandchildren's hide and seek (we had five before we left). This meant that we did not have a private family room, but on the first floor Eliza had a small workroom. We grew to love the house, although I disapproved of two people living in such a vast place. (Bishop Barnes, despite being a socialist, lived there with ten servants, including the chauffeur for his Rolls: Eliza had morning help twice a week.) It seemed to me ruinous to heat, and I insisted on a thermal efficiency survey which greatly reduced the heating costs.

Uncertainty about the future of the house meant that repairs had been postponed. The roof leaked terribly: we had to hang a pail above the gracious staircase to catch the rainwater. The Church Commissioners refused to put things right until I had signed a piece of paper saying I would live there for as long as I was the diocesan Bishop. After unsuccessful attempts at plans for a new house in the paddock, I signed up. A new roof was installed, and to my horror I discovered it was being covered with best quality lead. Later on it was found necessary to replace the bath in the bathroom attached to our bedroom (which contained a small plaque to the effect that a Prince of Wales had once slept there). The refurnishing of the bathroom took the Commissioners a whole calendar year! Apparently the bath was iron and extra long and had to come from Germany, and when it did come it had to be returned because it was the wrong colour, and so on. The plumbing system of the house was past finding out. When we needed a new washer on a tap in the bathroom, no way could be found of turning off the water, and the water in the pipe had to be frozen.

I found that not only was the Bishop's house in need of repair, but also the cathedral in the centre of the city. This was a splendid building on classical lines, built as a parish church, and its churchyard was one of the very few open spaces in the city centre. It did not look like a church, and a survey of the many Brummies who ate their sandwiches in the churchyard at lunchtime in the summer showed that few of them even realised it was a church. It had been designed by Thomas Archer, who also designed St John's Smith Square in London. St Philip's Cathedral was built in the eighteenth century at a time when the city was expanding rapidly, and the churchyard was even more necessary for burials than the church for worship. The building had grown very dilapidated, and a successful appeal fund was already under way. However, this was a period of rampant inflation, and it came to me that the real value of the money raised was actually being reduced despite the interest it was earning. I therefore arranged a date for its rededication as soon as possible, even before all the money had been gathered in or the work begun. The strategem worked well. I invited Princess Alexandra (my 'pin-up' Royal: I had known her when I was Bishop of Kingston, as she lived in my area, in Richmond Park) to come to the dedication, and we even entertained her to a lunch at 'Bishop's Croft' after a suitable survey had been made of security.

The diocese of Birmingham was a recent foundation. This is because originally it had been a city dominated by the Free Churches, and there had also been a large influx of Irish Roman Catholics. (There was even an annual Hibernian ball.) Free Churchmen and Roman Catholics very naturally did not see why they should contribute to the endowment of an Anglican diocese. Various attempts to found a diocese failed until Charles Gore, who was at that time Bishop of Worcester (within which the city of Birmingham lay) gave the whole of his patrimony to found the diocese in 1905, and became its first Bishop for a few years until he moved on to Oxford. Gore was succeeded by a London churchman, Russell Wakefield. He allowed clergy to do more or less what they wanted, and as a result when he was succeeded by Ernest Barnes in 1924 trouble broke out between him and the Anglo-Catholics.

Barnes, a former Cambridge mathematical wrangler and don of Trinity College, had come from the Temple Church in London. He was a well-known modernist. As a Bishop he only kept residence for the periods of university terms, as he had done as a don! He liked only to ordain men from Ripon Hall (a very liberal theological college) or those with first-class degrees. When I mentioned Barnes once in a sermon, a lady came up to me afterwards and said: 'I was confirmed as a girl by Barnes. His sermon was all about the sterilisation of the unfit. I was so angry I went straight home, and said "Daddy, I want to be confirmed again."' Barnes was said to have begun a sermon at an institution with the words: 'I would have thought that the patrons of this living would have chosen a man with intellectual capacities equal to those of his parishioners; but evidently they thought otherwise.' For all his acerbity, Barnes was popular in the city because he cared about the welfare of its citizens, and he was rather annoyed when they rescued him from crippling damages awarded against him for libel about an alleged cement cartel raising the cost of cement for wartime air-raid shelters. (He refused to pay himself and rather wanted to go to prison.)

I mention Barnes at such length because his shadow still lay over Birmingham even in my time. He had a vendetta against Anglo-Catholic clergy, which became so serious that there was virtually a schism in the diocese. He even tried to resort to illegal means to prevent their institution unless they promised not to break the law. Their parishes refused to pay their diocesan quota, and Barnes refused to confirm in their churches, so they imported colonial bishops on leave to do the job. It was a situation not wholly unlike that of those parishes today who will not accept the bishop of the diocese if his hands have been 'tainted' by ordaining women priests, and so 'flying bishops' are used instead. Barnes's radicalism extended to the Holy Communion. He wanted to send consecrated bread from Holy Communion to a laboratory for analysis! So there was understandably a legacy of opposition by the Anglo-Catholic churches towards the Bishop.

Barnes eventually retired after nearly thirty years, and Leonard Wilson succeeded him in 1953. One of the heroes of the Japanese occupation of Singapore, he had not only been imprisoned but tortured there. His strong personality revivified the church, and he engaged on a grand strategy of churchbuilding to meet the rapid growth of the city. Unfortunately this was the era of flat roofs, and Wilson would not build a new church that held fewer than five hundred people. This gave rise to problems by my time. Wilson in turn was succeeded by Laurie Brown, my beloved predecessor, in 1969, and nine years later I appeared as the city's sixth Bishop.

Not long after my enthronement the Lambeth Conference took place at Canterbury in the summer of 1978. This was a meeting of all the diocesan bishops of the Anglican communion, which takes place every ten years. I had been invited to contribute to a book of Preparatory Articles for the Conference called *Today's Church and Today's World*. The subject of my article was 'Nationalism and Internationalism'. I found this a fascinating subject. It was a period when people seemed almost ashamed of being British, and when patriotism seemed to be overlooked in the current denunciation of nationalism. On the other hand without nationalism the new countries of the Third World would never have thrown off the constraints of colonialism, to say nothing of their further educational and commercial development. At the same time the coming shortage of natural resources, and the complex interrelationships of nation states demanded a growing internationalism, not least because nuclear warfare threatened global peace. I could find no one who had previously tackled this subject theologically; and so I found it very interesting. I came to the conclusion that, as with individuals, until a nation had sufficient feelings of self-worth, it was not possible for it to be in good relationships with others.

The Lambeth Conference consultation lasted a month. For the first time Mrs Coggan, the Archbishop's wife, had arranged a short conference for bishops' wives in Canterbury. However, the two conferences were quite separate, and we were put up in different buildings. We hardly saw our wives! The bishops were accommodated in various colleges of the university. I remember one notice being given out: 'Will all Primates please go to Darwin College?' This referred not to a class of animals which formed part of Charles Darwin's theory of evolution, but to a meeting of the senior bishops of the various churches of the Anglican communion.

I do not recall much about this Conference over which Donald Coggan, the Archbishop of Canterbury, presided. He had been appointed Archbishop there not long before, and few preparations had been made. But it was moving for us all to worship according to the different rites of the Anglican churches, and to meet so many bishops from all over the world, many of them with problems so different from ours. I found myself sitting at breakfast next to the Bishop of the Arctic on one side and the Bishop of Mashonaland on the other. The conference was an enormous encouragement to those who came from isolated areas. The most important question concerned the ordination of women to the priesthood. Already the Churches of Hong Kong, USA and Canada had ordained them. In a typically Anglican manner we endorsed both those who had ordained them, and those who would not. We urged churches to remain in communion with one another and we encouraged members of churches, despite their different views on this subject, to remain in communion with one another and with the bishop. Whether the Anglican communion could overcome the stresses and strains involved remained for the future. At least the bishops had been able to listen to one another's views on the subject.

I had begged Elisabeth to find us a cottage when she returned from her short meeting with other wives which she greatly enjoyed, while I was still involved in the main Conference. We had sold the Old Vicarage at Abergwesyn, and we had nowhere to go for our holidays, or indeed as a refuge from 'Bishop's Croft'. This was before the era of 'faxes', and recording machines were not yet popular. I determined that I would not go ex-directory in Birmingham, because bishops ought, in my view, to be available. This was in some ways a nuisance, because Brummies had a tendency to ring their bishop when they were annoyed about something; but I think it was worth it. Occasionally at night I would be awakened by the phone ringing, and a gruff and blurred Irish voice saying 'Is that you, your Grace?' and I realised that this was a drunken Roman Catholic trying to ring his archbishop. I did not tell him the archbishop's number, but simply rang off! In order to be free from the phone, I had to escape from the house on my day off; and for that reason I badly needed a refuge on the Welsh border to which sometimes I could resort for twenty-four hours on my day off. I took my day off on a Saturday, because my secretary did not come on that day, and I liked the house to be empty so that I could feel free to roam around in my pyjamas and get breakfast in bed on this one free day.

Elisabeth succeeded brilliantly. She lost one delicious-looking cottage by only half an hour, but since it was in the middle of nowhere, and situated in the centre of a large field whose hedges and grass I would never have been able to control, this was a blessing in disguise. She bought the end cottage of a group of three on the outskirts of the village of Bucknell, a few hundred yards on the English side of the Welsh border, five miles from Knighton and in delectable country. There was one living-room, one double bedroom and another upstairs room in which you could only put up a second bed when the door was shut. It suited us admirably, and we had very happy times there, even in our first year. There were at least six lovely walks which we could take from the house, and a charming brook ran through the village. It was an hour and a half's drive from 'Bishop's Croft'. We liked it so much that by way of a joke we called it 'Lizzie's Folly'.

Back from the Conference, I realised that the diocese needed something to keep it together and to give it fresh heart. The next year was the seventy-fifth anniversary of the diocese, but there was little enthusiasm for large-scale celebrations. In fact we arranged a fascinating exhibition in stalls on the cathedral green, with liturgical dancing, etc. Bob Runcie was by then Archbishop of Canterbury: he spent the night with us, and graced the occasion which was somewhat spoiled by rain. I felt that the parishes did not feel much loyalty to the diocese as such, and did not look on the cathedral as their mother church.

I began a campaign for faith and commitment, and had meetings for representatives of parishes. Before I came it had been decided to run down the numbers of clergy in the diocese somewhat, for fear that there might not be enough money to pay them. I decided to reverse the process. How could the church blossom without enough clergy to lead and serve the laity? I did not see how we could prosper without some specialists, and I gave six months' notice of my proposal to appoint several non-parochial clergy. The proposal went through. I had to appoint a new chairman of the Board of Finance, and I invited Sir William Dugdale to take it on, and I was delighted that he agreed. He came from an old Warwickshire family which was fortunate enough to have a coal mine on its land: he was a good churchman, and in charge of the Severn and Trent Water Board. He was also an entrepreneur, and I think that the Church would be wiser to appoint good entrepreneurs rather than good accountants to its key financial positions.

As I knew there would be, there was a financial crisis. We ended the year 1981 with a thumping deficit during a time of high inflation, and there was an amendment being moved to the next year's budget which would have increased the deficit. I realised this was the time for a strong lead, and told the Synod that of course they must do what they wished, but they needn't think that I was prepared to preside over a diocese with deficit accounting. This hint of resignation worked a treat. So much money came in for the next two years that we actually returned a 'divvy' to parishes. We never had any more problems over money. Brummies are very good givers when they know what it is for and how it is being used. We borrowed money from a rural diocese, which at that time had big credits in their pastoral fund from glebe, and this enabled us to buy houses for the extra curates and non-parochial clergy; but we soon paid it back. One diocese in the south of England, feeling sorry for us in our troubles with so many inner-city poor parishes, actually opened a special fund for us, which was greatly encouraging. This fund, however, had to be closed hurriedly in a couple of years when it was realised that as a result of all our efforts we were now paying our clergy more than theirs. However, closing a fund in the Church of England when once it has got into the system is more easily said than done. We were highly embarrassed when money continued to come in from parishes in this southern diocese.

I introduced many of the ways of doing things to which I had grown used in Southwark diocese, not because I wished to continue that regime, but because I thought that they best suited our Birmingham circumstances; a new institution service, a joint baptism and confirmation service, and so on. I also set up a Liturgical Committee to advise me on liturgy, and we published a substantial 'Supplement to *The Alternative Service Book* authorised for use in the Diocese of Birmingham', including Holy Week services. Some of these were later overtaken by the publications of the Church of England's Liturgical Commission; but at the time there was no official guidance for incumbents for these and similar occasions. We also introduced a calendar of local saints for diocesan commemoration, who included such people as Samuel Johnson, Richard Baxter, Charles Gore, John Henry Newman and Brooke Foss Westcott.

I experienced some difficulties with my staff meeting, with senior staff unwilling to change their ways, and sometimes I used to emerge from these encounters feeling like a wet rag. I initiated the custom to which I was already used in Southwark of making a visitation of parishes, which I carried out jointly with Mark Green, the suffragan Bishop. Never could a new diocesan have had a more loyal or effective suffragan than Mark, who could not altogether have approved of all these innovations; but he willingly co-operated. It was not until some time later that I discovered that he had been the other candidate of the two names put forward to the Crown for the bishopric, and that he had been apprised of this information, which ought to have been kept secret; and this increased my admiration for his loyal and willing co-operation.

I do not delude myself that all the clergy (or even their congregations) approved of all the changes that I made, or of my personal style. I hope that too many were not offended. No bishop dares court popularity, but every bishop ought to be friendly, supportive and available to his clergy. I used to say that any priest could see me within twenty-four hours (providing I was in Birmingham), although, like Nicodemus, he might have to come by night.

I paid an interesting visit overseas on behalf of the Church. I was invited to form part of an international Anglican team to visit the Church in South Africa as part of their programme of self-appraisal. We were led by Archbishop Scott, the Primate of Canada. The day I arrived in Johannesburg, five clergy including the bishop, had been imprisoned for a demonstration on behalf of an imprisoned Methodist minister. I went to John Forster Square to the police headquarters, and said I must see the bishop, as I had come from another diocese. I was told I could see him from afar in court next day. After prayers attended by some two hundred people outside the court, led by the Methodist chairman

of district, we went in. The authorities were obviously frightened
of a riot. They adjourned the case, and asked Desmond Tutu
who was there, to get the young Africans out quietly. He said
to them: 'Now, boys, I want you to show your pride and discipline, and walk out in silence with your heads held high' – and
they did.

We split into teams, and I was with a party which went to
Durban and Zululand. My appearance at the court house had
marked me out, and I and my baggage were searched even for
an internal flight. In Zululand Bishop Lawrence Zulu (who had
attended my lectures in Cambridge) gave me a stout carved walking stick which I still treasure. Zululand was peaceful then, and
parts of it were very beautiful; but girls had to walk sometimes for miles to get water, which they carried back on the
top of their heads. The teams met up in Johannesburg at the
Mirfield house there. Two men who said they came from the
press asked if they could interview me. A Mirfield Father asked
if he could be present too. I was asked a lot of searching questions
unsuited to a press interview, and after they had gone the Father
said to me: 'You did realise that they were secret service men,
didn't you?'

After Durban (where electronic listening devices meant that
the police with earphones were in a truck outside listening in
to our conversations at a church centre) and after the secret
police at Johannesburg I felt somewhat under surveillance. But
it was nothing to what the Blacks were suffering. I was certain
that nothing could end apartheid except bloodshed, and even
then success would be doubtful because the Black townships had
been sited in vulnerable positions so that the Blacks in any trouble would be at a great disadvantage. The present reality of
peaceful majority rule after elections seems miraculous. I think
people don't realise what a tremendous revolution of opinion has
taken place among the majority of the white population in South
Africa.

Back at home my day started with a brief walk in Harborne
from 7 to 7.30 am, followed by the Eucharist and matins, and a
period of silence, before breakfast at 8.30 am. I had a mountain
of mail, usually some thirty letters, which I read over breakfast,
and glanced at the papers. I made a rule that answers to the
letters had to be put on tape by 10 am, (unless research or
enquiry was needed) so that a copy typist could start work at
10 am. The rest of the morning was usually free for interviews or
meetings. In the afternoons I usually had some time for sermon or

lecture preparation, before diocesan or city events in the evening. Elisabeth once again undertook to entertain all the clergy and their wives, and we held regular parties for some twenty or twenty-five people in order to achieve this.

I was fortunate so far as matters of clergy discipline were concerned. All the time I was in Birmingham there was only one case of marriage breakdown among the parochial clergy (and in that case the poor girl got *anorexia nervosa* when she lived with her husband). There were some accusations of misconduct about others, but without proof. I do not believe that bishops should be looking through the bedroom keyhole in the vicarage. Sexual matters, unless they bring the Church into disrepute, are a matter between a priest and God. The clergy are a naturally hard-working, conscientious and clean-living body of men. Among the ten thousand in the Church of England there are bound to be some who are 'unsatisfactory', but only in one case was it necessary for me to invoke the Ecclesiastical Jurisdiction Measure, and that for something that had happened before I arrived.

The most difficult case I had concerned an assistant curate, who decided to take 'drag weddings' in a church between homosexual couples. The first I heard of it was a warning that this had occurred, and that the press was upon me. I told my secretary I could not speak to them before I had seen the curate: 'Tell them that I have diarrhoea or anything.' I managed to speak to the curate on the phone, and told him I had no real idea of what had actually happened, but that I must suspend him. I then told the press that I could say nothing, as the man had been suspended: the matter was *sub judice*: anything said now could prejudice the case. I then got the man out of the city as quickly as possible. I am glad to say that, so far as I know, he is now happily exercising his ministry overseas in his country of origin.

I can never understand why a clergyman should be ruined for life because of some foolish act, especially when he is inexperienced. Good heavens! I thought that Christianity is about forgiveness and a fresh start. I rejoiced to take clergy who had been in trouble in other dioceses, and to give them a job. I always took the parochial church council into my confidence. On one occasion, when I asked them about receiving a divorced priest who had remarried in very extenuating circumstances, I discovered that all but one of the PCC were themselves remarried!

I took some thirty-five confirmations a year, and so did the suffragan bishop. These would take place on weekday evenings, or, as I preferred, on Sunday mornings or evenings, when those being confirmed could feel the whole local church behind them. I found that well over half of the people to be confirmed were adults. I usually asked them what had brought them to take this step, and as a result I heard heart-lifting stories about how God had become real to them. We were always anxious to increase the number of suitable people offering themselves to ordination. Every diocese has a Director of Ordinands, and with Canon Lorys Davies I was most fortunate in this respect. My domestic chaplain, Christopher Boyle, initiated a group of younger people considering offering themselves and this was most rewarding. When I arrived in Birmingham I found only two women in deaconess orders: I set myself a target of twenty-five before I left, which was just achieved. I had the pleasure of ordaining these women to be deacons (and 'clergywomen') just before I retired. We also instituted a new way for the selection and training of Readers; that is to say, lay men and women licensed to officiate at morning and evening services, to read lessons and to preach. As at Southwark, these comprised a splendid body of men and women.

I was anxious to encourage the clergy to think and to read. I had an enormous admiration for their ministry – I really did think with good reason that we had the best body of clergy of any diocese – but I knew that the pressures of vicarage life left little time for thinking and reading. So I started a bi-monthly little diocesan magazine called the *Bishopric* (named after Bishop Hensley Henson's earlier magazine in Durham), and I edited this myself, with articles on topics of current interest, awkward texts in the Gospels, etc; and I invited clergy to contribute on subjects about which they had special knowledge. I also held every year a non-residential Bishop's Summer School for two days for clergy and their wives, at which I went out of my way to entice the best possible lecturers. I remember Bishop Michael Ramsey when he came in his retirement struggling with a large suitcase on Birmingham New Street station until I was able to rescue him. Every third year, instead of this, we held a clergy residential conference at Swanwick Conference Centre, which was not far away in Derbyshire.

I was anxious also to involve the lay men and women of the diocese in training; and in the last few years of my time in Birmingham I initiated a three-year scheme of Know, Learn and Live Your Faith. I hope that, in doing this, as in other matters also, I did not allow the committees involved in these matters to feel that they were being outflanked or disregarded. I think that it did help to mobilise the enormous resources that any diocese has in its lay men and women. It is always difficult to know how much initiative should be taken from the centre, and how much parishes should be left to get on with on their own. We had to try to strike a middle way.

The Bishop's Council assisted the Bishop in the making of policy of the diocese, whereas the weekly staff meeting was a more informal affair, taken up largely by personal pastoral matters and appointments. I began by chairing the Diocesan Synod; but there was a complaint – very justified, I am sure – that I was too intrusive in contentious debates, and I decided that in future I would invite the Chairman of the House of Clergy or of Laity to take the chair for these, leaving me free to speak my mind from the floor. It was not easy to chair the Synod (or any meeting for that matter) in such a way that time was not wasted and yet people could feel that they had been able to say what they wanted. I always believed in starting dead on time, and on being brisk: the quality of decision-making seems to deteriorate after more than two hours of debate. But this does not find favour with everyone.

The media used to inform me from time to time that I was about to be moved from Birmingham to some other see – 'translated', to use the technical phrase. Thank goodness they were wrong, because I wanted to stay in Birmingham. What they did not know was that when Archbishop Coggan was to retire, my name was originally one of the two to be submitted by the Crown Appointments Commission to the Prime Minister from which she would choose Coggan's successor at Canterbury. I tell the story here because it is already in the public domain – for example, two people who have interviewed me had heard about it, including Lord Runcie's official biographer. And I think it is important that people should realise that, even if it is true that no Prime Minister has broken the formal agreement about the appointment of Archbishops, there are still ways open to them under the present arrangements for them to exert strong pressure if not positively, at least negatively.

The Patronage Secretary on the second day said that I would be too abrasive for Mrs Thatcher; and as a result it was decided (not without protest) that my name should be removed and another one substituted, so that she could make a real choice. This really made no difference to the result, because the Prime Minister would never have chosen me. 'Bishop, you are always so controversial' she said to me once when I was introduced to her one evening at the National Exhibition Centre (*she* of all people said that); but she was once heard to describe me elsewhere as 'that perfectly *dreadful* man

from Birmingham'. Yes, I probably would have been too abrasive
for her. I do like to call a spade a spade, and my style would
certainly have been different from Bob's. But my hide was just
not thick enough. Apart from my other failings and deficiencies,
I am far too sensitive for that job. I have no doubt that Bob was
the right choice. Despite his tendency to sit on the fence, he was
a very distinguished Archbishop, displaying wisdom and diplomacy
as well as graciousness and goodness. He stood up to heavy flak
magnificently both from some Anglo-Catholics and from most of
the media.

I realise I have not said anything as yet about ecumenism. It has,
I think, least influence at the international level. With Elisabeth I
went in 1979 to a large conference at the Massachusetts Institute of
Technology in Boston, USA., called 'Faith, Science and the Future'
called by the Department of Church and Society within the World
Council of Churches. Dr Paul Abrecht, head of the department,
provided the inspiration behind it. There were 450 participants,
a host of stewards and interpreters; and a parellel conference of
young people who mingled with ours. I was invited to be one of
the Presidents of the Conference, and I was also appointed Press
Officer, so I had a busy time.

Of course it was pleasant for us both to have a 'freebie' in Boston,
and we enjoyed it. And it was stimulating to meet scientists and
theologians from all over the world, and to hear the views of
developing countries about Western technology, which we all too
seldom hear. It was good to listen to world-famous speakers. I
was, however, appalled at the way in which the students, many
of whom had been conscripted to their conference regardless of
qualifications, voted with the main delegates, and indeed swung
the vote against nuclear energy. It was also sad to witness their
mindless anti-Westernism and uncritical attitude towards the as yet
unreformed USSR. Worst of all, when I came home, fired with
enthusiasm to economise on energy use, no one in Birmingham
wanted to hear. Meetings about the conference had to be cancelled
for lack of interest.

As for more local ecumenism, I think that Birmingham was
the only city in Britain which employed a full-time secretary
of its Council of Churches. There were three Presidents of the
Birmingham Council (which was really an umbrella body which
included all the local councils in the district). I think that the effect
of these councils was often marginal, but they did help to keep some
co-operation alive. I much enjoyed the regular meetings of the three
Presidents. Christopher Hughes Smith was the Methodist Chairman

of District, and he and his wife Jean were good friends. When I first arrived Patrick Dwyer was the Roman Catholic Archbishop of Birmingham, a man of real devotion with twinkling eyes. He was succeeded by Maurice Couve de Murville, who came from the Cambridge Roman Catholic chaplaincy. He, like me, had to live in a huge bishop's house, and his aunt, who was living with him before she died, was, I think, rather lonely and used to visit Elisabeth at 'Bishop's Croft'. Maurice was great fun, although we did not see eye to eye on theological matters. He also kept a very good table, and was rumoured to have sent the nuns in his household on a *cordon bleu* course in Paris.

It will be interesting to see whether there is any ecumenical advantage in the new arrangements of 'The Churches Together in Britain', which is a co-ordinating body of component churches rather than a decision-making body. While the old British Council of Churches sometimes used to act as if it was a church in its own right, I rather doubt if much progress towards unity will come through these new bodies. Indeed, I am doubtful about a lot of time being spent on ecumenical affairs, where again and again one seems to be up against brick walls. I hope, nonetheless, that the decision in 1994 to reopen Anglican-Methodist talks will come to something, as the scheme we rejected is the best we shall ever get.

What is undeniable is the marvellous improvements in relationships between individuals of different churches at every level; episcopal, clerical and lay. Institutional barriers no longer seem so important. But they *are* important. While organic unity is a long-term goal, there seems to me no chance of its realisation in the foreseeable future, and I would like to see some reconsideration of federal union, rather like Stage 1 of the Anglican-Methodist scheme, in which there would have been a reunification of ministries, and a commitment to work together for organic union in the longer term. But this is regarded as rank heresy by the stricter ecumenicists.

In anticipation of moves towards greater reunion some churches seem to have jumped the gun in 'local ecumenical projects'. In these there is a joint church building, and members of more than one church make up a single church fellowship, with ministers from each coming regularly to celebrate the Holy Communion according to their different rites. In Birmingham we had several such projects; and at these churches I used to confirm jointly with the Methodist Chairman of District. Those confirmed were welcomed both into the Church of England and into the Methodist Church (or United Reformed Church), and formed part of the one local Christian fellowship. This might seem to work admirably so long as they lived in that area; but if they moved, they would obviously have to make up their minds whether to worship in an Anglican or Methodist church or whatever. This kind of ecumenical project presupposed Stage 1 of the Anglican-Methodist scheme, and such projects are now left somewhat hanging in the air after its failure. They are a concrete reminder to the whole Church that we cannot stand still in ecumenical matters. (In Birmingham the only inequality about such projects was that the Anglicans owned the buildings.) Altogether in England there are some three hundred of these projects, which are of course greatly disapproved of by the stricter Anglo-Catholics.

Birmingham was twinned with the French city of Lyons, the second city of France, as well as with Turin and a Russian city I have never been able to spell or pronounce. One year I was invited by the Archbishop of Lyons to pay a visit there during the Week of Prayer for Christian Unity. This was initiated by a schoolmaster of Lyons, the Abbé Couturier. It was interesting that the Roman Catholic Church opened relationships with me, rather than with the Roman Catholic Church in Birmingham: this is typical of the Gallican church, which has long had affinities with the Church of England. Finding out before I left what formal sermons I was due to give, I wrote them beforehand, and had them translated into French for me by a non-stipendiary priest in the diocese who taught French at the Birmingham Polytechnic. My spoken French was a bit rusty, but fortunately after leaving school I had spent that term in Lausanne, where I had once been fluent.

Here is an excerpt from my diary for 16 January 1981:

Met at airport by Père Michalon while press take photos. Met Archbishop, less than month in office. I take to him – spare, alert, sixty. Michalon takes me on pilgrimage to crypt where Irenaeus' body lay until Calvinists violated crypt. Preached at Mass for Unity in modern church housing estate, 1,100 present, mostly (but not all) middle-aged women. By Bishop's wish all who wished chalice helped themselves to it. Twenty-eight priests concelebrated – none wore dog collars or soutanes except me, Archbishop and Père Michalon. Great lay participation and singing. Standing throughout. Archbishop in simple chasuble and skull cap, no cope or mitre, simplicity reigns. Reception afterwards with kir. Dinner with Archbishop hilarious. He has one thousand priests (plus one hundred worker priests) and 3,500 women religious in his diocese. Perked up. It was like home from home when bread ran out at HC. But I couldn't see in England photographers running up and down taking flash photos during

Mass. I didn't see *any* young priests present. There are now only one hundred ordinations a year in the whole of France

Again, here is another extract from the next day:

. . . reception by Reformed. More kir. Speech by president. I have to reply impromptu in French, with press present. Reception in anteroom of huge bare church with vast pulpit standing twenty feet above contradiction, and small holy table (? never used). Ground floor only full for Reformation Sunday . . . on to Vêpres Anglicanes, turns out to be Anglican evensong translated into French. Taking part Archbishop, Greek Bishop, Armenian priest with 'coal-heaver's' hood. Incredibly I am asked to preside. Nine hundred present, including Anglicans from Grenoble. I preach, I hope all right, but said to be 'daring', but as lesson about Jesus befriending publicans and sinners how could I pull my punches?

And for good measure, the following day:

. . . met in Greek Orthodox Church, horrified by arrival of TV team, asked the relevance of ecumenism to the world, replied 'remplir la vide spirituelle and pour la paix and le justice'. Felt v. nervous, couldn't get my genders right. Enormous Greek lunch follows – how can my stomach ever recover? . . . shown round town hall, absolutely fantastic. Mayor's parlour was Napoleon's waiting room, Chief Executive's room was his bedroom. Decorations, wall paintings, chairs, chandeliers; all out of this world. Presented with red and gold bound book. I have to reply in French . . .

It was certainly a busy few days.

Back in Birmingham much of my time was spent in the ordinary run of interviews, answering letters, preaching at services and other diocesan affairs. After consulting with a peer (I went to see another bishop for advice every year) I decided it would be right to spend one third of my time on the diocese, one third in the city, and one third on national affairs. I rather enjoyed these sessions: he always told me to do less!

Birmingham is easily the second city of Britain, vast in extent, and yet it is so much smaller than London that it is easy to get to know it as a whole. It is at the centre of the West Midlands conurbation of some six million souls, although the population is gradually decreasing as people move out to new towns nearby, and into the countryside. It is not one of the ancient cities of Britain. From the seventeenth century onwards it developed its industries, helped in the nineteenth century by its central position for transport. Ironwork gave way to steelwork and hardware, leading to bicycles, motor cars and electrical goods. Finance and trading services grew correspondingly, and so did metal manufacturing; while in the twentieth century light industries developed. A population of 71,000 in 1801 had grown to over a million by 1931. More and more workers were needed, which led to immigration. Earlier, people had come from other parts of the West Midlands, then there were also regular flows from Wales and Ireland, and after 1945 also from the West Indies, India, Pakistan and Bangladesh. Those from the New Commonwealth only numbered some 50,000 in 1951, but in the 1980s they accounted for 15 per cent of the total population and some 55 per cent of the population in the older inner city. It will be a predominantly coloured city by the year 2050.

In the 1870s Birmingham gained an international reputation as being the best governed city of the world. Civic pride was known then and since as 'the civic gospel', in the spreading of which non-conformist ministers, who were then dominant in the city, took a pre-eminent part. Unitarians and Congregationalists ruled the city in the days of Joseph Chamberlain (who was Mayor from 1873–6), while Anglicans and Roman Catholics played little part. Significant traces of this old civic spirit remained a century later when I was Bishop. No comparable city still alternated its mayors between Conservative and Labour councillors each year. The city council was more interested in the welfare of Birmingham than in party political advantage. This led to the development of the Birmingham Exhibition Centre outside the city, and more recently to the Birmingham Convention Centre. During the time of recession, when I was there, the city fathers were insistent that if Birmingham's traditional manufacturing industries were failing, new wealth must be sought from developing service industries. They built up the City of Birmingham Orchestra, and attracted the ballet and the D'Oyly Carte. Birmingham, with its fine art galleries, its two universities, its music and theatres could no longer be regarded as a cultural desert.

It was predominantly a working-class city, with many highly skilled workers who worked with their hands. The countryside nearby still contained the traditional squirearchy. For example there was a charity, which ran almshouses, founded in the seventeeth century, at the ancient hamlet of Temple Balsall, a few miles outside the city, and the present trustees came predominantly from the same titled families as the original ones. I used to make a point of attending their annual lunch, where a very rich sweet was served, strangely called 'Lady Catherine's bones' after the foundress. There were no titled people in the city. When I entered the House of Lords, I discovered that at that time there was only one person debarred like me from voting in a General Election; and she was a Labour life peer. Perhaps because Birmingham has always been a city of immigrants, past and present, there was a great friendliness to be experienced there. It is a place where nobody wants to go, and which nobody wants to leave. I have never been so happy anywhere else, and I treasure my memories of the warmth of its people of all classes and colours.

In an industrial city like Birmingham it seemed important to make myself known in the factories of the city as much as possible. Accordingly I used to set aside time, and my chief industrial chaplain would kindly arrange visits to factories. I recall going round very different kinds of works, from poisonous chemicals to electronic gear, from rubber tyres to materials for motor cars.

When I first arrived in the city it seemed as though the Austin Rover factory at Longbridge had a death wish. There were constant strikes. I was struck by the fact that few of the workforce seemed to use British cars themselves! The first time I went over the factory was a Friday afternoon. I could hardly believe my eyes. Most of the men were playing backgammon. When I enquired the reason, I was told that they had finished their quota for the week. The unions refused to allow them to exceed it, while the employers naturally would not let the men go. The men told me that the employers would engineer a strike when there was overproduction of cars: the management told me that they had a list of professional troublemakers. Perhaps both were true, perhaps neither. I was allowed a private talk with 'Red Robbo', the men's leader, and of course with me he was all sweetness and light. But shop stewards would ring me up and tell me that the situation was very different. At mass meetings men were frightened of voting against the union line, as photographs were taken, and the 'dissidents' could be spotted.

I had a great admiration for the courage with which Michael Edwards, the new man in charge, tackled the situation. At one stage there was a strike, about a tea break of all things. Since the whole of Birmingham's welfare hung on the continuance of its motor car industry, I thought this was absurd, and I issued a public statement, saying so. I announced my intention of visiting the works, but I was prevented by the management, with the excuse that if I came, it would look as though I was coming to carry out a requiem mass. When I see the dramatic change that has now come over the factory, I am amazed. When I was in Birmingham a whole night shift was found asleep on one occasion. Now it has one of the best records in Europe. The privatisation of the plant, which I opposed at the time, was in fact a good thing; and the introduction of Japanese methods of work has helped even more. But it is very sad that this great plant is now owned by Germans. It was a source of national and civic pride which has taken a knock with the buyout.

Oddly enough, it was in Africa that I made friends with many Blacks. The diocese of Birmingham had a special relationship with the two Anglican dioceses in Malawi, the landlocked country round the huge Lake Malawi in central Africa until recently presided over since its independence by the ageless President Banda. This relationship had come about because Susan Cole-King, the daughter of Bishop Wilson, my predecessor but one, was a doctor who had gone out to work there. (Susan was later working for Save the Children Fund in the USA and was ordained priest in the Episcopal Church before she returned to England.) Our diocese raised funds for the Malawian dioceses which were very poor: indeed, most of their priests' stipends came from this source. However, we were more than repaid by the enthusiasm and spirituality of their church, which was inspiring to members of the long-established Church of England.

Malawi is Livingstone country, and the majority of its inhabitants are Presbyterian or Roman Catholic, with some Muslims, who are by no means 'fundamentalist'. There was an abortive attempt in Livingstone's time to begin an Anglican mission there led by Bishop Mackenzie, who at one point advanced with a crozier in one hand and a rifle in the other. But this collapsed. However, the Anglican Church was planted again later, and thrives. As Bishop of their companion diocese, I was invited out for a visit and given a very strenuous month's tour. Elisabeth decided, rightly I think, that it would be too strenuous for her, and so I went alone. I had a wonderful welcome wherever I went, usually with singing and dancing women from the Mothers' Union. My experiences were very varied, as my diary records:

We looked in at M'karta Bay fiesta, just missing traditional dances, but saw the schoolchildren perform. On to Chombe Church, on tea estate, self-built, with voluntary priest James Chifisi, medical assistant on the estate, who had built up huge congregation from six. Chichewa Mass, I absolved, blessed, preached, blessed seventy-five children who were in wide-eyed silence throughout, wearing only alb, trousers and mitre. Dusk at 5.30, and we could only just read the missal by candlelight. Afterwards handshakes, speeches, presentations (eggs and huge stick of bananas). Singing terrific, and all very moving. Then on to D, old style tea planter.

We may complain about the NHS, but consider the Malawian hospitals: 'Medical assistant had performed Caesarian before breakfast: hospital in poor condition. Some beds without mattresses, no dressing room, sterilisation with primus stove, roof has holes so mosquitos can give children malaria.' Or again elsewhere: 'Two doctors, two medical assistants, 60,000 patients p.a., 120 beds, some patients on floor under beds. Measles is a killer, 40 per cent infant mortality rate, often gastro-enteritis from powdered milk and contaminated water or undernourishment after weaning.'

Nkhota Khota was the focus of the slave trade in the bad old days, before the British came. It was an evil place. But it had historic associations. 'After lunch we visited places of interest – the fig tree under which David Livingstone in 1863 gave an umbrella to a Big Chief, as well as another tree where he made a treaty with the chiefs, then to the jetty [from which the slaves embarked across the lake], then to the hot springs, with Africans doing the washing, then to abandoned bishop's house.' I got mild sunstroke through dedicating a new church as the old one was too small for the congregation. A stone was there, and I had to lay two bricks on either side. I could not wear cope and mitre for this, and an hour in red chimere without head covering in the heat of the day was too much for me. I retreated next day into the Roman Catholic hospital in Lilonge, the capital, and fortunately only stayed there for twenty-four hours. It did not interfere with the plans for the rest of the visit; and when I finally departed for England, I had amassed so many presents that it cost the equivalent of a full passenger fare to get them home (I left behind hundreds of eggs and a monkey). I still wear the ivory pectoral cross which the Anglican Council of Malawi so kindly gave me. I think that the visit was worth while. Our link with Malawi means a lot to us; and we in turn help greatly with their finances, and their clergy come over to Birmingham to visit us.

So far as the black people in Birmingham were concerned, I found that I had a goodly heritage. When West Indians first came to the city in increasing numbers Bishop Leonard Wilson appointed Paul Burrough (later a Bishop) as their chaplain, and he used to take his caravan to various parts of the inner city to befriend them. For this reason they were less estranged from the Church of England than was the case elsewhere; but nonetheless there was prejudice against them when they first arrived. In my time they accounted for no less than 10 per cent of the Church of England's electoral rolls in the diocese. Many West Indians were members of other 'Black churches', with non-stipendiary ministers. (I once entertained all Black church ministers in the West Midlands at 'Bishop's Croft': I rather liked it because when it came to free prayer, the Lord was invited to give me a 'crown of glory'!) At the same time there were no Black ordinands coming forward. We appointed someone to stimulate vocations among them, and a Black clergy group emerged nationwide.

I made a point of attending meetings of the Black community in the Council House, and I treasure the leaving present that they gave me. The Provost of the Cathedral at that time, Basil Moss, was chairman of the Birmingham Community Relations Council. In this way we had many contacts with the coloured communities. I would visit a Sikh Gurdwara if it were in the area of a parish during a visitation. The Muslim Central Mosque on one occasion kindly invited me to look over it, and I saw that not only is there separation of males and females in worship, but also for those awaiting burial. I was touched by an Imam ringing me up to ask for my help to enable Muslim girls to wear pyjama type clothes when nursing, and one vicar told me he had been invited to join the social committee of the local mosque. His vicarage was one of the few places where Muslim wives were allowed to come on their own. On the whole Muslims liked their children to go to our church schools until puberty, because they felt they would learn something about God; but I was impressed by the way in which Muslim children after school went on to the Muslim school to learn about Islam. There were also Hindu temples and of course well-established and well-regarded synagogues. There was an inter-faith council where representatives of the different religions could meet and discuss together. The Roman Catholics took a splendid initiative in arranging inter-faith discussions among groups of lay people.

I know that there were riots in Handsworth which received a lot of publicity. In fact they were mostly incited by drug dealers, but that of course does not excuse them. On the day on which they occurred, I was on a diocesan pilgrimage in the Holy Land, and happened to be at that trouble spot Hebron, a site sacred both to Jews and Muslims, where there has been more recently a massacre of Muslims by a Jewish settler. It was pointed out to me in strong language that I could hardly complain about Hebron after what was happening in Handsworth.

Towards the end of my time at Birmingham, I encouraged diocesan pilgrimages. They were a good way of bringing together lay people, and enabling them to encourage one another in an enjoyable but also spiritual journey. I had long known J. G. Davies, the Birmingham Professor of Theology, and I asked his advice. He became so interested that he researched the subject and produced one of the very few theological and historical surveys of the subject in his *Pilgrimages Yesterday and Today*. We advertised a pilgrimage to the Holy Land for 1985. The Roman Catholics from Birmingham were also making a pilgrimage there at the same time. Although we did not have a joint venture, we did join up together several times. Canon Ronald Brownrigg is an expert on the sites of the Holy Land, an old friend right back from Westcott House days (his Mark was baptised alongside our Janet). I invited him to lead it, and a clergyman in Birmingham kindly agreed to arrange it. I was surprised at the large number of people who came – two coach loads. People found it very moving to see the sacred sites, many of which are genuine.

Three things in particular in Galilee stand out in my memory. One is when we were hearing the Gospel at our open-air Eucharist overlooking the Sea of Galilee on our first day, and a small fishing boat passed by just as we reached the very point where Jesus called Andrew and Peter from casting their nets. On another occasion we were at the north end of the lake at Caesarea Philippi where the Jordan enters the lake. We all retook our baptismal vows, and I was enjoying myself asperging the Roman Catholic and Anglican pilgrims with water from the Jordan. As I was doing that, a dove suddenly flew over us, and we were inescapably reminded of the story of Jesus's own baptism. The third occasion was near the Mount of Beatitudes, in what we called 'Sower's Bay' (from the parable of the sower). Ronnie and I walked out in the shallows of the lake and read the parable, as the pilgrims gathered on the bank some distance away. We read out in an ordinary voice the story of Jesus teaching from a boat: it was a vivid reminder of how Jesus on one occasion spoke at that very point in an ordinary voice, yet all the people on the bank could hear. The acoustics there are remarkable. We saw all the main sites; but I insisted that we see something which belongs to today rather than to the past. We went to Neve Shalom, a wonderful experiment in inter-faith community where Jews, Christians and Muslims all live together. It was a fine pointer to what we all hoped and prayed might come to pass.

The following year, in 1986, I invited Canon (now Archdeacon) Lorys Davies to arrange another pilgrimage on which more people could come at less cost to their purse. We went to and from Canterbury. Numbers increase with the telling, but I think I am right in saying that over one thousand came. Certainly we filled the cathedral, so that there was only just standing room for everyone. I had hoped that we would all be able to go by pilgrimage train; but unfortunately all special trains but one had been booked for away football matches that Saturday. At least we had one special train – taking pilgrimage prayers in a carriage against the noise of the railtrack was a severe strain on one's vocal chords. The rest went in a fleet of coaches. We made the cricket ground our headquarters, where there was a match between teams from the two archdeaconries. And then we processed to Canterbury Cathedral for the Eucharist. Bob Runcie, the Archbishop, welcomed us with a splendid sermon which certainly cheered up the Brummies, and he presented me with some stained glass which I greatly cherish. It was a good occasion, and this is the kind of activity which greatly sustains morale and gives pleasure. I was presented with a greatly valued photographic record of the day.

I must not give the impression that life was all work and no play. I did take holidays, usually in September if possible, which gave me the chance of doing some writing in the usually quiet month of August. We would drive to Southampton, take the night ferry to Le Havre, and then drive across France to the Dordogne or Burgundy (alas, my Chambertin on one occasion was stolen from the boot); once we put the car on the train to Avignon, to explore the countryside around and to see the wild horses in the Camargue. On another occasion we went to Brittany. I had had an idyllic holiday there in my childhood, painting the fishing boats with their delectable blue sails; but now, alas, the romance had gone, all was mechanised and grey. One Easter we hired a car in Greece, and spent the Greek Easter at Delphi, and drove on to Thessalonica and also visited a curious monastery, the Great Meteora, up a steep rockside where the only access seemed to be by rope or ladder. One summer we also had a Greek holiday, this time taking a return flight to Rhodes without any plans, island hopping by the many boats sailing in those parts. I particularly remember the happy time we had revisiting Patmos, and also in Samos, overlooking the Turkish coast.

One year we took a package tour to Moscow and Leningrad, travelling by train through the birch forests between the two. We returned to Moscow a few years later to visit one of our daughters.

Janet, a lecturer at Kent University, and now married to Patrick Cockburn of the journalist family, had taken leave to be with her husband; and he was correspondent in Moscow for the *Financial Times* at this period. The only way we could really visit Janet was by package tour to Moscow (the USSR discouraged individual visits). This was of course before the fall of communism, and their block of flats, shared between diplomats and journalists, was naturally bugged, and so the open air was needed for frank speech. The car registration numbers were organised in such a way that any policeman could instantly recognise that our car belonged to a British journalist; and I noticed that we were stopped, without apparent reason, on the way home from an expedition to Gregorsk, the Orthodox Church centre some fifty miles out of town.

Back at home life continued as usual. My job was to look after the Church as an institution as well as the Church as a movement. Christianity started as a movement, but for any movement to continue over the centuries, it is necessary for it to be institutionalised. All institutional religion is bound to be corrupted, because all human institutions inevitably get corrupted, and are in need of reform. For example, the Church exists not primarily for the benefit of its members but for those who are not yet its members. However, if the institution is to flourish, and if the Church is to be able to continue to help non-members, one must safeguard it. As I understood it, I had to administer the institution in such a way that its future was assured, but at the same time leave room for the Holy Spirit to promote creative activities reaching out into the community which we rightly associate more with a religious movement.

In some ways the tensions between the two press hard upon the man at the top, the more so because his job is inevitably lonely. I was glad of a domestic chaplain (and all three of them served me very well) because then I could blow off steam to them from time to time: they were people in whom one could confide. Jonathan Tinker was a great help as I established my routines and my style for the first few years of my time in Birmingham; Chris Boyle gave me devoted service in the middle years, and David Columba SSF kept me company (and helped me to keep my cool) during the last period of my episcopate. However, more company among my peers was desirable. David Sheppard suggested to me an Urban Bishops group, and we asked David Young (Bishop of Ripon) who enthusiastically agreed. So we set up a group of some six or seven urban bishops and we used to meet regularly during Synod week, with one residential meeting a year in the diocese of one of our members; and our wives came too. One or two of us would introduce topics which needed airing or about which we needed help. This group was an enormous support, and in some ways transformed my episcopate.

Once Bob Runcie, the Archbishop of Canterbury, asked us if we would consider an idea put up to him by Eric James, previously a Canon of Southwark, then of St Albans, before he went on to direct Christian Action. He thought that a commission was needed to investigate the situation in the inner cities of the land, which had suffered grievously under the Thatcher regime. I recall we considered this in some detail, and suggested names of possible commissioners; and I also remember saying that the venture would gain in prestige if it was the Archbishop's personal commission, rather than one set up by urban bishops. This was the origin of the Archbishop's Commission on Urban Priority Areas which produced in 1985 the report 'Faith in the City', rubbished on publication by a cabinet minister as 'communist' propaganda, but which in fact was a very sober analysis of what was happening in these areas, with proposals not only for the state but also for the Church.

Although the commission had made a residential visit to Birmingham, we were only one stop among many, for the whole of England was included in its remit. I was deeply distressed at the situation in the country as a whole, and addressed the many people who participated in the March for Jobs from the Cathedral Green as they passed through Birmingham. I was particularly distressed at the effect of the recession on the West Midlands conurbation, which was the worst affected of any region. I recall ceremonially barricading Birmingham houses in order to draw attention to their dreadful state. On one occasion at a Birmingham civic dinner, when I had to reply to the perennial toast to the City of Birmingham, I drew attention to the shocking housing, in the knowledge that a government minister was present. When he challenged me afterwards to justify what I had said, I took him on a later occasion on a tour of bad housing areas, including an outer city housing estate where the window frames had been removed and sold, and the floorboards used for firewood. To be fair, he was deeply shocked, and ordered their demolition. I remember on a visitation to another parish in the outer city discovering that almost every one of the inhabitants of a tower block was out of work. The Black community was worst affected.

I decided to set up our own Birmingham commission, and persuaded the Bishop's Council to sponsor it. I was fortunate in that I persuaded Sir Richard O'Brien (who had chaired the Archbishop's Commission) to chair this also; and the city council generously gave us some facilities. The national report had been rightly criticised for its failure to produce an adequate theological critique, and I was determined to avoid this. Fortunately Bishop Lesslie Newbigin had retired to Selly Oak in Birmingham, and he had published with me some correspondence we had had over the 'Ten Propositions'. He agreed to chair a group which produced a theological chapter which 'offered an interpretation from a particular perspective of what is happening in a cosmopolitan, economically divided city, as it strives for unity and renewal'. The report 'Faith in the City of Birmingham' was not published until after I had retired from the city, but I believe it made a real contribution locally.

I did not have much time left over from all my other activities to concentrate on environmental matters while I was in Birmingham. I managed to have a small informal group which met on transport matters (which included, incidentally, John Prideaux, later in charge of Inter-city and then the Channel Tunnel services). I did, however, try to do something about lead-free petrol. It has now become so much part of the landscape that we forget that it has only been about for a dozen years or so. Dr Stephens of Birmingham University had done useful research on the lead contents of the milk teeth of children who played in the streets in the neighbourhood of Spaghetti Junction where the motorways straddle the city. Dr Nedelman, a German research professor, had shown that lead from petrol can slow down the developing IQ of growing children. I did what I could to publicise the matter, and to show up the greed of the big petrol companies who refused to take an initiative of their own in this matter. I also tried to help Des Wilson in his public speaking on the subject. I had a great admiration for Godfrey Bradman, a Jewish property tycoon who personally financed the lead-free petrol campaign which in the end convinced the government that something had to be done. I kept my links with the Friends of the Earth, and during the latter period of my time in Birmingham I was invited to join its trustees. It was difficult to find time to attend meetings in London, but I decided I should join.

My concern for the environment stimulated my interest in the natural sciences which had been kindled during the time when I was a Fellow of Caius College. I had long had doubts about the adequacy of neo-Darwinism, which is taken for granted by the British. It has attained the status of a scientific sacred dogma by the entire scientific establishment which has actually banished as heretical works that dare to contradict it. I had started collecting references and other relevant material on this and kindred subjects. I managed to find time to read *The New Scientist* when it came out every week. One day, as I was glancing at one of its reviews in my study at 'Bishop's

Croft', I came across an account of Jim Lovelock's book called
Gaia, and I decided to read it. Lovelock put forward the thesis
that Gaia is alive in the sense that it has developed (without any
outside interference) self-assembling cybernetic mechanisms which
maintain its atmosphere in such a way that it remains comfortable
for life, despite the increasing luminosity of the sun and the many
emissions that would otherwise disrupt it. Lovelock has suggested
many feedback mechanisms which contribute to the stability of the
planet and which enable it to support life on Earth.

Lovelock is a 'loner', and I regard him, together with Rupert Shel-
drake, as the most creative scientists today in Britain. Incidentally he
is a FRS. He believes that the institutionalisation of science has taken
the edge off its creative work, and he works alone in his laboratory
in rural Devon. When he asked for money to make a contrivance
to measure minute amounts of chemicals in the atmosphere, he
was told that it could not be made, and in any case it would need
full laboratory facilities to construct. So he made it by himself
and discovered the way to measure small amounts of CFCs in the
atmosphere, leading to the discovery of the ozone gap in the upper
atmosphere. He is greatly distrusted by his fellow scientists, because
they fear that his Gaia hypothesis introduces an element of teleology
into science, and teleology is their chief bogy. As a matter of fact
Lovelock himself is an agnostic, and bases his hypothesis entirely
on scientific grounds.

Nonetheless his thesis enormously excited me, because it produced, as I saw it, a missing link which was important for understanding the evolution of the cosmos as part of God's will, ending in the
emergence of intelligent life which could reflect on the universe and
also worship its creator. I wrote to Jim Lovelock to ask him whether
life on earth preceded Gaia, or Gaia preceded life on earth. This
was a question which interested him considerably, and as a result
we became friends, and eventually I have become President of his
Gaia Trust.

I now had enough collected material and I desperately wanted
to write a book from a theological perspective about the evolution
of the cosmos and the emergence of life. It seemed to me that
the Christian faith was becoming so Christological that it was
forgetting its origins in the natural world. Is God the creator
of the universe, or is it all ultimately meaningless? Christian
thinkers, it seemed to me, were ignoring the scientific challenges
of the day, as more and more becomes known about our world
from cosmology and the experimental sciences. Does all the new
knowledge make God improbable, or more probable? (I was

not so silly as to think that God could ever be the object of *proof.*)

I knew that I would never have the time and leisure to write such a book in England, let alone Birmingham. I needed to get right away for three months; and I came to the conclusion that I would better encourage my clergy to take sabbaticals (which for family reasons they were often loath to do) if I led the way myself. Where would we go? I had happy memories of the Anglican seminary at Berkeley in the Bay area near San Francisco. I had been offered a Chair there many years ago; and I had visited the area quite recently when I had been invited to preach at Stamford University, not far away, by Bob Kelly, its Dean, who was a former pupil of mine.

So I wrote off to the Dean of the Church Divinity School of the Pacific (the name of the seminary) because I knew that it had rooms for those on sabbatical. I was told that these were fully booked; but the Dean offered a flat in the basement of his own house. Bill and Joye Pregnall made us so welcome that we thoroughly enjoyed ourselves. I worked very hard, writing rather like Trollope to a schedule, armed by all my notes and references and helped by the marvellous libraries in Berkeley; and when the time came for me to return I had managed to complete my manuscript. It was published in 1984 under the title *The Probability of God*, and ran into two impressions. A lot of the material I used is now commonplace, such as the 'anthopic argument' and the various theories about the Big Bang; but in 1983 they were not. I particularly enjoyed writing one chapter, a 'Dialogue Concerning Natural Religion' in the style of David Hume but concerned with more contemporary material.

I was officially named 'Bishop in Residence', but so far as I could see, my only official duty was to eat meals in the college refectory, and so make myself known to the students. (It was a great disappointment to me that Elisabeth and I were having lunch in the underground refectory when the only 'decent' earthquake took place during my visit, and I did not even know that it had happened.) I was appalled at the degree of indebtedness which was necessary in order for American ordinands to pay their way through seminary and pass all the necessary examinations before they could be ordained in the Episcopal Church. There were no government grants, and no church grants for ordinands. The degree of commitment was very high, even if the average age was also high. There were almost as many women as men; the Episcopal Church has ordained women for a good many years.

The great delight of our sabbatical was for Elisabeth and I to be able live a normal life again together, free of all the stresses and strains of a grossly overloaded diary back at home. It was marvellous that we could spend time together and enjoy each other. Of course we made some expeditions while we were there: not only to Stamford, but also to see the wine growing in Napa Valley, and the sea otters at Monterey, and on to Big Sur down the Pacific Coast with the huge rollers on the shore. We had a lovely trip to beautiful Mendecino up north, and another one to see the graceful egrets in the Audubon reserve. Our best expedition was to Yosemite mountain park, passing en route by the ancient sequoia trees, some of which are two thousand years old, and one you could drive a car through its split stem. Yosemite itself is spectacular, with huge precipitous masses of striated granite boulders, a lot of snow, lakes and waterfalls. And of course we went nearer home, across the Bay Bridge to see the Golden Gate, and to San Francisco, where we even saw Freddy Macdonald, who had filled in at Caius in the interregnum before I became Dean, and was now in what the Americans call a retirement home but which seemed to us more like a four-star hotel.

Back at home John Robinson was mortally ill with cancer. In Cambridge we had seen a good deal of one another, and our families worshipped together at Great St Mary's. In Southwark I realised what a caring bishop he had been. I honoured him not just as a friend, but also as a fine scholar, one of the brightest sons of the Church of England. His books were always brilliantly argued with wide reading. They always had to contain 'radical' solutions to problems, whether of New Testament origins, or of Christian doctrine, or even of the Church of England. Even when in later life he had returned to more traditional conclusions, his solutions were still radical, e.g., *Redating the New Testament* all before AD 70, or asserting the *Priority of St John* over the synoptic Gospels. He was a man of transparent honesty, infamous for calling sexual intercourse 'holy communion' at the Chatterley trial, and for the phrase 'Our image of God must go', which was not his but an *Observer* headline about *Honest to God*. I particularly admired him after he returned to Cambridge as Dean of Trinity, when the Divinity Faculty declined to re-appoint him despite having previously been its most popular lecturer; and no one offered him an ecclesiastical post. He would have loved to be Dean of Canterbury, but efforts by friends led to the response 'His future lies in the academic world.' It didn't. (It was the same with Charles Raven when he retired from being Regius Professor in Cambridge: he offered his services to the

Church which ignored him.) John never complained. In 1983 he faced inoperable cancer with characteristic courage. I was glad to stay a night in November in Arncliffe with John and Ruth a week before he died. His funeral was a truly apocalyptic occasion, with drenching rain and flooded roads in the Yorkshire valleys, and the river outside the church in spate as his coffin with mitre on top was lowered into the grave. A good and noble man.

Troubles were looming for us too. Elisabeth's left hip was troubling her again. She had already had a hip operation once, and not long after we got home she had to have it again. It was really from this point onwards that her health began to fail. When she got out of hospital we had someone for a fortnight to help her. It was some time later that she fell in the dining-room. I was in my study working and my secretary was in the room next door to me: the house was so big, and the doors were shut, so she had to lie where she fell for rather a long time. Then they took her off to the accident hospital, but luckily no bones were broken. However, it was not long after that that more serious symptoms occurred.

Meanwhile I had many duties in London, so I had to be away a lot. As a Bishop I had to attend Bishop's Meetings, and meetings of General Synod. I had also taken on the job of chairing the Central Readers' Board, and trying to bring its procedures (and some of its members) into the late twentieth century. I had also been appointed to the Board for Social Responsibility, of which Graham Leonard, the Bishop of London, was chairman. I had a great respect for his chairmanship, even when we disagreed, as in the difficult matter of the report of the Yates Commission on homosexuality. The Board had set up this commission to look further into the matter and to report. When the report reached the Board, the majority of its members found it *simpliste* and unacceptable. The Board decided to publish it, but to make known its inability to endorse it and to explain the reasons for these reservations. There ensued a perfectly terrible debate in General Synod, which the Archbishop of York managed to terminate by proposing that the Synod passed to next business. But this left the Church in a very difficult position, in which it had pronounced neither against nor in favour of homosexual activity, and had nothing to say about homosexual orientation, a situation which badly needed to be resolved.

In other matters too I tended to disagree with Bishop Leonard (or Fr Leonard, as I suppose I should call him, now he has become a Roman Catholic). The Board for Social Responsibility had set up the Baker Commission to look into the morality of nuclear weapons used either in offence or in defence or as a deterrent. The

Commission, under the chairmanship of the Bishop of Salisbury, came out unreservedly against nuclear weapons of any kind. Bishop Leonard was in favour of them. There was to be a Synod debate at a time of national tension, when there was a considerable feeling in the country that CND was right, and we should do away with our nuclear weapons. The Prime Minister, Mrs Thatcher, was said to be very worried about the forthcoming Church debate, lest the anti-nuclear lobby should win and swing the country with them. It is one of the very few occasions when the Church of England held the attention of the nation. The BBC decided to televise the whole debate.

In this situation I deplored the polarisation between both sides. I thought that the true position lay in the middle. I proposed an amendment in which it was stressed that a country had a duty to defend its citizens, but that nuclear weapons were so dangerous that every effort should be made towards multilateral nuclear disarmament. These weapons should never be used first, but a country was justified in threatening to use them if they were used against that country. My amendment was more complex than that, but I have given its main gist. It easily won the day. It was regarded by the press as a compromise; but I think this was rather unfair, since the government's policy was (and for that matter still is) one of 'flexible response', and so 'no first use' was quite contrary to its nuclear strategy. My amendment, when put into the form of a substantive motion, still remains the official policy of the Church of England.

This was not the only occasion when I had found myself opposing Bishop Leonard. For example, in 1978 there had been a motion in General Synod that the obstacles to the ordination of women to the priesthood should be lifted. Previously Synod had agreed that there were no fundamental objections to their ordination: this was a more positive motion about their ordination. I was chosen to propose the motion, and Graham to oppose it. His speech, I noted, was actually in print before delivery under the auspices of the Church Union. I thought that mine was the better one but his won the day. The Church Union had organised its forces with extreme care, placing its members in particular positions, and forbidding them even to go out to relieve themselves during the debate! The result was, in a sense, a foregone conclusion after all that politicking. It was a sad day for the women, but the Anglo-Catholics were delighted. It was after this that some of us felt that some more enduring organisation was needed to promote the women's cause, and MOW, the Movement for the Ordination of Women, was born.

This matter continued to come up in Synod, with all the complex procedures which are necessary before a change in the law can be obtained. The same motion may not be raised again in the same Synod, but only after new elections have been held. A motion from Southwark diocese eventually precipitated further debate. I was strongly in favour of women's ordination; and at great speed I organised contributions to and edited a book called *Yes to Women Priests*. But as the debate continued it was clear to me that this would split the Church of England. Both sides were deeply entrenched; I was convinced that some compromise was necessary. I suggested in Synod that a Measure be promoted to enable women's ordinations to take place for a limited period of twenty years, which would function as a period of reception, after which another vote would be taken. If two thirds or more still wanted women priests, then the Church of England would continue to ordain them; but if a sufficient majority were not obtained, those already ordained would be able to continue to officiate, but no more would be ordained. In this way those women who had a real vocation could proceed to ordination; and it would be a real and valid ordination. But traditionalists who opposed their ordination would be able to claim that there had been as yet no permanent change in the doctrine or practice of the Church of England. However, nobody would take this compromise seriously. The pro-women lobby said it would be an insult to the women: the anti-women lobby said it would not be a fair trial, because once women had been ordained, it would be impossible to stop doing this. In fact each side was so prejudiced in favour of its own cause that it would not see the strong objections of the other side, and the coming threat to the very existence of our Church. I am convinced that, if Synod had adopted my suggestion, the Church of England would not be in its present state of virtual schism over this issue.

Synod also had to consider the reports of the Anglican Roman Catholic International Commission, which had reached such surprising and unexpected agreement on subjects on which no one could have imagined that this could happen. Reports had come out on the Eucharist, on the Church and two reports on Authority. There seemed to be a growing love affair on the part of the Church of England for Rome. People believed that a merger might soon be possible, providing that the papacy were reformed and the Church of England were able to function as a kind of 'uniate' church within a much less authoritarian form of catholicism. Although there was a miracle of convergence in the work of the ARCIC, it had to be borne in mind that the Church which they envisaged was an ideal

Church, far removed from the actual Roman Catholic Church with its strict dogmas, its refusal to admit the validity of Anglican orders ('absolutely null and utterly void'), and its growing centralism not only in senior appointments but also generally. It was also far removed from the actualities of the Church of England with evangelicals growing stronger with doctrines often rather distant from those of Rome. At the same time, some of us felt real difficulties in particular aspects of the joint reports, not least in the small say that lay men and women would have in the running of the Church.

I decided to write a book, stressing both the convergences and the difficulties that lay ahead. It was very hard to find the time: indeed I had to get up at 5 am. in order to get some quiet uninterrupted writing done before Holy Communion in the morning. I called the book *So Near and Yet So Far*. It was published in 1986. It was not very successful so far as sales were concerned, because the viewpoint I was putting forward was not at that time popular, since people really thought that a merger would be possible. But it was a marker laid down; and I am glad that David Edwards in•1994 has taken a critical look at the new Roman Catholic Catechism in the changed situation in which we now find ourselves nearly a decade later.

I was concerned about the differences in our sources of authority – for Roman Catholics both tradition and Holy Scripture come from the same fount and so have the same authority. I was concerned about the structures of authority: Roman Catholics have a pyramidical model, while Anglicans hold to a disseminated authority. I have already mentioned differences in the attitudes of the two Churches concerning the laity: it is profound. The Marian dogmas of the Roman Catholic Church about her Immaculate Conception and her physical Assumption into heaven are a grave stumbling block. Many Anglicans (including myself) believe that they are not true; and yet they have been infallibly defined for Roman Catholics so that there seems no way in which they can be relinquished. There are also real differences in matters of sexual ethics; and of course concerning the priesting of women. I went into all these subjects in considerable detail. Was it possible to find a convergence of faith behind these differences of dogma? Would such a convergence be considered a sufficient basis for the two Churches to come together? That still remains a question for the future; but the present signs under the present pope, together with the gathering strength of evangelicals, makes it a hope for the future rather than a present possibility.

I was greatly encouraged when I was made an Honorary Fellow of

St John's Oxford, my old Oxford college, and also when I was made Honorary Doctor of Divinity both by Birmingham University and also by Aberdeen University. The American Robert Macnamara also received his Honorary Degree at Aberdeen at the same time as I did. He had been awarded it a few years before when he was US Secretary of State, but he was told that it would be inadvisable to come in person to take it because of anti-American feeling on the part of the students. But when I was there he was President of the World Bank, which was politically acceptable, so he was warmly applauded by the undergraduates!

With this encouragement I made time to write two books based on the New Testament during my Birmingham episcopate. One was a short sketch of the life and teaching of St Paul. I produced this on the basis of some lectures which I had previously given at a summer school for Readers in Cambridge. I also put together a book out of the many learned articles that I had written about Jesus during the time that I was a Cambridge don. I called the book *Jesus Across the Centuries*, because I believed that the conclusions that I had reached had relevance to the Church today. Indeed I saw little point in the detailed study of the New Testament if this had no relevance for today. I can best explain what I mean by using the chapters of this book as an illustration.

Jesus had emphasised the Old Testament teaching that we should love our neighbour as ourselves. I believed that it was possible to show that while Jesus had interpreted as neighbour anyone who was in need, the primitive Church had inverted the meaning so that it referred to fellow members of the Church. I thought it was important to retain Jesus' interpretation. Again, the Church seems to regard the family as of supreme importance, and acts sometimes as though it has a prescriptive right to pontificate on this subject. Important as it is, nonetheless Jesus himself goes out of his way to give it a lower importance than the claims of God. I think that it is necessary to return to the priorities of Jesus. Again, there are scholars who say that Jesus taught that God was not the Father of everyone, but his heavenly Father and the Father of his disciples. I believe that it can be shown from the New Testament that Jesus taught that God is the Father of all people, and again this has important repercussions for Church attitudes today.

Another chapter concerned an examination of Jesus' use of parables. Nowadays it is fashionable to assume that Jesus only made one main point in each parable, and that this applied to the particular circumstances of his ministry. I do not think that this properly represents the teaching of Jesus, and from this I draw the inferences that we can both invent new parables and reinterpret Jesus' parables allegorically today so long as we keep their meaning within the drama of salvation. In yet another chapter I examined the crisis in Jesus' ministry, when he was faced with an abortive coup to make him king after the feeding of the five thousand in the desert; and I believed that his attitude then has an important bearing on what the Christian's attitude should be to the use of force to further the claims of Christ. Finally, Jesus' attitude towards the Temple Tax, when stripped of the various layers of accretion in the story as we have it in St Matthew's Gospel, has an important bearing not of course on the Jewish Temple which no longer exists today, but on the Church as an institution, and particularly on the many church buildings with which the Church of England has been entrusted.

I mention the contents of this book in some detail, because I wish to show what seems to me the important connection between the teaching of Jesus and the attitudes of the Church today. Not all would see such a direct connection; but for me the imitation of Christ is central to my discipleship.

These books were written under some difficulty at home. I found I had to be in London a lot, especially towards the end of my Birmingham episcopate. I learnt to loathe the journey from Birmingham New Street to Euston. This is the busiest stretch of railway track in Britain, and as a result there were many delays. Trains ran every half hour, and I used to have to catch an earlier train than the timetables suggested to ensure that I arrived on time to be present at a meeting.

I found meetings of the House of Bishops rather tame. People tended to make speeches rather than speak their mind. I suppose that this was inevitable in a meeting of some forty-five people, in which the Secretary General of the Synod was present together with other officers. All the same, these meetings were disappointing. In the first place, we did not really act as a college of bishops. There would be agreement on certain matters at our formal meetings, but this agreement was not always observed in the dioceses. A steering committee was eventually appointed, on which I found myself, but even this did not wholly meet the situation. I felt that the House of Bishops made a particularly bad showing over the Tulsa affair in 1986.

Bishop Graham Leonard evidently had great sympathy with one particular congregation in Tulsa in the USA. John Pasco had been parish priest of St Michael's, Tulsa. This congregation had received money from the diocese of Oklahoma (in which it was situated) to buy land and construct a church building. However, the building had been bought not in the name of the Episcopal Church, but in the name of St Michael's Church Foundation, a private charity over which the Bishop had no jurisdiction. As a result of false entries this remained secret for five years. The Episcopal Church of St Michael was reduced to mission status when the fraud was discovered. This enabled the Bishop to remove Mr Pasco as Vicar and appoint a new one. Mr Pasco refused to give up the church building. He recognised the validity of the orders of bishops and clergy of schismatic 'continuing churches'. These were Anglican congregations which had separated themselves from the Episcopal Church of the USA. Charges of fraud were brought in the ecclesiastical court and Mr Pasco was deposed. He thereupon sued the Bishop and Standing Committee for $2 million. Incidentally, he also threatened to sue me, but this came to nothing.

Underlying this row over property were questions of churchmanship, including the liberal bent of the Bishop of Oklahoma and the ordination of women to the priesthood. Bishop Leonard announced his intention of supporting Mr Pasco by going to Tulsa in order to hold a confirmation. This reminded me immediately of the earlier semi-schism in Birmingham when colonial bishops had held confirmations in Anglo-Catholic parishes without the permission of Bishop Ernest Barnes. This decision of Dr Leonard incensed all the American bishops without exception, both high church and low church, because in the past, before the Episcopal Church gained its own bishops (and that from Scotland, not from England), the Bishop of London had had jurisdiction over the whole of the Church of England in America; and so this looked like a return to ancient colonialism. Apart from this, it was contrary to the age-old tradition of the Church, reaching right back to the Synod of Antioch in AD 341, for one bishop to interfere in the working of another, except when there was rampant heresy; and such a judgement of heresy was not to be made by an individual bishop of another province, but by all the bishops of the province concerned.

For reasons that are not altogether clear to me, the Archbishop of Canterbury, although he asked Bishop Leonard not to go to Tulsa, did not invoke the metropolitan oath of obedience that a bishop makes to his archbishop, and order Bishop Leonard not to go. He persevered, and did go to Tulsa. I feared that individualism had infected even Catholicism, so that he felt justified in taking this unilateral action. I gave notice of a motion in our House of

Bishops, not naming Bishop Leonard, but criticising the action that had been taken. The reluctance of the House of Bishops to grasp this nettle suggested to me that it was acting like a club, in the sense that it seemed more important to shelter a fellow member than to align itself in this matter with the customs of the universal Church. As a result a watered-down motion was passed. The matter seemed to me important because the Anglican communion is held together not by strict canon laws which enforce obedience as in the Roman Catholic Church, but by adherence to custom and by brotherly bonds of affection, loyalty and spirituality. These can become badly strained when challenged by unilateral action. The same customs and bonds ought similarly to hold together the Church of England, and while a person must always act in accordance with his or her conscience, proper attention must be given to the welfare of the whole body, and in particular to the wishes of a Metropolitan. I believe that my fears were fully justified, and that the present somewhat fragile stance both of the Anglican communion and of the Church of England has been caused among other things by the Tulsa affair.

Also in 1986 the House of Bishops published their report 'The Nature of Christian Belief'. This was a statement made in response to a request from General Synod in a debate on the subject occasioned by the remarks of David Jenkins, Bishop of Durham, on the virginal conception of Mary (generally known as the virgin birth) and the Resurrection of Jesus. The report had been the subject of prolonged discussion by the bishops, and a draft had been prepared by John Austen Baker, the Bishop of Salisbury. This is hardly the place to comment on the original remarks made by David Jenkins. I realise that what he said stimulated discussion of religious subjects among ordinary people, and greatly encouraged many people who felt doubts about traditional doctrines. At the same time I personally was somewhat distressed about his style and by his apparent lack of interest in New Testament scholarship. Deep theological matters were raised, without, it seemed to me, sufficient attention given to the evidence, such as it is, that can be found there.

It was unfortunate that it was not possible for me, due to blizzards, to be present at the meeting of bishops in which the report was finalised. Although I could not object to any of its statements, I was greatly dissatisfied with the report as a whole. I did not think that it came clean so far as the bishops were concerned. It is one thing to say that so and so expresses the faith of the Church of England, and quite another to say that the bishops believed it. Many didn't. While I believe in the physical Resurrection of Jesus, I personally am agnostic about his virginal conception. I did not feel that the arguments against this doctrine had been properly expressed. The Archbishop of Canterbury naturally wanted a unanimous report, and there were several difficult phone calls. I was not encouraged by the Bishop of Durham, who had caused all the trouble, appearing to have no difficulty in signing up. I found myself in a grave dilemma. Should I or should I not write a minority report? I very nearly did; but in the end I decided I would go along with the rest, because a minority report would have been misunderstood (after all I could not actually disagree with anything in the report), and this was a time when the college of bishops needed to stand together. I would clarify my position later, as I did.

I was particularly distressed that when the report was actually published what seemed to me a significant change of two words was made to it 'for reasons of style'. We had agreed that the empty tomb was 'part of' the faith of the Church of England. In the published report the words 'part of' were omitted. If I say 'X is part of the truth', that leaves open the possibility of its being balanced by Y, another part of the truth. But the bare statement 'X is the truth' has a take-it-or-leave-it feel about it, which I thought was inappropriate to the empty tomb, even though I myself happen to believe it was empty.

Bishop Leonard had for some time been chairman of the Board for Social Responsibility. A strong lead was needed at the Board of Education, and he was asked to go there in place of the Board for Social Responsibility; and indeed he gave the Church signal service by his work there, not least in the House of Lords over an Education Bill. In 1983 I was invited to take on the chairmanship of the Board, which I did for the last four years before my retirement. This was a heavy job, because the chairman could be invited to comment, and often was asked to comment, on any national event which could be regarded in the sphere of social responsibility. There was a Board of some twenty people which met quarterly, and there was a staff of some ten people at Church House. I was fortunate to have John Gladwin (now Bishop of Guildford) as Secretary of the Board: he had a fund of good sense, and could not be rattled. I fear that I gave the staff a rather rough time, always suggesting new work to already overworked officers. In particular I set up an Environmental Panel of experts who could advise the Board on this subject, and it prepared a paper at one stage which formed the subject of a Synod debate.

I realised the extreme sensitivity of this job at the beginning of my time as chairman of the Board, when I was interviewed, in the presence of the Second Estates Commissioner (who is responsible for liaison between Parliament and the Church) by a Member of Parliament who felt that there was a bias against Conservatives in the constitution of the Board's Committees! The very idea had never even entered my head.

One of the difficulties of the Board was that its various committees, industrial, foreign affairs and social, had a tradition of making their own agenda, and publishing their own reports which were not necessarily endorsed by the Board. Sometimes it was necessary to form a special committee of people from outside the Board to report on a particular subject. It was clear to me that the scourge of AIDS, and the resulting fear of homosexuals, meant that we should re-open the Church debate on this subject, after the synodical debacle following the Yates Report. Although I got the Board for Social Responsibility to endorse this project, I thought I should consult the Steering Committee of the House of Bishops about such a sensitive matter, although I need not have done so. The Archbishop of Canterbury was only persuaded to agree to our going ahead, if our report was not published outright, as was our usual custom, but presented to the House of Bishops. This happened after my retirement. In fact the bishops refused to allow it to be published, but it was leaked to the press.

As chairman of the Board, I had to play a rather prominent role in the Synod. I was conscious that I was not always a very good synodsman. Question time always brought contentious matters concerning the Board which I had to answer. I realised that some of these were intended by conservative members to needle me; and they did. I think I spoke on occasion too vehemently for that strange body. It was at General Synod, just as at bishops' meetings, that I felt most out of tune with the institutional Church. I also sensed that I was not very clubbable, perhaps not even all that likeable. People loved gossiping with one another, but not with me; and I felt it badly. I felt an outsider; and sometimes very much a Jewish Christian almost alone in an overwhelmingly Gentile Church. I also disliked the way in which people drew free allowances to come to Synod, and then attended comparatively few debates.

In fact I tried twice to reduce the number of groups of sessions each year, with an optional extra one if needed for legislation. These meetings cost thousands of pounds out of church collections. Much business could have been speeded up, or never come to Synod. Other countries had one Synod every three years; we had three each year. Although I nearly got my 'private member's motion' through the second time (and that in a thin house, because few had bothered to turn up) I had the whole weight of the Church establishment against me. They said it would be impossible, and make business long drawn out. Surprise, surprise! When a new Secretary General arrived, the change was made within a year.

There were three matters during the time that I was chairman which are most vivid in my memory. One of these concerned the National Health Service and the Social Services. During the Thatcher regime there had been cutbacks, and it was evidently right that we should consider the situation and report. I confess that I did not like the report very much. It seemed to me that our members had not sufficiently taken on board the possibility of Christians holding views different from that of an earlier national consensus on these matters. Indeed, at the stage of a draft report I invited an independent opinion. It seemed to me unfortunate if the Board should in principle take a position closer to the Labour Party than the Conservatives. However, the report was altered sufficiently for me to endorse it.

The second matter concerned the Warnock Report on human embryology and fertilisation. By and large the Board endorsed the findings of the Warnock Committee, but the Synod rejected the Board's support of the Warnock proposal that research could be carried out on embryos up to fourteen days old for such purposes as the protection and prevention of inherited disorders or the alleviation of infertility. This rejection distressed me, insofar as I felt I no longer had the confidence of the Synod, and so I thought it right to tender my resignation to the Archbishops; but it was not accepted. The Synod had a further debate in July on this subject, and this time it agreed (by a small margin) to the Board's proposal that its report 'Personal Origins' be commended to the dioceses for study. Synod also recorded its belief that it was essential to create a national licensing authority, already welcomed by the Board, in order to regulate research and control infertility services. I informed Norman Fowler, whose constituency was in my diocese, and who was the Minister concerned, that it might be wise to postpone immediate legislation on these matters, in view of the division of opinion in the Church, which I believed represented divided opinions at that time in the nation as a whole.

The third matter concerned divorce. This led me into a frightful row with the Lord Chancellor, Lord Hailsham. I was fond of him, but he could be quite terribly rude, as I had experienced years before on 'Any Questions' over the matter of Concorde. The government was promoting a bill which would make it possible for a couple to begin divorce proceedings after only one year of marriage. This seemed to me not to give their marriage a chance, and to make other couples less inclined to persevere in their early difficulties of marriage and instead to seek immediate relief in a divorce. Unfortunately before I became chairman, the Board had been told of the government's intentions, but had made no reply. I did not know about this, and I could not hold myself responsible, for all that Lord Hailsham described me in the House of Lords as the 'Chairman of the Board for Social Irresponsibility'. I will forbear to quote the vitriolic correspondence I received on this matter from the Lord Chancellor.

I had already exchanged robust correspondence with Lord Hailsham on the subject of overcrowded prisons. (I used regularly to visit Winson Green prison in Birmingham. I remember beginning to preach there one Good Friday: 'In the name of the Father and of the Son and of the Holy Spirit' – slosh! An inmate had felled a prison officer, and the sermon had to be delayed until order was restored.) Taking advice from a professor of criminology the Board wished me to make representations about overcrowding to the Home Secretary, and I received from Douglas Hurd (as in all my dealings with him) a courteous and sympathetic reply. I thought it would be appropriate to send a copy to the Lord Chancellor, as the overcrowding occurred as a result of prison sentences given by judges under his supervision. I have another vitriolic series of letters from him in my files about this.

There was one occasion when Elisabeth and I were invited to dine at No. 10 Downing Street. I still have the seating list. It was when Shimon Peres was Prime Minister of Israel, and he was visiting our Prime Minister. Leading members of the Jewish community were present, and I suppose Mrs Thatcher thought it would be appropriate to invite me, as a member of the Jewish race. She could not have been more wrong! As a Jewish Christian I was not overpopular with the leading members of the Jewish community. When it came to grace before dinner, she called on both the Chief Rabbi and me to say a grace. When Lord Rabinowicz said his in English, the thought crossed my mind that it would be rather fun if I said mine in Hebrew; but I sensibly desisted. What I chiefly remember is the fine bearing of Leon Brittan. It was, if I remember aright, the night before he was made to resign from the government.

I have mentioned the Lord Chancellor. This leads me to recall the many contacts that as chairman of the Board I had with ministers of the Crown. Although it was useful to have the backing of the Synod on matters of public importance, I had come to the conclusion that we were more likely to influence ministers by quiet conversation rather than by simply issuing condemnatory reports and by Synod motions which they might feel that they would lose face in accepting. I had audiences with Michael Heseltine when Minister of Defence over 'no first use' of nuclear weapons, with ministers of the Foreign Office over sanctions against South Africa, with the ministers in the Home Office over immigration and the police bill, with the President of the Board of Trade over unemployment, and with the minister responsible for overseas aid. I can remember a particularly unpleasant consultation at the Home Office over what we regarded as the government's immoral policies over immigration, in particular difficulties over the immigration of dependents, and the dangers to family life involved. Today, years later, the position has not improved. Indeed in some ways it is worse so far as refugees seeking asylum are concerned. I suppose that it was due to the establishment of the Church of England that there was such ease of access to ministers. It seemed sensible to make use of the privilege, but I cannot say that the establishment can be justified on this account.

Only twenty-four bishops and the two archbishops can be full members of the House of Lords with speaking rights in the chamber. The 'prince bishops' – London, Durham and Winchester – are members *ex officio*: the other bishops become eligible by seniority of tenure in their see, and have to wait until death or resignation before they can be admitted. I had to wait an unconscionably long time, some six and a half years. However, I determined to make up for this long wait. The circumstances of my admission were particularly unfortunate. I suppose someone who is being admitted to the national legislature ought to come to the Lords by taxi: we came by Underground. At Westminster underground station, Elisabeth slipped as she left the coach, and fell on the track beneath. I shrieked to prevent her being run over by the train as it left the station. The transport police arrived very quickly and she was taken to Guys just over the Thames. The accident was reported in the national news bulletins, but it might have been much worse. She was in shock, but not hurt, and I was able to take her home the next day. But the lunch party I had arranged to celebrate the occasion fell a bit flat. I fear that this accident was a pointer to what was to come.

A little later I made my maiden speech. There are strict conventions about this. It must last for a certain time, and it must not be controversial. At any rate, all was well. One of the more charming aspects of the House is that it is customary for later speakers to congratulate the maiden speaker. This was the occasion when Harold Macmillan, by then the Earl of Stockport, made his famous speech about selling off the family silver; but naturally I treasured most his kind congratulatory words. It also happened to be the first debate in which the House of Lords was televised. There was therefore considerable national interest. Unfortunately many of the 'noble lords', relishing the prospect of being televised, decided to put down their names to speak. A maiden speaker is expected to stay in the chamber until all have spoken. The House did not rise until after midnight; and I had to be in the House from 2.30 pm until then. I was somewhat swimmy by that time.

I greatly enjoyed the atmosphere of the House of Lords, in which *la politesse* reigns supreme. Indeed, I thought that the sharp barbs of polite comment were more effective than the heavy rhetoric of the 'other place'. 'I must congratulate the Noble Lord on the brilliance of his speech', an opponent might say, 'But I only wish that its content had matched the distinction of its style.' Or again at question time, someone might comment on the minister's reply with some such remark as 'I thank the Noble Lord the Minister for his answer, even though it fails to give a reply to the question that I asked.' I was surprised how greatly the bishops were made welcome in the House, even though one of their changing rooms had been converted into 'The Bishops' Bar' (which was of course open to all). Everyone could walk about in normal dress except the bishops: they had to wear a rochet and black chimere if they were to enter the Chamber for debate. Noble Lords only got their attendance and other allowances if they actually attended the House, so there was a large number present for the half an hour set aside for question time, and usually a very sparse attendance for debates.

It is sad that the Labour and Liberal Democrats have said that when they are in power they will introduce an elected chamber. This will mean that elections will be bound to be politicised, and if they take place at the same time as the Commons; we shall get second-rate politicians in the Lords instead of world-renowned experts. If they take place at a different time we shall get a different proportion of political party representation than that in the Commons. At present it is hard to make a speech in the Lords without the presence of someone who is a guru on the particular subject under debate. The Lords themselves proposed their reform, under which the present hereditary peers (except for a very few) would be able to speak but not vote, and in future such peers could have the use of the House, just as I do as a retired Bishop, where I can eat in the restaurant, use the library, and sit on the steps of the throne (which are rather hard). But they would not be able to speak in debate, and future appointments would all be for life peers and baronesses. This idea was actually promoted in a bill under a Labour government, but it was dropped, because there was a marked lack of support from MPs who were frightened lest the House of Lords should thereby increase in importance at the expense of the Commons. They prefer the present situation in which they can pour scorn on the Upper House as an unelected chamber.

Unfortunately the Conservatives, who have a built-in majority in the House, are content with the *status quo*. A chamber of experts with independent minds, and the power to slow up legislation, seems to me an important check on an arbitrary even though it be an elected government. I would hope that some bishops remain in a reformed chamber. They have been there as long as any hereditary earl. At the moment they are the only people who can talk as it were from a constituency. One could wish that more Free Church ministers could be offered life peerages; but there is difficulty in tying a peerage to an office, because theirs are annual appointments. Furthermore, no member of the legislature ought to be a peer purely by reason of an *ecclesiastical* appointment: Anglican bishops can only participate because of their appointment by the Crown. This is the difficulty about official Roman Catholic representation, although it is believed that Cardinal Hume has turned down a life peerage, and in any case Roman Catholic priests are not encouraged to take part in political activity. However, the Duke of Norfolk organises the Roman Catholic lobby admirably.

During the comparatively short time that I was a serving Bishop, I took as full a part as I could in the Lords' proceedings. I opposed the Shops Bill, and moved a 'reasoned amendment' to the government's proposal to deregulate completely the legal limits of shop opening. It is not 'done' to oppose directly at second reading a bill introduced by an elected government, so I moved that 'the bill be read six months hence', which comes to the same thing. There ensued a long and difficult debate, and I found myself opposed by Lady Trumpington whom I had known of old in Cambridge. She rubbished the bill, using rather unworthy arguments, such as the custom of cathedrals selling Bibles on Sundays, which is strictly speaking illegal. We who opposed total deregulation were prepared for any reasonable compromise; part-time opening on Sundays, restrictions on the basis of square footage or the number of employees, etc. But the government was adamant: total deregulation or nothing. They won in the Lords. Large numbers of usually absent peers appeared from the shires, and I noticed that they remained in the bar, and only entered the chamber in order to vote! However, our delaying tactics enabled the mobilisation of effective opposition in the 'other place'; and when the vote was taken there, Mrs Thatcher suffered her largest defeat during the whole time that she was Prime Minister. Unfortunately this took place on the same night as American bombers used British bases to bomb Libya and to attempt to kill Colonel Gadaffi, so much of the publicity value of this defeat was lost. Since then a compromise has been reached and passed into law which gives those in favour of total deregulation most of what they want.

I was very concerned at the government propaganda about AIDS, since the concept of self-restraint never entered into any of their advertisements. If people were chaste AIDS could never spread. This obvious fact was totally ignored by government. I even went so far as to commission some strip cartoons which showed how my viewpoint could be expressed in popular form, and sent these to Lord Whitelaw, who chaired a committee on the subject. I also raised this matter in the debate on the Speech from the Throne, which sets out government policy. I took part in other debates, such as those concerned with new techniques of human fertilisation, and the question of British citizenship for Indians in Hong Kong after we had returned the concession to China. It was difficult to see a bill all the way through its Second Reading, Committee Stage, and Third Reading, because arrangements for debate are only made a month ahead, and bishops' diaries are made up a year ahead. However, I managed to see the bill about animal experiments all the way through.

The situation about abortion in the country was scandalous. The law had been unwittingly devised so that abortion was virtually available on demand. In General Synod the government minister John Selwyn Gummer taunted the bishops for not doing something about it. (What had *he* in government done about it?) They should knock on the door of 10 Downing Street, he said. So I did. I wrote to Mrs Thatcher. She replied, saying that these moral matters were left to the conscience of MPs, and the government was neutral.

In Birmingham I found myself visiting maternity hospitals where I cuddled premature babies which it would have been legal to abort at the very stage of development at which they had been born alive. This seemed to me intolerable. I remember going to Lord Denham, the government's Chief Whip, and asking him whether it would be possible to find someone who would introduce a bill on the subject. He said 'Why not do it yourself?' I had never thought of that, and

I replied: 'Bishops don't introduce bills.' 'We will see about that,' he answered and sent for the Clerk of Parliaments, who confirmed that a bishop had indeed introduced a bill. It was a good many years ago, I think it had something to do with drains and church buildings. 'There you are,' he said.

So I took his advice and decided on 'DIY'. I had to get a legal adviser to draft my bill. I took advice from the junior ministers Lady Trumpington and David Mellor – bad advice, actually. I was told it would be impossible to amend the Abortion Act itself, as that would open up a hornet's nest. I was advised to attempt to amend the Infant Life Preservation Act, according to which it was illegal to kill a child born alive. It was bad advice because this Act was rubbished in the Lords on the grounds that it was originally devised to prevent girls from killing a child in the process of birth.

The title of a bill is important, because all amendments must be relevant to the title, so I decided on the Infant Life Preservation Act Amendment Bill. I also decided on a one-clause bill, because only that clause could then be amended, and none could be added. Under the Infant Life Preservation Act, it was stated that, for the purposes of the Act, evidence that a woman had been pregnant for a period of twenty-eight weeks or more was *prima facie* proof that she was at that time pregnant of a child capable of being born alive. I said that things had moved on since 1929 [when the Act was passed], and my bill was simply to reduce that time limit to twenty-four weeks. I had received support for this from most of the professional bodies concerned. My sole object was to prevent the abortion of a foetus which was capable of being born alive. The whole issue of abortion is a very difficult one. I do not myself believe that in all cases it is wrong to abort. I am not in that sense a 'pro-lifer'. There is a gradual period of development in the foetus, and while it is always a human being distinct from other beings and must therefore always be treated with respect, it is hard to say at what point it actually becomes a human person. Birth is a somewhat arbitrary (if useful) moment to choose. But, even in the case of a misformed foetus, it must always be wrong to kill a foetus that is capable of being born alive. That, indeed, is tantamount to murdering a newborn babe.

I was ill-supported by my brother bishops when the bill came up for Second Reading; but that was no surprise. I was well supported by the Duke of Norfolk and the Roman Catholic peers. Lord Beaverbrook said, to my great surprise, that, although the government would not impose a whip on the subject, government ministers in the chamber would vote in favour. To my enormous surprise my bill was passed on Second Reading.

But then the trouble began. Two or three peers went to Lord Whitelaw, the Leader of the House, and threatened a filibuster. Lord Whitelaw sent for me, and told me that this would upset the government's business timetable, and would keep peers and servants in the House late at night when it would be difficult for them to get home. 'We must get this bill off the floor of the House.' His idea was that I should recommend that it be sent to a Select Committee. I demurred at first, but then I realised that bishops, who in a sense were only in the House on sufferance, must not interfere with government business. I agreed that a Select Committee be set up. It was normal for a promoter of a bill to be on such a Select Committee, but by this time I had retired from Birmingham, so I could only give evidence. The Select Committee was packed with those against my bill, and the net result at the end of the day is that all limits are now removed: an abortion may take place at any time during gestation until full term. My gallant effort was not only a failure: it actually helped to make the situation worse.

These matters could only take up a small proportion of my time, most of which, naturally, was spent in Birmingham. I found more and more demands were made on me by the media. Perhaps it was unfortunate that I was only ten minutes away from the BBC studios at Pebble Mill, and not much further from Central TV studios, not to mention the local radios. I found that I was often asked to speak on the *Today* programme, and on other programmes on many matters of social responsibility. I think that the most interesting TV programme was *Lovelaw*, a consideration of marriage in different cultures; and the last programme concerned us here in Britain. The BBC took over a private hotel near Worcester, and a group of us were invited to stay for a couple of nights. As the programme was about marriage, and I did not want to leave Elisabeth alone at 'Bishop's Croft', so she came too. I thought, considering the subject of the programme, that it was decidedly odd that I was the only person to be accompanied by a spouse. It was an interesting group of people, including Germaine Greer, Sue Slipman and Ken Livingstone.

I was getting more and more worried about leaving Elisabeth alone in 'Bishop's Croft' at night, as happened when I went on a visitation, or when I had to be late in London, and stayed overnight. We had a bell by her bedside connected to the chauffeur's house, but that was a couple of hundred yards away. We never had a break-in, but the security of the house was minimal, and there were large French windows which would have easily afforded access. Elisabeth's health was now going downhill. My daughters first noticed that she was no longer interested in cooking – she had been a superb cook. She resigned from the chairmanship of her Clergy Wives group. She could no longer work in the garden, which had been her delight. Her memory was beginning to fail. Entertainment had to be cut to a minimum, and when it was necessary we used to get meals brought in, whereas before it had been her pleasure to provide lovely food. Her doctor sent her to hospital for examination, including a brainscan. The specialist told me that there was no sign of shrinkage of the cortex, which, we were informed, could be a symptom of Alzheimer's. It was the first time that that word had been used, and I tried to find out just what it meant. Finally Elisabeth told me that she felt she could no longer carry on much longer. I agreed. I was then aged sixty-seven, and my length of service was such that I could retire on full pension. I think that if Eliza had been well I would probably have carried on until I was seventy, which was the age at which I would have had to retire. But in retrospect I am exceedingly glad that I did retire at sixty-seven.

Oh God, what next? Where should we go? The answer seemed to come even as the question was being asked. By great good fortune the tenant of the house where we had lived on Wandsworth Common, which I had let while we were in Birmingham, had given notice that he would leave. If Elisabeth did have Alzheimer's, it would be good to be somewhere which she could still then remember, and in an area like London where there are good facilities. I had not even visited the house for nine years, and I knew that a lot of single people had been living there, and the building would be in a terrible mess. It was. Moreover the builders found dry rot where the diocesan surveyor, when I first bought the house, had authorised plastic sheeting to be installed. A great deal of work had to be done on the place. Elisabeth had very rightly said that she could not face the two steep steps down into the original kitchen, which was a sort of corridor along the side of the small garden. So we had the old dining-room turned into a kitchen/breakfast room; a great improvement. The house had to be redecorated and painted throughout. It was a major operation to supervise from Birmingham, and it took several months. I could not go before Christmas, and I was determined not to try to move house during the winter. I announced my retirement for 1st April 1987. All Fools Day seemed a good date to choose: I felt it would prevent me from taking myself too seriously.

It is interesting how the situation changes when one's retirement is announced. People knew that I would no longer be in a position of influence in a few months' time, and this made a subtle difference. But there was still much to be done. I was sorry that I had not been able to complete the programme which I had sketched out in my mind: after 'Know, Live and Learn Your Faith' I would have liked an opportunity to tackle a kind of Birmingham mission. I had been encouraged by diocesan officers to do this, but the town hall was not available on the dates which were convenient before I left; and already there was talk of the Birmingham Council of Christian Churches having a celebratory event with someone like Bishop Tutu of Johannesburg visiting the city. I had always felt guilty that I had not put up a tent outside Austin Rover's Longbridge works, and held open meetings about the Christian faith to Brummies as they left the factory. Although few of them attended church, many of them felt that in a sense they belonged to it through their wives. In the West Midlands it is not natural for working men to get down on their knees. However, I was leaving, and it was not to be. Man may propose, but God disposes.

A great farewell was planned for me at the Birmingham Exhibition Centre. Colin Buchanan was my suffragan Bishop who had taken over from Michael Whinney when he became Bishop of Southwell He took up the matter with characteristic energy. First he published a fifty-page booklet *Bishop Hugh – with Affection by some of his friends*. I was really touched by this. The many contributors covered most sides of my activities. I was particularly struck by a contribution from an assistant curate, who recalled when I came for confirmation at his church. I had forgotten my pastoral staff and to the consternation of the rector I seized hold of a Victorian churchwarden's ebony wand as a substitute. Coming into the church building, I had said I knew the way well, opened a door and walked into a broom cupboard. I fear all this has the ring of truth.

Colin also organised a great farewell Eucharist at the Birmingham Exhibition Centre. The largest hall was taken. A huge table served as altar, a back cloth had been specially designed for the occasion, and there was liturgical dancing. The mayor was there, the Roman Catholic Archbishop and the Free Church President of the Birmingham Council of Christian Churches. To my enormous surprise, over seven thousand people came. I had been asked if there was anything I specially liked, and I said 'balloons'. At the end of the service I was ceremonially stripped of my cope, mitre and pastoral staff, and walked out with Elisabeth as three thousand coloured balloons were loosed from the ceiling. I gather that the occasion was featured on the BBC TV nine o'clock news, and I have a wonderful video of this never-to-be-forgotten occasion. We had friends who came for the occasion, and what should we do afterwards? I could not ask Elisabeth to produce food. We all went to a Bakti Indian restaurant in the inner city where delicious curry is served in metal bowls which you eat in your fingers with nan (special Indian bread) which is served alongside. We still had the hassle of leaving Birmingham in front of us, but my ministry there had ended.

Chapter Ten

RETIREMENT

I had made no arrangements for retirement. In the interviews I had given before leaving Birmingham, I had said that retirement gave an opportunity for *contemplatio mortis*, preparation for death. I had not realised that I had retired young enough to begin another chapter in life. When I said 'Oh God, what next?' I did not know what life was to bring. Surely it would be a long progression downhill. How wrong I was! Those who fear retirement ought to take heart, it is to be strongly recommended. Just think of it, two-thirds of one's stipend is given for doing nothing! Well, not quite. Once a priest, always a priest; but at least one has control of one's own diary.

At first I had to get the house in order single-handed, because Elisabeth was not really able to help. I struggled with curtains, carpets, pictures, furniture, not to mention pots and pans and blankets and beds and so on. This kind of thing was new to me. After nine years the garden was practically non-existent. Eliza could help here a bit, and she did. And there were the books – oh! the books. The house was full of them. I suppose my theological library by now is well over three thousand books; right up to the ceiling of my study, and then an attic full of them. How would it ever be possible to sort them out? And the rest of the house was full of other books collected over fifty years. Some people regret that they cannot take their money out of this world. For others there is an even more distressing thought – there will be no books in heaven, no, not even in purgatory. They really ought to be glad, because sorting out one's books is a nasty form of purgatory.

The neighbourhood where we lived had utterly changed. Most of the old shops in the road had gone, or had had a face lift. Some of them now seemed more like boutiques than shops. Fortunately the banks and the post office and chemist and other necessities were still there. Wandsworth Common had become a kind of Chelsea-over-the-river. The older inhabitants had sold their houses, made a killing and moved out. How quickly London neighbourhoods can change! The same was true of the parish church. When we were here ten years previously it had an exiguous congregation. Now there was a new vicar, and it was burgeoning with new middle-class families who seemed to increase weekly. On one occasion there were over seventy in the Sunday school. Not that attendance was regular. Off they went for the weekend to Granny or to the dacha. The Church Commissioners could not have been more wrong about my house. I found myself with a most desirable little residence, rather large in fact for a retirement home, with a lovely view overlooking the Common.

But inside me there was a strange emptiness. My diary had been choc-a-bloc, now it was empty. Previously I had been in demand: now I was not. How salutary for the soul! I decided that I was suffering from a bereavement syndrome; and I waited for the various phases to pass. I started reading again, novels, biographies, books from the public library. It was not a phase which lasted very long, but long enough to give me pause.

The important point was that I was with Elisabeth, we were on our own, that was the great thing. But it would not last. She was not well. We found a good doctor for her, and the first thing she did was to impound her many medicines for various small complaints in Birmingham; and she seemed the better for that. (Encouraged by this example, I did the same with mine, sleeping pills, the lot. No medicine now for seven years!) But there was obviously something very wrong with her. Was it Alzheimer's? Through St Luke's Hospital (the clergy hospital) she went to the National Hospital in London, which specialises in nervous diseases, and stayed there a couple of nights. Back came the verdict – yes, it was Alzheimer's. No, they could not say how it would progress, only that it was a deteriorating illness. I discovered that, if you do not die first, you end up as a jellyfish, or a cabbage, or however you like to express it. All through the overloaded diaries of the last twenty or thirty years, I had told myself and told her: 'At least we can be together when I retire.' Yes, that was true, but what sort of a together was it going to be? Meanwhile, what? We decided there was no point in trying to paint the town red while we could. Holidays, yes; but let us enjoy as much as we could the many blessings of ordinary life which we usually take for granted.

Later, I read in the papers of a supposed cure at the Maudsley Hospital in London, and, determined to do what I could for Eliza,

I made contact with the consultant geriatrician who kindly arranged for an all-day session for her. The same diagnosis: Alzheimer's. If she joined in the experiments on the new medication, I was told that the very best that could happen would be some remission for up to six months *and no more*, and during that time she might remember what she had forgotten, so that the last state would be worse than the first because that awful process of knowing what was going to happen to her would start all over again. I get so angry with newspaper headlines alleging cures for Alzheimer's. There are no cures. The doctors are slowly finding out more about the disease; but no one knows even how it is caused.

She had cared for me so wonderfully and so loyally through all the difficulties of my ministry. In Birmingham at least we had shared our ministry more than anywhere else. She had provided the emotional support that I so badly needed. I was *déraciné*; an exile from the Jewish community and, I felt, not really accepted in the Christian community. I was sensitive about criticism; I realised that I was not altogether likeable, otherwise my peers would talk to me more and befriend me. I felt I always had to take the initiative. I might appear to be brash and self-confident (I was certainly impetuous); but this often hid an interior feeling of unacceptedness. Elisabeth always accepted me, and she provided that calmness and serenity which my impetuous nature craved. Had I been able to provide the same complementariness for her? In some ways, perhaps: she always called me her 'ideas man'. At least we helped one another out of our shyness; but I was very conscious of my many failings towards her, of which I will only say here that I now regret not having been more at home.

We had loved one another since we met in Oxford all those years ago. That heady feeling of falling in love had ripened into a more mature loving and caring, and now we belonged to one another in an indissoluble way. She was so beautiful. So gifted. So talented as a mother – you have only to read that wonderful book of hers *Half Angels* to realise that. One clergy wife in Birmingham told me that she had modelled the bringing up of her family on that book. She was an expert with her needle, whether it were clothes or church embroidery or knitted wear. She was a wonderful cook. She had been an English scholar with a great knowledge and love of English literature. She was a bird expert, an expert on flowers and gardens. She was a social worker, with a marvellously kind and caring voice. For fourteen years she had been a member of the Liturgical Commission, and by now she knew a lot about the subject. She had suffered from depression, as so many people do;

but she had also enjoyed life. She was wise and she was loving and she was clever. And now, and now, it was all going to go. She would remain alive, but her talents, her memory, her feelings of self-worth (achieved with such difficulty) would be taken from her. Someone once described Alzheimer's as a house in which the lights were on, but there was no one at home.

However, life must go on. I hate self-pity. We must make the best of it, and if God permits Alzheimer's, then we must accept it. Not that it was all that easy to understand why God did permit Alzheimer's. Surely steps could have been taken to see that this particularly nasty kind of illness either didn't occur, or would be phased out on Darwinian principles? But no, it hadn't been, God created the universe so that it would evolve without interference from him; and if everyone asked to be a special case, where would we all be? We all ask the question: 'Why does it have to happen to me, or to my loved one?' but it's a fruitless question, really. It's the luck of the draw. Providence is not primarily about what happens to each one of us, but about the resources that God gives us to cope with what happens. All the same, I couldn't help telling God from time to time what I thought of him.

There were some jobs that I carried over from Birmingham. I was still a trustee of the Friends of the Earth Trust. Jonathan Porritt was becoming a nationally known figure, interest in the environment was catching on, membership was increasing by leaps and bounds, and so was the number of staff employed. I had also been for the past few years chairman of the Luthuli Memorial Trust. This was a charitable body set up through the African National Congress to find money to educate young Africans, either abroad or in South Africa. The need was very great, as the new Africa would need educated Blacks, and there was a great shortage because of the school and college embargoes of the past few years. It was, however, very difficult to raise money for this kind of charity in Britain. We had to rely to a great extent on a proportion of the budget which the ANC itself got from government agencies more generous than in Britain. Finally we did get a most helpful grant from a Scandinavian country, but then we were landed with a scheme of funding hundreds of African young people in Nigeria. At the request of Oliver Tambo I had been glad to chair the Trust (which brought me in touch with most interesting Africans and others) for five or six years. Now, after three years of retirement, I felt I could make way for another; and I was delighted that the present Bishop of Leicester, Tom Butler, took on this important job. Now that apartheid has miraculously ended in South Africa without violence, the work of the Trust over here is finishing, and the London office is to be closed. Of its African Trustees, three are now in the South African cabinet, and Thabo Mbeki is Vice President of the country. They were always an impressive body of men, but never did I dream that this metamorphosis could take place.

I was also invited to become chairman of Transport 2000, as a result of my earlier interests in transport and the environment. Transport 2000 is an umbrella body whose board consists of representatives of other environmental or social agencies which are concerned with transport. Our core funding had come from British Rail, the NUR and ASLEF, I believe the only project on which three bodies readily co-operated! We were a small body (it still is), with a director, an assistant, and two clerical staff. However, they were exceedingly competent, and at a time when transport issues were coming more and more to the forefront, its services were much in demand. Our director disappeared into British Rail, and we appointed in her place Stephen Joseph, who has been pre-eminently successful in this role.

I cannot say, however, that we have single-handedly turned back the policies of government on transport matters. These have been lunatic, as one looks back over the years. One of our problems has been that there are masses and masses of civil servants whose jobs concern the planning of roads, but very few whose task is to oversee the railways. Right back at the time of 'Changing Directions' and the Independent Commission on Transport, we had called for restrictions on the use of motor cars, and the result? An increase of 44 per cent in the decade up to 1981! Transport 2000 carried out a users' bus survey, and found that there were more buses after deregulation, but they were carrying fewer passengers. We have protested long and loud over the running down of British Rail, and the unfairness in the way in which money is allocated to roads contrasted with rail. For roads, investment is permitted on cost benefit analysis calculated in terms of money saved through the saving of journey time, while railways have to show a profit of 8 per cent before investment can be approved. We have protested long and loud not about the privatisation of the railways in principle, but about the way in which privatisation is being carried out, which is bound to produce more expensive fares, dislocation on journeys because of a lack of through ticketing and the lack of an integrated timetable on the part of different franchisees, and decreased spending on safety.

The road lobby, which has been immensely powerful in preserving what Lady Thatcher called 'our great car economy', has won the battle so far. Furthermore, ministers seldom travel by rail, they go by official car. (Mrs Thatcher almost never travelled by rail.) We have pointed out the dangers children suffer from the roads when going to school, the lack of facilities on the roads for public transport, the difficulties people encounter, especially in rural areas, if they cannot afford to run a motor car or if they do not have access to the family car. We have explained why traffic now moves in the big cities at the same pace as it did when there was horse traffic.

It is only now, at long last, becoming apparent that there is a change of heart beginning to take place at the Ministry of Transport; and that not because they do not want to favour the car, but because it is beginning to be realised that we cannot physically provide roads for all the cars which will congest them unless steps are taken to control them. And then, in 1994, came two reports; one from SACTRA pointing out the illogical way in which cost benefit analysis has been used to justify road building, and the other from the Royal Commission on Environmental Pollution. This is a splendid, long, authoritative and detailed document which if implemented would give us most of what we have asked for. But will it be? I fear it will be a long time before transport improves in this country, and by then more and more of the countryside will be despoiled, more and more towns will be congested beyond endurance, more and more railway tracks will be closed, more and more carbon dioxide will help to heat up the planet's atmosphere, more and more cases of asthma will develop, and minute particles from diesel released from the exhaust will lodge in the lungs and cause more and more cancer. It is not an attractive prognosis. Even if we have not been successful in Transport 2000, at least we have succeeded in engaging the sympathy of the public. A recent TV programme made by the organisation was shown on BBC TV, and attracted in response forty-three bags of mail!

After chairing this organisation for five years since my retirement, I felt that this too was long enough, and someone else should take over. We formed a trust, so that we could attract grants from charitable bodies for education and research, and I have become chairman of the Transport 2000 Trust instead of the parent body which is a compaigning organisation. When I stepped down from Transport 2000 I warned that rail privatisation could unseat the government at the next General Election. It will be interesting to see if my prophesy comes true.

I have also for the last four years taken on the chairmanship of the Friends of the Earth Trust, which performs a parallel function to the transport trust. It has been an interesting time of transition after the departure of Jonathan Porritt. The recession has meant a decrease of interest in environmental matters, which is picking up again as the recession eases. I have always had a great admiration for the Friends of the Earth, because it always researches its facts properly before undertaking any campaign; and it has a happy knack of campaigning in such a way as to catch the imagination of ordinary people. Heaven knows where we would be without these voluntary organisations opening our eyes to matters which officials would prefer we should not know about, and countering the powerful efforts of large vested interests to maintain the *status quo*.

I was also invited to become the chairman of what used to be called the Homes for Homeless People Trust, but which is now known as the National Trust for the Homeless. We concentrate on helping hostels for single homeless to get off the ground and to continue to keep going. Our chief activity is an annual National Sleep-out in December, but as we only keep 10 per cent of the proceeds (the rest goes to local projects in the various places where the sleep-outs are held), we have to try to obtain sponsorships as well. The whole position about housing in this country is most unsatisfactory. There is much homelessness, much substandard housing, little building of cheap rentable accommodation. This situation causes much suffering and impairment of home life. Most tragic is the position of the young single homeless. The numbers, both men and women, who leave home and become homeless, increase annually. Some 1,700 young people between sixteen and twenty-five arrive in London in each year with nowhere to stay, no gainful occupation and no close family to turn to for support. Increasing numbers are arriving now in provincial centres. One in four are women and one in ten come from ethnic minority groups. In 1988 there were about 5,700 young people between the ages of sixteen and nineteen in temporary accommodation, mostly in board and lodgings, but others squatting or in hostels or short-stay properties.

The interim report (1994) to the Mental Health Foundation about these young people is an appalling indictment on family life in Britain today, and on arrangements for looking after young people in care. Of the sample of young homeless in this interim report, almost half had run away from a care establishment before they had reached the age of sixteen, almost half showed marked lack of care in early childhood, and 38 per cent had experienced at least one instance of sexual abuse or severe physical abuse. Half of the sample suffered from a treatable psychiatric disorder, the majority of these suffering from both mental illness and substance abuse; and only 15 per cent of these have ever received psychiatric help. A third had attempted suicide at some point. These are surely some of the people in our society most in need of support. I do not grudge the time I have spent chairing the National Trust for the Homeless. Surely on any showing, the work to help these young people is very worth while.

However, chairing these organisations does not take up a great deal of my time. What else would I do? After those few months of quiet when I first retired, offers came along. I found myself, to my enormous surprise, engaged on a writing career. It was something that I enjoyed, and something that I could do at home, while Elisabeth was still able to occupy herself in the same room with what I suppose could be called occupational therapy. She enjoyed tapestry, and for some years she was able to make chair cushions from coloured designs – the house is now full of them.

The first offers came from Scotland. Would I give the Barclay Lectures in Glasgow in 1988 on 'Communicating the Gospel in a Scientific Age'? Yes, I would; and we enjoyed our trip to that noble city, even if there was a demo against me at one point by Presbyterian fundamentalists. The lectures were subsequently published. Again, would I give the Margaret Harris Lectures at Dundee University in 1988 in tandem with Jack Dominian? Again, yes, I would. I had an enormous admiration for Jack, whom I had known right back at the time when I was on the Root Commission on Marriage and Divorce. He was a senior consultant at the Central Middlesex Hospital and a very distinguished Roman Catholic marital consultant. This was the first time that lectures on sexual ethics had been shared between an Anglican and a Roman Catholic, and it was a very happy partnership, and our lectures were published under the title *God, Sex and Love*. We shared out our subjects: I took an 'Introduction to Sexual Ethics', 'Homosexuality', and 'Abortion and *in vitro* Fertilisation', while Jack took 'Masturbation' and 'Premarital Intercourse', and 'Marriage and Marital Breakdown'.

Both these sets of lectures required considerable reading and preparation, but not so much as the next course that I gave. Would I give the Drummond Lectures at Stirling University in 1989? Again, yes, I would. I was asked to lecture on the theme of Christianity and Politics, which was the title under which these were subsequently published. It was a subject about which I had already thought a great deal as chairman of the Church of England's Board for Social Responsibility; but I wanted to take a broader perspective over the centuries about the relationship of the Church to the state. I gave five lectures, one on 'Church and State', another on 'Theology and Politics', and a third on a subject which is not often broached, the 'Theology of Party Politics'. A further lecture was concerned with 'Environmental Politics and Christianity', and the last one concerned the 'British Churches and Politics Today'. As I was lecturing in Scotland, I had to do considerable research into the Presbyterian Church of Scotland's involvement in politics. Although this receives little national attention, it is in fact more trenchant and direct than that of the Church of England. And it was to the General Assembly of the Church of Scotland that the Prime Minister, Mrs Thatcher, had given her famous (or if you like, infamous) address on the relevance of Christianity to political life, when she made that extraordinary remark about there being no such thing as society. In the published version of my lectures, her speech is printed in one of the appendices to the book.

I had been invited to write a chapter in a book to be published the following year to mark the retirement of Bob Runcie from the Archbishopric of Canterbury. He had been much criticised in the press for statements which he had made and which were, in the eyes of the media, allegedly anti-Thatcher. I chose in my chapter to compare his statements with those of his predecessors, and my conclusion was that what he said was well within the broad stream of earlier archepiscopal utterances and that in his statements he has pressed for Christian principles rather than particular policies.

I had given a good many other lectures in this period in universities, colleges and elsewhere. Some of these have been published in other collections, but I gathered others of them together in a book published under the title *Reclaiming the High Ground: A Christian Response to Secularism*. They comprised such subjects as religious experience, love and marriage, our technological society, the environment, freedom, the evolution of life, the origin of species and 'the premature demise of the soul'. The point that I was trying to make was that Christian thinkers must try to reclaim the high ground of debate. Too much of Christianity has consisted of assertion rather than argument; and in today's world it needs to be demonstrated that Christianity has something to say in the secular debates of the day, and that it not only has something to say, but that it is impossible to make full sense of these matters of moment without a religious, and, indeed, a Christian, perspective. We need hard thinking and rational argument to show the inadequacy of materialism which is today so popular. It is a theme to which I believe the Christian Churches ought to pay far more attention than they do.

At the same time as I was writing books. I also began to write in a more journalistic vein. I had contributed articles now and again to *The Times*, and one summer I was surprised to be invited to write a regular column for the paper for a few months. This whetted my appetite for attempting to write about large subjects in a few hundred words, and in 1990 I started a 600-word weekly article for the *Church Times*, which I have done without a break since then for over five years. I have been grateful for this platform (I will not call it a pulpit) in which I can air my views every week on a great variety of subjects, in fact whatever I choose, whether this be religious, theological, ecclesiastical, political, environmental, scientific or whatever. It takes up quite a lot of time during the course of a year, but it stimulates me to pay attention to what is happening in the Church and in the world around me. It has also given rise to a considerable correspondence, often of an interesting kind.

To my great surprise I find that I am still in considerable demand in the media, usually but not always concerning current news. As an example, the day before brothels were due to be licensed in Holland (where they had long been tolerated), I was flown to Amsterdam for the day. The Mothers Union had suggested that licensing might be no bad thing. I was opposed, partly because it would be state recognition of vice, partly because of those who would live near a licensed area. Things were bad enough already in the red light area of Balsall Heath. (I had been embarrassed, arriving early for a confirmation, to find myself constantly accosted by prostitutes as I sat in my car.) I flew with Lydia Gladwin, wife of the new Bishop of Guildford, representing the Mothers Union. We interviewed prostitutes and a brothel keeper. (When I met Lydia later at her husband's consecration, I was able to say: 'We last met in a brothel.') Perhaps inevitably, the TV programme was called *The Bishop and the Brothel*. We insisted no clients be present, and that no nudity should appear on the screen. This was honoured, though it was somewhat distracting to see naked girls moving around in the background. I remember saying to the brothel keeper: 'You only have one life. Are you proud of your profession?', to which he blandly replied 'Yes, I produce a service.' One of the girls to whom I spoke, clearly a nymphomaniac, said that it would be an advantage to be registered, because she would be eligible for unemployment benefit if she left the brothel. When I pointed out that, as a registered prostitute, she could never get a respectable job, she said she did not want one. (Not all prostitutes were like that. Illegal immigrants, permitted to stay in the country but denied employment permits, were trapped in their work.) I remembered Josephine Butler in our calendar of saints, who successfully opposed registration and helped women regain their self-respect.

In an earlier chapter I have expressed the dissatisfaction that I felt with the report of the House of Bishops on 'The Nature of Christian Belief' which was published in 1986. Accordingly I had

promised myself an opportunity to examine the questions of the
virginal conception of Jesus and his physical Resurrection in greater
depth and in what I hoped would be a more fair-minded way than
had been done in that report. I published in 1992 *The Womb and
the Tomb*, a paperback in which I tried to look at every aspect of
these doctrines, and to give the arguments as fairly as I could both
in favour and against; and I did not disclose my own views until the
last chapter. Although this book received a very favourable review
from Professor Donald Mackinnon, it did not sell well. I find this
interesting. In the first place, fashions come and go, and the debate
moves on. Bishop David Jenkins had aroused great interest in these
doctrines; but that interest has died down. There is also, I fear, a
less reputable reason. In the world in which we live today, people
do not want to hear both sides of a question, and then make up
their minds. They prefer to hold strong convictions one way or the
other, accepting with enthusiasm a book which accords with them,
or expressing revulsion against a book which advances a contrary
viewpoint.

Earlier I had been approached about writing a book on the environment, in a series which consisted of sermons on different subjects.
Mine was on *Preaching for Our Planet*. Through the Friends of the
Earth I had been able to keep abreast of the environmental scene
(which is constantly changing), and I enjoyed the challenge of trying
to write popular sermons on subjects of some scientific complexity. I
find that there are comparatively few Christians in the environmental
movement. The Church as a whole hardly seems interested. To be
sure, there are one or two Christian pressure groups, but their
membership is not large. I could not understand, in my involvement
in the movement over the years, why the Church did not take more
seriously the assaults on God's created world which are the result
of human greed, modern technology and our thirst for 'progress';
so I was glad to write a book on this theme addressed specially
to Christians. The Duke of Edinburgh was kind enough to write a
Foreword, and I wrote a course of twenty-two sermons (to be read,
I hasten to add, not to be given from a pulpit). These ranged from
'Ozone' to 'Matter And Materialism', and from 'Acid Rain' to 'The
Kingdom of God'. It gave me great pleasure to find relevant texts
from which to preach such sermons. These ranged from the Song
of Solomon to the Parable of the Prodigal Son.

Meanwhile a considerable amount of time was being taken up on
a different project altogether. Way back in 1981 the British Council
of Churches had approved a large conference to be held in 1984
on the subject of the relationship of the Gospel and our culture;

but this had been cancelled because it was rightly felt that there had been insufficient preparation. Dr Kenneth Slack had chaired a continuation committee, and Bishop Lesslie Newbigin had written a small booklet called *The Other Side of 1984* which became a bestseller and which was translated into several languages. After Dr Slack's premature death in 1987 I was invited to take over the chairmanship of the committee. I was glad to do so, and I was fully committed to the central thesis that the presuppositions of our contemporary culture, of which we are often not consciously aware, greatly affect our ability to respond to the Christian Gospel. Indeed, now that a Decade of Evangelism had been declared, it seemed to me that this would be bound to fail unless this aspect of evangelism were more fully explored.

When I took over chairmanship of the committee, it seemed to me that we needed a definite goal to which to work; and so we there and then booked the Swanwick Conference Centre for a National Consultation on the subject in mid-1992, which gave us over four years for preparation. Fortunately we had Dr Beeby, former Principal of St Andrew's College in Birmingham, as part-time Director of the 'Gospel and Our Culture' project, which was therefore centred in the Selly Oak Colleges there, where an old pupil of mine from Caius, Martin Conway, was Principal, and very sympathetic to our project. It was decided that we needed to produce literature as part of our preparation, and in particular a book was planned which would explore the presuppositions ('root axioms', as some anthropologists call them) of a number of aspects of our culture, and see how these related to the Christian faith.

This was a major project. We were kindly lent the Jerusalem Chamber of Westminster Abbey for meetings. I got together groups of experts in these various subjects to discuss a specially written situation paper, and as a result of these meetings I invited someone from each group to contribute to our symposium. After a few years I resigned from the chairmanship of the committee, as with Elisabeth to look after it became too difficult for me to attend its meetings in the Birmingham Selly Oak Colleges. I concentrated on the production of the book which I found needed a strong editorial hand. *The Gospel and Contemporary Culture* appeared in 1992, and apart from my introduction there were essays on history, science, arts, epistemology, economics, education, health and healing, and the media. The National Consultation at Swanwick, sponsored by the Bible Society, was fully booked and a resounding success, and the book itself, despite the difficulties I had encountered in finding a publishing house willing to commit itself to a symposium, sold out two impressions. (The movement has since merged with the C. S. Lewis Society and is now known as 'Gospel and Culture'.)

I felt that what we had achieved in this book was important, but somewhat negative. It showed up the difficulties that the Christian faith has in establishing itself in a culture such as ours. But that culture will not change overnight; and meanwhile the Gospel is still to be preached. I felt that there remains a parallel task. The Gospel needs to be inculturated into our contemporary culture, however alien that may be to the Gospel. It is necessary to take seriously the new insights of the human and natural sciences. I was therefore sympathetic to David Edwards when he encouraged me to write a 'mini-systematic theology' which gave a broad view of Christian faith and life as it may be understood within our present contemporary culture.

Writing this book was a vast undertaking, and the resulting volume was far larger than any which I have previously discussed, some three hundred pages of close-printed type. I was able to write it very quickly, and I hope it does not sound ridiculous to put into print my strong conviction, as I wrote it, that I was receiving help and encouragement from Geoffrey Lampe and John Robinson. The book really brought together and summed up all my theological thinking over the past half century. It is in no sense intended as a 'final' theology. All theology by its very nature is provisional, for it needs to be expressed in ways suited to a particular culture; and cultures differ. *Credible Christianity* was published in 1993, with the subtitle 'The Gospel in Contemporary Society'. It encompasses the whole field of systematic theology, with chapters also on practical theology and spirituality. I am naturally delighted at how well it has been received, and the American edition has been chosen for the Episcopal Book Club in that country.

I have been surprised how frequently I have been called upon by the media of television and broadcasting since my retirement. Perhaps this is partly because I live in London, which is convenient so far as studios are concerned. I find that people are very understanding about Elisabeth. At first they were able to find someone to sit with her outside the studio, and more recently they are prepared to pay for minders.

I felt that we ought to take trips abroad as long as Elisabeth could enjoy them. When Susan Cole-King was in England she asked me whether I would preach and participate in her ordination to the priesthood in New York. I gladly agreed to do so. How could I refuse? After all, she was the daughter of one of my predecessors in Birmingham. Elisabeth and I went over on a short visit, and the ordination took place at the Church of All Angels just off Fifth Avenue. Since women were then not yet allowed to be ordained to the priesthood in England, this was for me a memorable occasion. I was also invited by the Anglican Institute in the United States of America to make a visit, preaching in parishes and (with the permission of the bishop) confirming. We were very hospitably entertained in St Louis, which was our base, by Ed Salmon (now Bishop of South Carolina) and his wife. We seemed to have engagements in very different parts of that vast country, from Denver City near the Rockies, to Seattle, near the Canadian border and a church in central New York.

The following year the Institute invited me again, this time to visit a variety of Anglican seminaries. It was not suitable for Elisabeth to come with me on this, so I left her behind, to be looked after by one of the 'Country Cousins' who specialise in this kind of help. I went to five seminaries altogether, from New York to Sewanee, preaching and talking. I managed to be in Berkeley and to participate in the farewell Eucharist for its Dean, Bill Pregnall, who had provided such magnificent hospitality to us both when I was 'Bishop in Residence' at the Church Divinity School of the Pacific. It so happened that I was to be in America at the time when the first woman Bishop, Barbara Harris, was to be consecrated in Boston, and I wanted to be present. I thought it right to tell Bob Runcie, as Archbishop of Canterbury, of my intention; and he begged me not to participate as a Bishop: it would, he said, create many difficulties for him. I honoured this, but I still wanted to be present. I wrote to *The Times* newspaper, and asked them if they would like me to be there as their special correspondent (it would not cost them anything); and they agreed. So I went, staying with a former priest of the Birmingham diocese, then working at the Old North Church. The consecration was an extraordinary occasion. We do not let loose balloons at a service for the consecration of a bishop in Britain.

We also made other visits. In 1988, after we had settled in, we went on our 'retirement holiday' in a boat down the Nile. This was most enjoyable, and the sights most impressive, although after a bit one could not help thinking that one Egyptian temple was much like another. Unfortunately there was not enough water for us to go all the way down to Cairo, and we had to turn back by Nag Hammudi. I was very disappointed by this place. The Gospel of Thomas and other gnostic manuscripts had been found in a field by one of the fellahin near Nag Hammudi, and I expected a small village; but I was astonished to see a big town with a factory. It was very sad to see the effects of the Great Dam up the Nile on the river as a whole.

Whereas in the past the river had fertilised the surrounding area, there now was a factory for artificial fertiliser. Most of the passengers had suffered from 'Gippy Tummy' and we too succumbed. Some people were really ill, on drips. We felt ourselves hard done by, until we found another steamer on which every single passenger had been ill.

In 1989 we had a lovely holiday in Cyprus in April, when it was warm, but not hot. We stayed a week at a nice old-fashioned Victorian hotel at Platres, up in the central mountains, where we hired a car and Elisabeth greatly enjoyed seeing a hoopoe, and then a week by the sea at Paphos, with expeditions to monasteries and medieval churches with wall paintings, when we could track down the Pappa digging his garden and persuade him to open them up. The following year we went on a trip down the Rhine. Elisabeth enjoyed this, but by this time her disabilities were causing other passengers to look at us somewhat askance, and I determined that this must be the last time that we went on this kind of corporate expedition. However, I did manage a trip with her to Copenhagen, by sea, which she enjoyed, and my daughter Catherine, with a friend, was kind enough to accompany us on a short trip to Bruges. After that, I felt it would be irresponsible to take her on any more trips away.

There was, however, another visit that we had been able to make before Elisabeth was too disabled to travel. I had been invited to visit the Anglican Church in Japan in 1989 and to give lectures in various centres by Rikkyo University in Tokyo. This is a university on an Anglican foundation originating from the Episcopal Church in the United States. I realised that Elisabeth, while she was still well enough to take part in conversation, was not well enough to remain on her own when I was lecturing. Ruth Robinson, the widow of Bishop John Robinson, whom Elisabeth had known well in Cambridge, of her kindness offered to come with us, and to help in taking care of her. This we most gratefully accepted; and we made preparations for a two-month visit, from mid-October to mid-December, when the climate is at its most pleasant.

The Anglican Church in Japan is small, comprising only 35,000 members and three hundred clergy, but these members support their Church with great loyalty. The religious basis of the university was fairly nominal, although there was of course a chapel and regular services. Our hosts were most welcoming and kind. We were put up in what seemed to us the largest house on the campus; it was formerly the Vice Chancellor's. Most houses in Japan are very small, and people, who are very conscious of such things, customarily entertain people in restaurants rather than lose face by bringing them to a small house. When I asked why this house was so large, I was told because it was one of the houses built for missionaries. We were on one occasion invited to dinner at a private house, but it was very difficult to find, as houses are numbered not logically but by their distance from the Emperor's palace. When we got lost and had to ring the bell of a house to find our way, even the inhabitants, who, it turned out, lived only half a block away, had to get out maps in order to guide us. It is said that if you see people walking around in a residential area after dark without a bottle of wine, it is the host looking for his guests; and if you see someone with a bottle of wine, it is a guest looking for his host.

I think and hope that my lectures were adequate, but it was difficult to be certain, because no one ever asked any questions at the end, although invited to do so. When I enquired why, I was told that people might be frightened of losing face if they could not phrase their question in proper English. But that may also have been another example of extreme Japanese politeness. I lectured in Sendai, Omija, Kobe, Osaka and Kyoto; I also preached in St Luke's Hospital, Tokyo, at a school and at the Anglican church there. Japan is a very beautiful country, and journeys by bullet train are very fast and comfortable (although ordinary trains are somewhat slower than ours). We stayed in Hiroshima where there were vigorous signs of life despite the terrible havoc of the nuclear bomb: it was interesting to see laughing schoolgirls going into the museum there with its awful exhibits. (It was strange to see schoolgirls in sailor suits as their uniform, and the boys in what looked like Prussian uniforms. The boys and girls are grossly overworked at school, and the modern generation of students, as a result, is now tending to drop out at university, to the dismay and incredulity of their parents.)

The Anglican parish of Hiroshima kindly entertained us to dinner, and it was humbling to meet three ladies who had been in Hiroshima when the bomb fell, fortunately for them living on the outskirts of the city. As I wrote before, this visit led me to remark to a Japanese Anglican chaplain of a school how ashamed now some were in Britain at having connived at the dropping of those two nuclear bombs; but he demurred, saying that without this the Japanese would never have given up fighting, even if they had been dropped out at sea.

We grew quite used to raw fish and chopsticks, and we even stayed once at a Japanese inn, with its communal bath and rice for breakfast. When we were shown to our room, there was simply a bare floor. When we asked where we sat, we were told the bedding was kept in the cupboard. We were somewhat embarrassed that, although the Anglican Church was so small, it was apparently necessary for us to be accommodated in the most luxurious hotels, or our hosts might have lost face. I was impressed by the Zen monks. We were entranced by the Shinto shrines, and it was interesting to see businessmen frequenting them, and leaving written prayers on trees. We learnt that while the Shinto priests preside over birth ceremonies, and Buddhist priests over funerals, church weddings were very popular, and couples sometimes flew to America to be married, as Japanese churches tended to be strict. Unlike Britain, opposition to women priests came not from the laity or the clergy, but from some of the bishops.

I was moved to meet Dr Kigawa, who had been in Hong Kong during the Japanese occupation, and insisted, as a Christian, on attending worship at the cathedral, and who had tried to mitigate some of the hardships of the British in prison. I was also delighted to meet a retired priest who had been in Akyab during the war: Akyab was an island which we failed to capture during the abortive Arakan expedition in which I was involved (see Chapter 3). After my experiences in Burma, I knew that until I went to Japan I would never feel really able to get over my prejudices and be in a proper relationship with Japanese; and I was right. Although no Westerner can ever really read the oriental mind, I was overcome by their friendliness and warmth, and made many friends.

I have always enjoyed debating. I remember when I was at Rugby going to Stowe School to debate there, and being offered sherry by Roxburgh, the headmaster. (It is the sherry I remember most.) When I was at Birmingham I took part in a good many debates at the Oxford and Cambridge Unions, as I still occasionally do. I found myself debating in a new kind of way during my retirement; it seems to have become a novel way of launching books. I debated at St James, Piccadilly, when Jim Lovelock launched his *Ages of Gaia*, and again when my own *Credible Christianity* was published together with a book publicising the views of the new trendy theology which insists it is Christian while no longer believing that God is real. I have been involved with Richard Dawkins in two debates about God; one in the old Divinity Schools at Oxford for TV, and the other at the Royal Society in 1992, when Professor Paul Davies came over from Australia to launch his latest book, *The Mind of God*. On my side was Russell Stannard, lecturer at the Open University, and on the other were Sir Herman Bondi and Richard Dawkins. I will always remember that when I or Russell (I forget who) asked why there was something rather than nothing, Richard Dawkins dismissed the question, saying it was illegitimate. Illegitimate! What he meant was that on his presuppositions it could not be asked. There could scarcely be a better illustration of how scientists step outside their boundaries when they make statements like that. Dawkins was expressing not his science but his atheism.

Meanwhile matters did not stand still at home. It had become apparent that the cottage in Bucknell was too far away for us to use it for holidays. It was over two hundred miles distant. Elisabeth could no longer enjoy herself there; she could not walk very far, there was only one living-room, and there was nothing for her to do there. I determined to sell it, but during the recession that was more easily said than done. It was on the market for over a year. Then there was the terrible problem of sorting out the furniture and other objects that were there, sharing them among the family, and bringing back to London what we needed here, for there was no point in keeping a workroom for Elisabeth any longer, and it would be better to turn it into a bedroom.

Once more Catherine came to the rescue and looked after Elisabeth, while I took a train to Birmingham, got a self-drive van and drove out into the night to the cottage. My former domestic chaplain was kind enough to come out to Bucknell the next day to help me load the van. All went well, without any accidents, and I arrived back in London with the booty.

All the time Elisabeth was growing more disabled. It became apparent to me that it was vital that I should keep fit, as otherwise she would have to go into a residential home; and so I managed to lose a stone and a half in weight, and I took great care over a balanced diet for us both. (Alas, I have had to take it all off again since then.)

It soon became apparent that Eliza could not cope with the cooking; and I took over, first one meal a day, and then the lot. She could no longer cope with money, and although the local shops had been very good in helping her with her change, it became obvious that she should no longer carry any cash. I had got her to sign an enduring power of attorney. Her spelling had already been affected before we left Birmingham, and she found it progressively more difficult and then impossible to write. It was the same with reading. Cheques were out of the question, and then, sadly, letters. As I have said, she could do tapestry for some years, but then she could not distinguish between the different colours of the design. She could still do the drying up! But even that become impossible. She could then dress herself, but that too became more difficult, and then impossible.

The really terrible time was when she was finding things difficult, and realised what was to come. I would find her upstairs in the bedroom crying her eyes out, saying 'I know what's happening to me.' She felt 'I am nothing, *nothing*.' What could I say? It only caused stress and frustration for her to fight against this terrible illness; better just to let go and accept it, but who was I, in full possession of *my* faculties, to say such a thing to *her*? Well, I did, occasionally. The best thing was just to hug her tight and to go on hugging her until the moment passed. She preferred not to discuss the future with me, so we didn't. We used to have a daily Eucharist together (we had made a lovely chapel in one of the attics); but in the end I had to give that up, because she really didn't understand what was going on at all. The vicar kindly comes to breakfast once a week, so I can still have a service.

I had to learn new skills, which I never thought that I would possess; washing clothes, washing her, cleaning, shopping, cooking, sewing. (You can hardly go wrong with cooking if you follow the recipes.) I have a growing admiration for women, who manage to use all these skills, bring up children and do a paid job into the bargain. How *do* they do it? How foolish we men are not to realise their superior abilities (and, research now suggests, their superior intellect). I have good help with a cleaner who comes once a week. The first one seemed only to pat with a duster, and the second used a Hoover and did nothing else, and even I could see that this was insufficient; but now I have got a Philippino, and everything *shines*. My daughters are kind in keeping a good eye on me.

There is a day-care centre on Saturdays and on Sundays (so I can still go out to preach and take services). Social services send a home carer now to come in twice a week to help to bath her. Joan and Louise take turns as two devoted carers for six hours a day on weekdays: they take a week on and then a week off. That leaves me with eighteen hours a day on my own with her, and nights are a little disturbed; but so what? The local hospital gives me respite care of a fortnight every three months, so I reckon that, however much other people complain, I do very well by the NHS and the social services. I have managed to get abroad during this fortnight's break. I can take on lecturing outside London during this period, and I have holidayed in Barcelona and been to Washington twice to see my daughter Janet. (Her husband, Patrick Cockburn, was then a foreign correspondent for the *Independent* in Washington, and she engineered leave of absence from Kent University.) On one occasion I got to Moscow for an ecumenical conference to commemorate Fr Alexandr Men, the Jewish Orthodox priest who took over the spiritual leadership of the country after the death of Sakharov, and then was murdered, it was thought, by the KGB.

As I look back I am grateful for God's grace and providence which have brought me to this point. People sometimes tell me how sorry they are, and all that. I am grateful for their sympathy, but I wish they wouldn't. I have had an easy life, so far as outward conditions are concerned, and I have always felt rather guilty about the family money I have inherited, and which my father took steps to see that I did not give away. In fact I even used to ask God to send some difficulty into my life, to help to make me more mature. I never thought for a moment that this is what would come; but now it has come, I am content.

Sometimes I think back to what Elisabeth was, and I have been reduced to tears when I have left her for respite care in the hospital ward with the human wrecks who are its permanent inhabitants. But then I recollect myself, and realise this is only self-pity. I can no longer feel really bad about how she feels. Now that she no longer has any idea what is happening, and certainly can't remember anything at all of what she once was, she is really quite happy for most of the time, once one gets the medication right. Her myoclonic spasms are more alarming for me than for her. The sweetness of her temperament is still apparent. She still looks beautiful, with a lovely figure. I am grateful to the saints, whose prayers I have so often invoked on her behalf, and grateful of course to God for these blessings which he has given us. He has not changed her condition but he has certainly made it bearable for her and for me. It is good looking after her: I actually like doing it. For over forty years she looked after me so lovingly and so caringly. Why should I not spend a far smaller number of years looking after her? I *like* to do so.

I get rather angry when people tell me about excellent residential homes for Alzheimer patients. I am sure that some are excellent, but by the nature of the case they cannot offer the one-to-one care that we can give her. I realise that for many people, circumstances are such that parents or spouses cannot be looked after at home. Sooner or later it may come to that, but at least I seem still blessed with good health and energy, and while I have the physical strength to do so, I want to keep her here at home. She cannot speak much now, although occasionally there are flashes of the old Eliza, and she can still use those admirable 'cover up' words which she employed to hide her inability to answer questions – 'Perhaps' or 'Possibly' or 'Probably'. She no longer knows my name, but she can still smile, and occasionally she says 'I love you'; or more probably she gets her pronouns confused and says 'She likes him'.

Oh God, what next? At least I am a little less immature than I used to be, but I am very far from perfect, and I am sure that a pretty sharp spell in purgatory awaits me. I suppose I am not yet fully in touch with myself. No doubt I will learn that there, if not before. This year is in a sense my *annus mirabilis*. I will have been twenty-five years a Bishop, married for fifty years, and seventy-five years old. I no longer ask myself 'Oh God, what next?' I shall find out when it comes. At the moment I am content with the present.

INDEX